TURKS AND ~~CAICOS~~ CHAOS

RYAN WATSON

FOREWORD BY
SENATOR MARKWAYNE MULLIN

I've spent my life as a fighter - in the ring, in business, and now in the United States Senate. But some of the hardest fights aren't the ones you choose for yourself. They're the ones thrust upon innocent people who find themselves trapped in impossible situations, far from home, with everything on the line.

Ryan Watson's fight was one of those.

On April 12, 2024, Ryan and his wife Valerie were arrested in Turks and Caicos for accidentally having ammunition in their luggage - a mistake any American hunter or sportsman could make. What should have been resolved with a fine became a nightmare of indefinite detention, threats of a twelve-year prison sentence, and a legal system more interested in making examples of Americans than serving justice.

My office was notified immediately, but it wasn't until April 25th that Ryan and I began working together directly. From that day forward, we spoke almost daily. I've worked on many constituent cases over the years, solving countless problems, but this one was different. This wasn't just about navigating bureaucracy or applying diplomatic pressure - though we did plenty of that, forming a Congressional Delegation (CODEL) Task Force and relentlessly pressuring the State Department. This was about a man's soul, his family's future, and whether faith could truly sustain someone when everything looked hopeless.

During our calls, as we strategized about available options and ways I could assist him as his Senator, I found myself praying with Ryan. I prayed for his heart - that it would have the strength to endure what no man should have to endure. But here's what struck me: Ryan didn't need me to prop up his faith. He was already standing firm on the Rock.

While I was fighting for him in Washington, Ryan was fighting a different battle on that island. He ministered to other detainees. He submitted himself completely to the Lord's plan, trusting that God's way was better than any outcome he could engineer himself. In every interview, in every interaction with authorities, he praised the Lord. Not with the forced optimism of someone trying to convince himself, but with the genuine confidence of a man who knew whose hands he was in.

When our CODEL finally flew to Turks and Caicos and I met Ryan in person for the first time, we immediately started joking like old friends. I gave him grief about wearing a cowboy hat on a tropical island - leave it to an Oklahoman to bring the ranch to the Caribbean. But beneath the humor was something profound: a bond forged through fire, prayer, and shared purpose.

I won't sugarcoat my feelings about what happened. The Turks and Caicos authorities acted with political motivations, not justice. They imprisoned Americans to make a point, to flex their power, to extract votes. It was wrong. It was cruel. And it demanded a response from the United States Congress.

But this book isn't primarily about the failure of a foreign government or even about the advocacy work we did - though both are part of the story. This is about what happens when a man of faith faces his darkest hour and discovers that his God is faithful.

After Ryan came home, he and Valerie joined me and my wife Christie for dinner, along with their children Van and Ellie. We celebrated. We gave thanks. We marveled at how God had moved. Since then, Ryan and I stay in touch, occasionally sharing words of prayer and support. And here's what I know: Ryan's case has helped other Americans caught in similar situations. His witness didn't end when he left that island. It's still echoing.

In the pages ahead, you'll read about a vacation turned into a nightmare, about corruption exposed, about a justice system that failed, and about political intervention that succeeded. But more than anything, you'll read about unshakeable faith - the kind that doesn't crumble when circumstances turn dark but instead becomes a light for others.

Ryan led others in their walk with faith while he was detained. Now, through this book, he's leading again.

This is a story that needed to be told. Not just so we remember what happened, but so we remember what's possible when we trust God's plan even when we can't see the way forward.

Read this book. Let it challenge you. Let it inspire you. And let it remind you that even in the chaos - especially in the chaos - God is sovereign.

Senator Markwayne Mullin represents Oklahoma in the United States Senate and served as a key advocate in the Congressional effort to secure Ryan Watson's release from Turks and Caicos.

FEBRUARY 13TH, 2024

The pages crackled like dried leaves between Michael Grim's fingers, swollen fat from the humidity that hung in the air like a wet blanket. He turned another page of

The Gulag Archipelago

The book's spine was limp and barely held the pages together. Mosquitoes droned through the cell bars—a constant, maddening whine that burrowed into his skull. The tropical air carried their song along with the thick smell of salt water and rotting vegetation, a scent that had long ago soaked into his skin, his clothes, the concrete walls around him.

Less than seventy-two hours remained. Seventy-two hours until his six-month sentence ended, but time had betrayed him. Instead of sprinting toward freedom, it crawled. Dragged its feet. Each second stretched like taffy. Each minute felt like an hour. His fingers traced the patchy stubble on his jaw—rough, uneven, grown wild. Seven months ago, he'd been clean-cut, sharp-dressed, chasing political dreams with the confidence of someone who'd never tasted failure. Now, long hair hung greasy over his ears. His cheeks had hollowed out, carved away by prison food and constant vigilance. He looked like something that had washed up on shore.

A shipwreck survivor.

Until now, he hadn't given his appearance a thought. Survival took priority. But his family would be seeing him soon—for the first time in months—and the image of his mother's face when she saw him like this made his chest tighten.

The distance between them wasn't her choice. It was his. Michael had learned fast in here: a worried family was blood in the water. The sharks circled. Guards smelled desperation the way dogs smell fear. Inmates smelled money. The prison allowed two five-minute phone calls per month—made from guards' phones or from contraband cells smuggled in by fellow inmates who'd pay a guard to look the other way. Either way, the math was simple. You dial your family, their numbers pop up in a call log, and suddenly everyone has direct access to the people who'd empty their bank accounts to keep you breathing.

Michael needed extra caution. He was the only white face in the prison. The only American accent bouncing off these concrete walls. To everyone inside, that combination meant one thing and one thing only.

Money.

But Michael was sharp. Sharper than most gave him credit for. His knowledge wasn't limited to political science textbooks or the philosophical volumes gathering dust on his shelf back home. He'd studied survival. Trained in psychological endurance. Learned weapons and hand-to-hand combat. That knowledge kept trouble at arm's length when it came sniffing around his cell—and it came sniffing regularly, testing him, probing for weakness. The thirty-five thousand dollars in cash his parents had stuffed into the local attorney's pocket probably didn't hurt either.

Insurance.

~❖~

Seventy miles away on that same chain of islands, the Hagerich family reluctantly stuffed beach towels into suitcases and packed away half-empty bottles of sunscreen. This was their third trip to Turks and Caicos—they'd officially fallen in love. The manicured all-inclusive resorts with their perfectly raked sand. The crystal-blue waters so clear you could count fish from the shore. It was the perfect antidote to Pennsylvania's gray, wet winters that seemed to last nine months out of the year.

The airport assaulted the senses. Small. Hot as a furnace. Chaotic with bodies pressed together in lines that barely moved. Not the ideal way to end a week in paradise, but Ashley's phone held a thousand photos—their sun-kissed babies playing in the sand, building castles, splashing in the surf—and that made the sweaty wait bearable. Their two kids chased each other between rows of chairs at the departure gate, their laughter somehow cutting through the din of a hundred conversations, crackling intercoms, and the constant hum of inadequate air conditioning.

Bryan was a complete sucker for those kids. His decorated days as a minor league baseball player—the newspaper clippings, the trophies, the dreams of going pro—all of it paled next to watching his daughter's gap-toothed smile or his son's silly knock-knock jokes. He'd traded cleats for a corporate badge years ago and never once looked back. Healthcare paid the bills. Kept the lights on. Put food on the table. That was what mattered now.

But he'd kept one piece of his old life. Hunting. Trudging through freezing pre-dawn woods, breath fogging in the air, tracking deer through terrain that tried to break your ankles. Ashley never understood the appeal—why anyone would willingly wake up at four in the morning to sit in a tree stand in sub-zero temperatures. But she didn't need to understand. He was a good husband. A good father. Everyone needed something that was just theirs.

They kept one eye on the kids—making sure neither one face-planted into a chair or knocked over someone's carry-on—and another eye on the window, watching for their plane to taxi up to the gate. It would be a long flight. Hours of are we there yet and I'm bored and I have to go to the bathroom. Snacks needed to be strategically deployed. Tablets needed to be at full charge. The intercom crackled every few minutes with last-call boarding announcements, that particular brand of airport white noise that most people had learned to tune out completely.

Ashley was mid-scroll through vacation photos—her thumb swiping past images of her sun-browned babies building sandcastles—when one announcement made her finger freeze on the screen.

She lowered her phone slowly.

"Did they just say Hagerich?"

Bryan's head swiveled toward the old speaker mounted in the corner, its black mesh cover dusty and cracked.

Bryan Hagerich, please report to the security area for a bag inspection.

"Oh yeah, I guess it did."

He stood, brushing pretzel crumbs off his shorts.

"Hang here with the kiddos. I'll be right back."

The oversized hunting bag had been perfect for this trip—big enough to swallow beach toys, pool floaties, snorkel gear, and all the random kid detritus that somehow multiplied on vacation. Bryan figured one of the kids had probably stashed away a pocketful of seashells they'd collected, maybe some sand dollars. probably saw something weird on the X-ray.

No big deal.

The security area smelled like recycled air and stress sweat. An overweight local woman waited for him, arms crossed, face set in that particular expression of bureaucratic boredom that airport security officers seemed to master on their first day. No warmth. No smile. Just dead eyes and a job to do.

"Are you Mr. Hagerich?"

Her voice was flat, mechanical.

"Yes, ma'am."

"Boarding pass and bag ticket."

Bryan dug into his pocket, fingers fumbling past receipts and loose change until he found the crumpled pile of baggage claim tickets. He handed them over along with his boarding pass, slightly damp from being clutched in his sweaty palm.

"I just need the ticket for this bag."

She jabbed a finger toward his hunting bag and thrust the tickets back at him like they were contaminated. Bryan sorted through them—squinting at the tiny numbers—and handed her the correct one. She glanced at it. Gave a curt nod.

"I'm going to perform a luggage inspection."

She moved to the metal table where his bag sat like evidence at a crime scene. The zipper screamed as she yanked it open. A heavy sigh. A theatrical shake of her head. She pulled items out one by one with the energy of someone who'd done this dance a thousand times and resented every repetition—dirty t-shirts. Sandy swim trunks. Deflated pool floaties. A plastic shovel. Beach toys that left a trail of sand across the table.

The pile grew. The bag emptied.

She picked up the hollow shell of the bag and shook it hard, the fabric snapping like a flag in the wind. She wasn't done. Not even close. Her hands dove into the interior, feeling along seams, jamming fingers into every pocket with the intensity of someone searching for contraband.

Then she stopped.

Her fingers had found something. Bryan watched her face change—the bored mask cracking as her eyes widened slightly. She dug deeper, her whole hand disappearing into a side pocket he'd forgotten existed.

Bryan's heart started to beat faster. Something was wrong. He could feel it in his gut, that primal warning system that predates language.

The corners of her mouth turned up.

Not a smile exactly. Something else. Something worse.

Satisfaction.

She pulled her hand out slowly, deliberately, like a magician revealing the final trick. Her fist opened.

A box of hunting ammunition. Twenty rounds. Copper-jacketed. The kind he used for deer season back home.

The air left Bryan's lungs.

"Oh God."

"I'm so sorry. I don't—I don't remember leaving those in there. That must be from a hunting trip. Months ago. I completely forgot—"

"Mr. Hagerich."

Her voice cut through his rambling like a blade.

"You need to stand right there while we notify the authorities."

The room tilted slightly. Bryan's mouth went dry as sand.

"That really isn't necessary. This is an innocent mistake. Can you just—just throw them away? Please?"

She shook her head, that satisfied smirk still plastered across her face like she'd just won the lottery. She brushed past him, clutching the ammunition box like a trophy, her shoulder bumping his as she headed toward a back office.

The next few minutes blurred together. Suddenly, there were officers. Three, then four, then five. Uniforms everywhere. Radios crackling. Voices sharp and rapid-fire. They surrounded Bryan like he was dangerous, like he might bolt for the exit. His hands started to shake.

"Please. My wife—can you bring my wife over here? I need to explain what's happening. My kids are with her. Please."

The officers exchanged glances. Finally, the female security officer gave a nod and trudged off toward the departure gate.

Bryan's heart hammered against his ribs. Sweat pooled in the small of his back.

"My kids are here. Please—please don't arrest me in front of them."

No one responded. No one even looked at him.

Minutes crawled by. Then the security officer reappeared with Ashley and the kids in tow. Ashley's face was pale, confused, her eyes darting between Bryan and the circle of officers. The kids sensed something was wrong—they'd gone quiet, clinging to their mother's legs.

Bryan tried to explain. Tried to keep his voice steady, tried to make it sound less terrifying than it was. An honest mistake. Forgot to check the bag. Everything would be fine. But his voice cracked on that last part, betraying the lie.

The officers allowed him one last hug. He knelt down, pulled his kids close, breathed in the smell of their hair—sunscreen and saltwater and innocence. Then rough hands grabbed his arms and pulled him away.

His kids started crying. High-pitched wails that cut through every other sound in the terminal.

Ashley stood frozen, her arms around their sobbing children, watching her husband get dragged away like a criminal.

She turned to the female officer, desperation naked on her face. Searching for reassurance. For comfort. For someone to tell her this was a misunderstanding that would be cleared up in an hour.

The officer offered nothing. No sympathy. No warmth. She simply shrugged—a gesture so casual it bordered on cruel—and delivered her verdict in a voice completely devoid of emotion.

"Your husband is going to prison for twelve years."

Then she turned on her heel and walked back into her office.

The door shut with a soft click that sounded like a cell locking.

Word traveled fast through the Royal Turks and Caicos police department. Another American arrested. Another fool caught at the airport. The guards talked about it in low voices, half-amused, half-satisfied. Like they were keeping score.

Michael was making his way across the courtyard toward the prison yard—his muscles aching for that precious hour of sunlight and space—when one of the guards approached. Michael greeted him with his usual friendly hello, the performative warmth he'd learned to deploy as a survival tool. This guard was one of the few he'd managed to win over. But the expression on the man's face told Michael this wasn't the usual small talk.

When they reached the yard—away from cameras, away from other guards—the man pulled out his phone.

He handed it to Michael without a word.

It took Michael a moment to process what he was seeing. A WhatsApp message thread. The TCI police department's group chat. Messages flying back and forth in that casual shorthand cops use when they think no one's watching.

His eyes found the relevant line.

American arrested for possession of ammunition at Howard Hamilton Airport.

Michael's heart dropped into his stomach like a stone into water.

His attorney's words came flooding back, spoken in that courtroom months prior, delivered with the weary certainty of someone who'd seen this play out before:

Michael, I know you think you got it bad, but you only got your tail clipped as you made it through the gate. You got lucky. The next American? The next American is about to get it really bad.

Michael handed the phone back, his hands numb.

Somewhere on this island, another American family was being destroyed.

And there was nothing he could do to stop it.

Same day, back in Oklahoma.

Tanner Dyer and Trey Marler were two of my best friends from college—the kind of friends who knew all your worst stories and still picked up the phone. Miles separated our towns now. Tanner had ended up in Pampa, TX. Trey was outside Tulsa. Family commitments made getting together a logistical nightmare. But text messages kept the friendship alive—stupid memes at two in the morning, fantasy football trash talk, the occasional deep conversation at midnight when one of us couldn't sleep.

All three of our birthdays fell within the first couple of weeks of March. For years, we'd talked about planning a joint trip for our fortieth birthdays—some epic celebration to mark four decades of survival. But busy kid schedules, conflicting work obligations, and wildly different ideas about what constituted a dream vacation had kept it firmly in the realm of someday.

Then someone—I think it was Trey—had a genius idea.

We created a new group message that included our wives.

The shot callers. The ones who actually made decisions in our households.

Valerie and I had fallen in love with Costa Rica over the years—zip-lining through cloud forests, surfing in Tamarindo, hiking to waterfalls that felt like something out of a movie. We were eager to share that adventure, to guide our friends through the kind of vacation that left you sore, sunburned, and completely alive. But the other two couples had different ideas. They wanted relaxation. Beaches. All-inclusive resorts where someone brought you drinks with little umbrellas. The kind of vacation where the hardest decision was whether to read your book by the pool or by the ocean.

Time was running out. Our birthdays were approaching. Valerie and I looked at each other across the kitchen table and made the call.

We conceded. Caribbean it was.

After all, the destination didn't matter nearly as much as the company. Getting everyone together—that was the whole point.

The Marlers had visited Turks and Caicos before and wouldn't shut up about it. Best restaurants they'd ever been to. Clearest water you could imagine. You could see fish swimming thirty feet away. The Dyers were immediately sold. Within an hour, someone had found the perfect place—a beachfront Airbnb with enough bedrooms for everyone, right on the sand, with a view that looked photoshopped.

The group message exploded with enthusiasm.

Book it!

The replies came in rapid-fire succession. Everyone typing at once. Thumbs-up emojis. Celebration GIFs.

And just like that, a trip we'd talked about for years was suddenly real. Dates on a calendar. Money down. Plane tickets to book.

We were going to Turks and Caicos.

None of us had any idea what we were walking into.

APRIL 7TH

3:15 a.m.

My hand slapped blindly across the nightstand, searching for my phone. The alarm chime—that sound I'd grown to despise over years of early mornings—didn't grate on me today. Today was different.

Today was vacation.

Valerie and I moved like we were on fast-forward, brushing teeth with one hand while pulling on clothes with the other—outfits we'd laid out the night before like careful planning could save us from our perpetual lateness. We needed to be at the airport in forty-five minutes.

"Hey, babe, we need to be pulling out of here in six minutes."

I counted down the minutes like a countdown clock while loading luggage into the car. Valerie was notorious for taking every second she was given to get ready. With a wife that beautiful, helping her manage time was safer than complaining about it.

With the car loaded and both our coffee mugs full—mine black and hot as the sun, hers with two ice cubes to cool it down just enough—I started the engine. A subtle nudge. It worked. She came hustling out the door, makeup bag clutched in one hand, purse swinging from the other.

"You look great, babe."

I patted her thigh as she slid into the passenger seat and threw the car in reverse.

I was halfway down the driveway when Val stopped digging through her makeup bag and looked at me with that expression I'd learned to recognize over thirteen years of marriage. The one that meant I wasn't going to like what came next.

"Did you think my bag was over the fifty-pound weight limit?"

"I think it's fine, babe."

"I know I overpacked. I'm worried it's over the limit."

"If it is, I'll just pay the fee. We're running behind. We need to get to the airport."

She turned in her seat, eyes pleading.

"If you pull back up to the house, I'll run in real fast and grab that duffel bag. I don't have a carry-on and I'd like to have a change of clothes in case something happens to our luggage. Please?"

I smiled and put the car back in drive. I couldn't tell her no. She knew it. I knew it. This was our dance.

When we pulled back up to the house, Valerie darted out like she was running a hundred-yard dash, disappeared through the front door, and emerged thirty seconds later with a canvas duffel bag. She slid back into the car and kissed me on the cheek.

"Thank you."

I smiled back. "Can we start this vacation now?"

"Yes! Go! What are you waiting on?"

She was grinning now, that mischievous smile that had gotten me in trouble over the years.

Disregarding most traffic signs and at least two stop lights that were technically still yellow, we pulled up to Will Rogers Airport at 4:35 a.m. The parking garage was nearly empty—just a handful of cars scattered across levels designed to hold thousands. Valerie immediately started picking through her suitcase, rearranging outfits and swimsuits, playing Tetris with clothes and toiletries.

"Do you want me to throw a pair of swim trunks in here for you?"

"I'm willing to risk it, babe. We need to go."

She zipped up the duffel and handed me both bags. I slung them over my shoulder, and we hustled toward the terminal, our footsteps echoing in the concrete structure.

The terminal was quiet at this hour—fluorescent lights humming overhead, a janitor pushing a mop across already-clean floors, the smell of burnt coffee wafting from a Starbucks kiosk that wasn't open yet. We made our way to the Delta check-in kiosks when we heard a familiar southern drawl cut through the silence.

"Hey there, Watsons!"

Amy's voice carried across the terminal like she was calling hogs. Tanner trailed behind her, weighed down with luggage like a pack mule, his expression somewhere between exhausted and amused.

"If it ain't the pride of Pampa, Texas!"

I hollered back as she trotted over to hug us. Amy had that West Texas energy that never quit—up at 3:00 in the morning and acting like she'd just had three cups of coffee and won the lottery.

We did our best to catch up on the past several years while printing boarding passes, checking luggage, and navigating our way through the nearly empty terminal. One perk of flying out at the crack of dawn—security was a ghost town. No lines. No waiting. Just sleepy TSA agents who looked like they'd rather be anywhere else.

I bounced on one leg, then the other, struggling to pull off my cowboy boots while simultaneously trying not to face-plant onto the dirty airport floor. Tanner couldn't resist.

"Watson, you might be the only guy on this planet who travels to a Caribbean island dressed like you're going to a rodeo."

Valerie passed by me, slipping off her sandals with the grace I clearly lacked.

"Aww, I love my handsome cowboy."

She placed the duffel bag on the conveyor belt with a smile.

With my boots and belt finally in the bin, I looked up at the TSA agent and pointed at my cowboy hat—a silent question about whether I'd need to send it through the scanner too. He shook his head and gave me a thumbs-up. OKC had enough cowboys flying through that they knew better than to mangle a good Stetson in an X-ray scanner.

Tanner's harassment continued as I hopped around trying to put my boots back on without falling over. I just gave him a big smile and settled my hat back on my head. Truth be told, I'd missed this. The jesting. The easy rhythm of old friends.

We grabbed our bags from the belt, nodded our thanks to the TSA agents, and made our way to the gate. The girls immediately pulled out their phones, scrolling through photos of their kids, swapping stories about volleyball games and dance recitals. Tanner and I settled into our familiar routine: making fun of Trey.

"What's the over-under that Trey actually shows up to the island on time?"

"Are we sure he even knows we're going on vacation?"

"Crap! You didn't call to remind him?"

"I knew I should have gotten the number of the driver picking us up!"

Despite Trey having built a small empire in the medical imaging space—offices across multiple states, enough money to retire tomorrow if he wanted—we never let him forget we knew a different version. The college, Trey. The guy who once walked all the way home from the bar before realizing he only had one shoe on. The guy who showed up two hours late to everything but somehow still made it worth the wait.

His success made it clear he'd outgrown those days. But we took pride in being able to tease each other about our past lives. It was an homage to how long we'd stayed friends. How many versions of ourselves we'd survived together.

Our plane touched down in Turks and Caicos at 12:45 p.m. The cabin door opened, and Caribbean heat rushed in like opening an oven—thick, humid, carrying the smell of salt and jet fuel and vacation.

After we filed down the airstairs, Valerie stopped and dug her phone from her purse. She held it up, leaned into me and cheered, "We made it!" as she snapped a selfie.

Much to our surprise, Trey and Jill were waiting at the gate. After hugs and the obligatory 'you look great' and 'how was your flight?' we made our way through customs. The line moved slowly—tourists from a dozen flights shuffling forward, passports clutched in sweaty hands. One by one, each couple got their passports stamped. The officer barely looked at us. Stamp. Next. Stamp. Next.

When we grabbed our luggage off the carousel, I looked up and saw the airport exit only twenty yards ahead. No additional screening. No bag inspection. Just glass doors leading to the outside world.

I turned to Trey.

"Is that it? They don't scan bags upon entry here?"

He shrugged, already halfway to the exit.

"It's the Caribbean, Watson! Everyone's worry-free here, buddy!"

I laughed and followed everyone toward the doors. Worry-free sounded pretty good.

The exit doors parted, and we were hit with sensory overload. Whistles. Shouting. Car horns blaring. Taxi drivers competing for tourists like street vendors hawking watches. The heat was oppressive—not just hot, but thick, wrapping around us like a wet towel. We weaved through the chaos, searching for the back of the pickup line.

"Trey, Reuben did confirm the pickup time with you, didn't he?"

Jill's question hung in the air. Trey shrugged with the casual confidence of someone who absolutely had not confirmed anything.

"He just liked the message when I sent him the flight info. He'll be here."

Trey looked at Tanner and me with a big grin—the kind that said he knew exactly what we were thinking and was enjoying every second of our doubt.

"I don't want to mislead you guys. We might not be riding in style, but my boy Reuben is always on time. At least he is when you actually give him a time."

We knew he was just egging us on. Classic Trey.

A few minutes later, a black Chevy Suburban came rattling down the road—not driving so much as announcing its presence. The horn started blaring. A hand popped out the window, waving like it was attached to a windmill. The Suburban crossed lanes, nudging its way partially into the taxi line. Other horns erupted in protest. The Suburban came to a sudden halt, blocking two lanes of traffic without apology.

Reuben slid out of the driver's seat and waddled over to us, his smile so big and genuine it was impossible not to smile back.

"Welcome to the beautiful Turks and Caicos Islands!"

He hugged Jill just as another taxi driver grew impatient and laid on his horn. Reuben didn't flinch. Me, Tanner, and Trey all moved to help him load the bags—his hobbled stride told a different story than the smile he wore, and we couldn't just stand there watching him haul our luggage.

He swatted our hands away with a chuckle.

"Please allow me. I am much more experienced in this game of Tetris."

True to his word, he had everything loaded in half the time it would have taken us, bags stacked and wedged with the precision of someone who'd done this a thousand times. Once we were all crammed in—knees pressed against seats, someone's elbow in someone else's ribs—Reuben beeped the horn, waved cheerfully at the angry drivers behind us, and pulled away. Traffic flowed again. It was clear this wasn't his first time making that sort of entrance.

We rolled down the windows. Reggae music poured from the speakers—Bob Marley, maybe, or someone who sounded enough like him that it didn't matter. The warm air whipped through the car, carrying the smell of ocean and flowers and something frying from a roadside stand. It transported all of us back to younger versions of ourselves. College road trips.

Spring breaks. That feeling of infinite possibility that seems to evaporate somewhere around thirty when mortgages and kids and responsibilities pile up.

This was what we'd been chasing. Not an escape, exactly. More like pressing pause on the jobs, schedules, and carpool lines back home. A chance to flip back to the chapter of our lives we'd all left bookmarked.

It all seemed innocent enough.

We figured we'd press play on our real lives again in five days.

We had no idea how wrong we were.

APRIL 12TH

Grains of sand scratched against my sunburned skin as I stretched and yawned, the sheets feeling like sandpaper. A reminder that sunblock—like most responsibilities—had slipped away over the past several days. I panned the room, blinking sleep from my eyes, trying to orient myself in the morning light filtering through the curtains.

Was it already time to go home?

The empty suitcases on the floor said yes. Five days' worth of clothes scattered everywhere—swim trunks draped over chairs, sundresses hanging from doorknobs, flip-flops kicked into corners—all of it screaming that paradise was over.

I crawled out of bed and made my way downstairs to start a pot of coffee. The sputter and hiss of the machine coaxed Valerie and the Dyers out of their rooms. We drifted outside to the covered patio—me hiding from the sun like a vampire, nursing my hoarse voice with hot coffee while we recounted the trip. The best meals. The funniest moments. That one night that got a little too wild.

We were bummed the Marlers had missed the last night. Some work emergency in Florida had forced them to cut their trip short and fly back to the States a day early. The group felt incomplete without them.

Valerie finished her coffee and set down the mug.

"What time is Reuben picking us up again?"

"Nine-thirty."

Tanner stood up from his chair, the universal signal that playtime was over. We had just under an hour to pack up and start the trek back to reality.

Right at 9:30, Reuben's knock echoed through the Airbnb. We were mostly packed but still scrambling to straighten up—wiping down counters, checking under beds for forgotten socks, trying to leave the place better than we'd found it. The cabinets and refrigerator were still stocked with sundries we'd accumulated over the week. Unopened bags of chips. Half cases of water. Condiments we'd bought and never used.

We offered it all to Reuben, who accepted with his usual gracious smile.

Once we were loaded up—bags crammed into every available inch of the Suburban—Reuben drove us to what he promised was the best brunch spot on the island. A local place, he said. Not the tourist traps. He dropped us off at the entrance and told us he'd take the groceries home and be back around 11:30.

Everyone at the restaurant seemed to be operating on island time—which is to say, not operating at all. We stood next to a Please Wait to Be Seated sign for twenty minutes, staring at empty tables throughout the restaurant, watching servers walk past us like we were invisible. When someone finally deigned to seat us, it took another fifteen minutes for anyone to take our drink order.

"Has it been like this all week, and we were just too distracted by each other's company to notice?"

I asked the table.

"Maybe. I don't think I've been paying attention until now. But these people are flat-out ignoring us."

Tanner's frustration was starting to show.

When the food finally arrived—lukewarm and clearly sitting under a heat lamp for who knows how long—we asked for the check immediately. We didn't want Reuben waiting on us. The check took another twenty minutes. By the time we paid and rushed out to the parking lot, we all felt terrible.

But Reuben just shrugged it off when we apologized.

"Everyone here is on island time."

His smile never wavered.

We pulled up to the airport right at noon. Lines of travelers spilled out into the streets—a chaotic mass of sunburned tourists dragging overstuffed suitcases, kids melting down in the heat, couples bickering about who forgot to print the boarding passes.

"Uh, guys... we might not make our flight."

Tanner's voice carried a note of panic as the car came to a stop.

"If you have the Sky Pass, then you should be just fine."

Reuben tried to offer some assurance. The Sky Pass—an upgrade we'd all purchased when booking the trip—was supposed to let us skip to the front of the security line—a VIP fast track. Worth every penny, the Marlers had said when they convinced us to buy it.

We quickly grabbed our luggage and went searching for the end of the line. The problem was, it wasn't really a line anymore. More like an angry mob of irritated travelers, all jockeying for position, no one was sure where to stand or what was happening. We joined what we thought was a line and stood there for thirty minutes without making any progress. Not a single step forward.

I ducked through the crowd to see if I could make sense of the chaos. Near the front, I overheard an airport attendant tell a frazzled traveler:

"If you're on the 1:30 Delta flight, you can go over to this line."

She pointed to a roped-off area.

I hurried back to the group.

"Follow me."

We wove through the crowd with our luggage, wheels catching on other people's bags, elbows bumping shoulders. People started shouting. We couldn't tell if they were shouting at us or the airport officials, but we didn't have time to find out or apologize. Our flight was boarding in less than an hour.

With bags checked and boarding passes clutched in sweaty hands, we made our way back through the crowd to the Sky Pass section. They gave us each a pink wristband—our golden ticket—and escorted us to security.

You could feel the people in the regular line glaring at us as we walked to the front. The resentment was palpable—we were cutting, skipping ahead, playing by different rules. They handed each of us a bin.

"Have a nice trip."

Then they walked off, leaving us to face the hostile crowd.

The people behind us made their annoyance crystal clear. They began pushing in front of us, placing their bins on the conveyor belt to block us from putting ours down. Our attempts to avoid further upsetting the mob caused us all to get separated in the chaos.

Somehow, I ended up being the first one through security.

I stepped through the metal detector. No beep. Grabbed my bin from the other side. Started pulling my boots back on, trying not to tip over while standing on one foot.

The terminal beyond security was packed—a sea of tourists and families and business travelers, all moving in different directions. Too many people. Too much noise. I hate crowds. Always have. That feeling of bodies pressing in from all sides, the inability to find space to breathe.

I spotted a small duty-free shop just beyond the security checkpoint and ducked inside to escape the chaos. To catch my breath. Despite the noxious combination of perfumes—competing scents battling for dominance—being out of the crowd for even a moment allowed my blood pressure to drop.

I got distracted browsing overpriced, gaudy jewelry displayed under glass when I realized the others should have made it through by now.

I looked through the shop's glass front and saw Valerie. She'd made it past the metal detectors but was standing off to the side, waiting. Something was wrong.

I exited the shop.

"What's going on?"

"I don't know. They're saying they need to rescan the duffel bag."

Her voice carried an edge of worry.

"Isn't that where you put your makeup kit? I bet there's a liquid or something in there."

We stood there watching as the TCI airport security officer ran the bag through the scanner again. And again. The belt moving forward, the bag disappearing into the machine, emerging on the other side. Repeat. Each pass taking longer than the last.

By this point, the Dyers had made it to the gate and walked back to check on us. We all started teasing Valerie, trying to lighten the mood.

What are they going to find in there? Something nefarious? Something embarrassing?

Valerie rolled her eyes, but I could see her hands fidgeting with the strap of her purse—nervous energy.

The security officer began pulling items from the bag one by one, running each piece through the scanner individually. Makeup containers. Clothes. Toiletries. One item at a time. Methodical. Thorough.

Then they ran the empty bag through the scanner.

"Dang, Val! They're really looking for something."

Tanner's voice carried a note of disbelief.

A female agent brought the bag over and set it on a table in front of us. She pulled at the zippers. Shook the bag. I was confused—what could she possibly be looking for in an empty bag?

Then she reached inside and tugged on something I'd never noticed before—the zipper of the lining.

It looked like the teeth had separated, creating a small hole. I hadn't even known the lining zipped out. She kept pulling until the zipper finally broke free and unzipped completely.

Her hand disappeared between the lining and the outer shell of the bag. Felt around.

I watched her facial expression change.

Her eyes widened slightly. Her lips pressed together. She snatched something from inside, turned quickly, and walked over to the other security officers huddled near the X-ray machine.

Val turned to me.

"What was that?"

"I have no idea. I didn't get a good look at it."

The agent showed the package discreetly to another customs officer standing a few feet away. A quick flash. A nod. Then she walked back over to where Valerie and I stood.

She held it up.

Four rounds of 6.5 Creedmoor ammunition in a clear package.

The world tilted slightly.

I recognized the packaging immediately—the small store back home where I bought hunting ammo. But I couldn't make sense of how or why it was in that bag. The hunting trip to Tanner's ranch last fall. I used that bag to carry my clothes. I always carry my ammo in my rifle case. Did I inadvertently throw the rounds in there when packing to leave? How did TSA not see them when they scanned the bag in Oklahoma City? My mind searched for the answers before Val or the security officer asked a single question.

Val turned to me, her voice rising with panic.

"Ryan, what is that?!"

"Babe, I think that's my hunting ammo."

The words came out flat, matter-of-fact, as if I were identifying a lost set of keys.

"Babe, why in the world is that in the bag??"

Her voice cracked.

"I don't know. They shouldn't be in there. I only use that bag to carry clothes, NOT to carry ammo. Maybe from the hunting trip I took to Tanner's ranch in the fall?"

I looked back at the security officer, trying to inject confidence I didn't feel into my voice.

"I'm so sorry. That's my mistake. I didn't know those were in there. You can just toss them in the trash."

I'd heard stories from hunting buddies back home—guys who'd accidentally left loose ammo in their carry-ons. They all got the same treatment: a stern talking-to, maybe a finger wag, and the rounds went in the trash. No big deal. Happens all the time.

So, I wasn't overly concerned. Not yet. I tried to convince Valerie she shouldn't be either.

A different security officer approached—older, more official-looking.

"Anyone caught with ammunition in our country must speak with the police. But don't worry about it. It happens often."

His tone was casual, almost bored. Valerie started to relax slightly. I felt my shoulders drop an inch.

As we stood there waiting, I noticed something that made my stomach turn. The security officer who'd discovered the ammunition walked over to the X-ray screen, held up the package of rounds, and took a selfie. Smiled for the camera like she'd just caught a trophy fish.

That wasn't normal. That wasn't good.

Twenty minutes crawled by. We stood there awkwardly next to the security line, tourists flowing past us, everyone else moving toward their gates while we remained frozen in place. Waiting.

Then a guy in a polo shirt and jeans walked over. Plain clothes. No uniform. He signaled to the customs agent, who nodded back, confirming we were the ones in question.

He took my passport and boarding pass from my hand. Looked down at the flight information. Then looked up at me with an expression that was almost apologetic.

"You're not getting on that flight."

The words were delivered matter-of-factly, like he was telling me the restaurant was out of the daily special.

It was the first time I lost confidence that this was going to be just a verbal reprimand.

"Gather the duffel bag. Both of you follow me out of the airport."

Val turned to Tanner and Amy, trying to inject some levity into the situation.

"Welcome to traveling with the Watsons."

I could see the concern on their faces. They were torn—wanting to stay, wanting to help, but also needing to catch their flight.

"Don't worry about us. We'll be on the next flight out."

I tried to sound confident. Casual. Like this was a minor inconvenience. But my voice betrayed me—just a little too tight, a little too forced.

"You guys need to get on that flight. Get back to your kids."

They nodded reluctantly and disappeared toward their gate.

Valerie and I were escorted outside the airport into the afternoon heat. The sun hammered down on the pavement. We stood on the curb, sweat already beginning to bead on my forehead.

A silver, beat-up old Nissan SUV pulled up next to us. Two people in street clothes climbed out—a man and a woman, both with the casual appearance of locals, not law enforcement.

They started questioning us. Where had we stayed? How long had we been on the island? Did either of us have a license to possess ammunition in their country?

I tried to explain that where we lived in the United States, a license wasn't required to own firearms or ammunition. The Second Amendment. Constitutional rights. But the words sounded hollow, meaningless here.

We still hadn't been shown a badge. Given the sketchy appearance of these supposed officers and their beat-up vehicle, I was extremely skeptical whether they were actually law enforcement or if we were being set up for something worse.

A few moments later, a marked police vehicle arrived. Two uniformed officers got out. The man and woman questioning us immediately broke off the conversation and approached the marked car—a brief exchange. Then the uniformed officers got back in their vehicle and left.

Val looked at me, eyes wide.

"What's going on?"

Before I could answer, the two plainclothes officers returned.

"We're taking you to our station to ask you more questions."

"Where is the station?"

"Not far. Get in the car."

They opened the back door of the small silver SUV. Valerie and I slid in. They tossed the duffel bag in my lap. The interior smelled like old fast food and cigarettes.

Valerie immediately pulled out her phone. Her fingers moved quickly across the screen, typing a message to Tanner and Amy.

We're being taken to a police station by two supposed police officers. This is super sketchy! We're sharing our location with you. Please track us.

We weren't entirely sure if we were being arrested or kidnapped.

I try making conversation with the officers. The male responds in monosyllables. My questions seem to grate on the female officer—her jaw tightens with each one.

"Can I call my mother? She is keeping our children."

"When we get to the station." The male officer's tone leaves no room for negotiation.

Silence fills the car. I try once more. "Are y'all believers?"

The bigger officer shifts uncomfortably. "I'm... spiritual. But not like that."

The female officer doesn't even blink. Just stares through the windshield like I haven't spoken.

"I'd like to pray."

No response.

I reach for Valerie's hand anyway. Her fingers are ice-cold. "God, thank you for always protecting us. Please lay compassion on these officers' hearts. Help them see this was an honest mistake. We had no idea those bullets were in that bag."

The car pulls into a parking lot. A white two-story building looms ahead, a large "Noxus" sign across the front.

This doesn't look like any police station I've ever seen.

Valerie's already texting Tanner and Amy: *"We just parked."*

Amy's response comes instantly—a screenshot of our GPS location. *"This is what your location shows. Are y'all sure this is even a police station?"*

No. We weren't sure of anything anymore.

The male officer appears at my window. I grab the door handle just as he yanks it open.

Snap!

The plastic handle breaks clean off in my hand.

"I... I'm sorry, I didn't mean to—"

He doesn't say a word. Just pulls me aside, tosses the broken handle into the backseat, and grabs the duffel bag. The female officer extracts Valerie from the other side. They march us up the stairs to the second floor.

The building is wrong. All wrong. Bare walls. Empty offices. The hollow echo of our footsteps.

A woman in office attire approaches, her Jamaican accent warm. "Would you like some water?"

We both nod, mute.

The officers lead us into a cramped room—maybe eight by ten feet—containing two chairs and a desk. "Sit."

We sit.

The Jamaican woman returns with two bottles of water. Something in her eyes softens as she looks at us. "I think you guys should be okay."

The door closes behind her.

"Babe, I'm freaking out." Valerie's voice cracks.

I force confidence into my voice. "We're going to be okay. God's looking after us."

The door opens. Both officers enter, each clutching a notebook. They move stiffly, mechanically—like actors who've over-rehearsed their lines.

"I'm Sergeant Charles." The male officer clears his throat. "This is Officer Markland."

"You're under arrest," Markland says flatly. "Suspicion of possession of ammunition."

The questions come rapid-fire. Why did we come to Turks and Caicos? How long were we here? Where did we stay? Who traveled with us? Were we involved in any crimes?

I explain everything. My fortieth birthday. Two other couples. An Airbnb on Turtle Tail—though I can't remember the exact address.

"Who possessed the bag?" Charles asks.

"It's mine. But Valerie put some items in it so we had room for wine bottles."

Markland leans forward. "If it's *your* bag, why is your wife's makeup and clothing in it?"

The question is so absurd that I almost laugh. What married couple doesn't share luggage space? I try explaining again, but her expression hardens. I'm not giving her the answer she wants.

"Are you licensed to possess firearms or ammunition in Turks and Caicos?"

"No. I've never been to your island before. I didn't intend to bring any ammunition."

"Do you have a license for the ammunition in the United States?"

"My state doesn't require a license. Our right to own firearms and ammunition is protected by the Constitution."

Her lip curls slightly, disgusted that such a thing could exist.

Sergeant Charles studies me. "With what reason did you own these bullets?"

"I'm a hunter. I think the last time I used that bag was on a hunting trip in Texas."

"What do you hunt?"

"Different animals. Those bullets are for deer."

Two hours blur past. Questions circle back on themselves. I ask if I can call my mother—our kids are expecting us home.

Charles straightens and grins. "You two don't get it. You're under arrest for possession of ammunition. You're not going home."

The words hang in the air.

"You're going to prison for twelve years."

The words rob every ounce of oxygen from my lungs.

My body turns numb.

Sounds instantly muted.

My eyes begin to blur.

It has to be an intimidation tactic. Some kind of scare tactic to make us compliant.

Valerie starts sobbing.

"We can't go to prison," she pleads. "We have to get back to our babies."

"This was a terrible accident," I say, heat rising in my voice. "You're upsetting my wife with these threats."

Markland's expression doesn't change. "This is not a threat. It's our law. Possession of firearms or ammunition carries a mandatory minimum of twelve years. Both of you are going to prison. Tonight."

The room tilts.

This just got real.

Valerie weeps harder. Charles leans in. "How did you travel to our country and not know our laws?"

"Because it was an accident! I had no idea the ammunition was in the bag. I was packing swimsuits and flip-flops. Why would I research ammunition laws for a beach vacation?"

"Your State Department issued warnings on their website," Charles counters. "Americans are warned not to bring firearms into our country."

The State Department. The Embassy. In every movie I've ever seen, Americans in trouble abroad call the Embassy first.

"Can I please call the Embassy? Let them know we're in trouble?"

Charles smirks. "They already know. They know exactly where you sit and why you're sitting here."

"How?"

"You're American. We always have to notify them."

Valerie wipes her face, trying to steady her breathing. "We've never been in trouble before. Never been to jail. I'm scared." Her voice drops to a whisper. "What is it like? Will I be cold?"

The question shatters something inside me. I'm her protector. I vowed to protect her at all costs. And I've failed.

"Nope."

Both officers snap to attention.

I sit up straight, my demeanor shifting. The meek tourist evaporates. "My wife is not going to jail. I don't care what has to happen here today, but my wife is NOT going to jail."

They exchange glances. Whisper. Charles motions toward the door— they need to talk privately.

The moment they leave, I pull Valerie close and kiss her head. "We're going to be okay. We're in God's hands."

We both grab our phones, typing frantically. I text the group chat with Tanner, Amy, Trey, and Jill: *"Situation just got serious. We're being arrested. We need an attorney."*

Trey responds immediately: *"I'll contact Reuben about finding one."*

Valerie looks up. "I'm texting my principal. She's offering to contact Senator Mullins and Governor Stitt."

I nod, not taking my eyes off my phone.

Trey sends a screenshot of an attorney. *"Reuben recommended him. I'll call and pay the retainer if you want."*

I type: *"Yes, please."*

The door opens.

Sergeant Charles perches on the edge of the desk. "I'm going to do my one good deed for the day. I'm offering you police bail."

Valerie and I exchange blank looks.

"What does that mean?" Valerie asks.

He explains: police bail is for people arrested but not yet charged. Since we're Americans—flight risks—we'll have to surrender our passports. Plus, we'll need to provide "surety" instead of cash bail.

"Surety?" We ask in unison. "What's surety?"

"A local Turk Islander puts up an asset—a car, house, business—equivalent to the bail amount. Reduces the likelihood you'll flee."

"How are tourists supposed to find a local willing to do that? We've been here four and a half days."

He shrugs, studying his shoes.

"We don't even know how much bail will be."

Charles looks at the ceiling, sighs. "Your bail will be set forrrr... five thousand dollars. Each. Ten thousand total."

He's clearly making this up as he goes.

"Can I just write a check?"

He shakes his head, chewing his lip.

So much for hoping this was about a bribe.

"How long do we have to find someone?"

He glances at his watch. "I've got something in about two hours. So we either get you to jail or finish the bail paperwork."

"Two hours. To find a local willing to put up over ten thousand dollars in assets. From this room?"

He raises his eyebrows—"good luck"—and leaves.

I call Trey immediately.

"Hey, man. The attorney's paid and on his way."

"Thanks. But now they're saying we need a local to put up ten thousand in assets for bail, or we're both going to jail tonight."

"A "local"?"

"Yes. A 'respected Turk Islander.'"

"Let me call Reuben."

"You think he'd do that?"

"Ryan, he's the only local any of us know. I'm calling him now."

The line goes dead.

I turn to Valerie. "Trey's calling Reuben. Our attorney's coming."

"You want to pray?"

She puts her head on my shoulder.

"Heavenly Father, thank you. Thank you for being with us in this room and going before us in this situation. You're sovereign. You're working in this. Please place compassion in Reuben's heart."

I don't trust that they called the Embassy. I search for the Turks and Caicos Embassy contact information. Turns out it closed—moved to Nassau, Bahamas. I call that number.

A recording answers. "You've reached us after hours."

After hours? I check the time: 3:13 p.m.

The recording continues: "Hours of operation are Monday through Thursday, 9 a.m. to 5 p.m., and Friday, 10 a.m. to 3 p.m."

Even the U.S. Embassy runs on island time.

The door opens. Charles and Markland return.

"Have you found anyone?"

"We haven't heard back from the only local we know."

"What happens if we can't find someone?" Valerie's voice trembles.

"Then we take you both to jail."

Valerie's composure breaks. "We have a seven- and nine-year-old waiting for us. They can't grow up without a mommy and daddy."

Markland walks out without a word.

Charles won't meet my eyes. He clicks his tongue, shakes his head. "It's all really sad, but..." Another shrug. Then he leaves, too.

My phone vibrates.

Trey: "*Reuben said yes! He's on his way.*"

"Thank you, Lord!" I show Valerie the screen.

"See, babe? God's watching after us."

Charles returns moments later. We tell him Reuben's coming.

"There will be stipulations. Including surrendering your passports."

"I'd like to wait for our attorney before agreeing to anything."

"Attorney?" Charles looks annoyed. "You're not even supposed to have phones in the interrogation room. But you Americans think you're above everyone's rules."

He left us alone to find surety, but now he's angry we used our phones?

"Who did you retain?"

I check my messages. "Nashwood Forbes?"

He sighs, shakes his head, and walks out.

Maybe his annoyance means our attorney is sharp.

Ten minutes later, footsteps approach. Casual conversation filters down the hallway.

Charles opens the door. "This is Nash Forbes."

Nash enters, shaking our hands. The first thing I notice: his pinky fingernails, grown out on both hands.

Something about him feels... off.

He gives us a brief overview of the court system in TCI, then leans back. "This is going to be pricey. Do you have access to money?"

"How much?"

"Didn't someone already pay your retainer?"

"Yes, but that's just initial. This goes all the way to the Supreme Court. Depending on my time, it could cost twenty, thirty, maybe fifty thousand. Do you have that kind of money?"

I thought the police were looking for a bribe. Now our own attorney is shaking us down.

"I don't have that cash on me, but I could arrange a wire."

I just want out of this building. I need to call our family.

Nash says he's already spoken with Reuben, who's agreed to put up his car as surety.

Fifteen minutes later, Charles returns with bail paperwork. The stip-ulations: surrender passports, provide our address, maintain contact with Reuben. Return Monday, April 15th, for a recorded interrogation.

"Should we sign?" I ask Nash.

"It's your best option."

We sign.

Reuben's distinctive laugh echoes down the hall. Markland walks him in.

Valerie jumps up and hugs him. I do the same.

"Thank you."

Reuben notices Valerie's tears. "Listen, you're going to be okay. Think of this as an extended vacation."

An extended vacation. How am I supposed to do that?

Thirty more minutes of paperwork. Copies of Reuben's car title. While they work, I search for hotel rooms on my phone. I find one at Ocean Club East—I can book it with credit card points.

Charles returns. "You're free to go."

I grab our luggage. We follow Reuben and Nash to the parking lot.

Nash says he'll be in touch. Reuben loads our bags in his car.

In the backseat, I hold Valerie. She's still in shock, repeating to Reuben that we're not bad people, this was just an oversight.

Reuben tries to reassure us. Suggests we enjoy the beaches this week-end.

"Reuben, I appreciate that. But our vacation officially ended. Our nightmare has begun."

We pull up to Ocean Club East. The bellman opens our door, expecting excited vacationers.

Instead: Valerie's tear-stained face. My blank expression.

Reuben shoos the bellman away and helps us unload.

"Call if you need anything."

We walk into the lobby. Everyone seems to be staring.

"Do they know?" Valerie whispers.

"There's no way."

At the check-in counter, I provide my license and credit card.

"May I see your passport?"

"I don't have it on me."

She frowns. "Oh. Let me talk to my manager."

She disappears. Valerie shoots me a look: *They know.*

We stand there. Forever.

The woman returns. "Would you like to have a seat? Some water? My manager just needs to make copies of your license."

They know. I'm sure of it.

We sit on the couch, avoiding eye contact with happy vacationers.

Finally: "Sir?"

She hands me my ID and the room keys.

It feels like a small victory.

We reach our room. I lock the deadbolt. Latch the safety chain.

Valerie and I move through the space like fugitives, closing every blind, drawing every curtain.

We sit on the edge of the couch in the darkened room.

I hold her. "I'm sorry. I don't know why we're in this, but God knows. He has a plan."

Our phones had died during the chaos. We dig out chargers, plug them in.

A few minutes of silence.

Then our phones power on. A flurry of buzzing and dinging.

We jump up, responding to concerned messages. Our network of friends and family has been calling local politicians, anyone with connections. Others have been scouring the internet for information on similar cases.

My mom calls. She's contacted someone at the Embassy. We need to print and sign a form for them to assist us.

Another call beeps in. "Mom, I love you. I'll call back."

I switch over.

"This is Lane from the U.S. Embassy. I'm calling at your mother's request."

"Thank you for calling! We need help."

"There have been other Americans in situations involving ammunition. But you're in uncharted waters—TCI recently changed its laws, instituting a twelve-year mandatory minimum prison sentence. There isn't much I can do except provide a list of vetted attorneys. I can't give recommendations, but..." He pauses. "Pay very, very close attention to the first attorney listed."

We hang up.

I sift through messages from friends and family. J.C., from our church's small group, has been sending articles about previous ammunition cases in TCI.

One common denominator: Oliver Smith.

I show Valerie. "I think we need to fire Nash and hire this guy."

An email from Lane arrives. I open the attachment.

At the top of the list: Oliver Smith.

"See? Oliver's our guy. I'm calling him."

"Babe, it's late. Should we wait until tomorrow?"

"The clock's ticking."

I hit call. The phone rings. And rings.

Just as I'm about to hang up: "Hello?"

His voice is soft, groggy. I've woken him.

"Oliver? My name is Ryan Watson. I got your information from the Embassy. My wife and I were arrested today for possession of ammunition at the airport. We need help."

Silence.

"Are you out now?"

"Yes. We're on police bail. Staying at Ocean Club East."

"Can you meet me at my office tomorrow at eleven?"

"Yes. Just tell me where."

He gives me the address.

"Thank you. Sorry for calling so late."

"I'll see you tomorrow."

The line goes dead.

The slightest bit of relief washes over me. This is the guy we need. And he's agreed to work with us.

I call Mom and my stepdad, Terry, back, updating them.

Then Mom asks the question we've been avoiding.

"What do you want me to tell the kids?"

Valerie and I look at each other, tears streaming.

"Tell them storms delayed our flights."

We hate lying to them. But they're nine and seven. It's the best way to protect their little hearts.

After all, we *are* in a storm.

~❖~

We're both numb, and it's late, so we decide to try and get some sleep. As we lie there with our minds racing, I look at Valerie, and the words spill out before I can stop them.

"We have to tell everyone it was my bag. That we only put your things in it to make room for the wine bottles we were bringing back. I will not let you go to prison too."

Valerie's heart is too pure to lie naturally. We need to practice the story so much that she begins to believe it's true. For hours, we lie there rehearsing every detail. I even role-play as an interrogating officer, trying to think of any line of questioning that could possibly trip her up. We go over it again and again until the words feel worn smooth, like stones in a river.

After what feels like an eternity, I feel Valerie's breathing deepen and slow. I look down at her in my arms, confirming she's finally asleep, and I feel like I can have my moment of weakness. I try to remain as still as possible while I cry and plead to God for help. The tears come silently, desperately. "*Please. Please help us. Please protect her. Please get us home to our babies.*"

My prayer is interrupted by the sound of helicopter blades churning in the distance. At first, it's just a faint rhythm, barely distinguishable from the ceiling fan above us. But the beating grows louder and louder, more insistent, until I'm certain they're hovering directly over our hotel. The blinds are occasionally illuminated by a floodlight sweeping the area, casting moving shadows across the darkened room.

Is this God answering my prayer? Is someone coming to rescue us? Or is this the Turks and Caicos police department, coming to rip us out of bed and drag us to jail? My mind spirals through every terrible possibility. Did they change their minds about the bail? Did Nash call them? Did we violate some condition we didn't understand?

I feel like I'm suffocating from the fear and adrenaline coursing through my body. I'm not sure how long I lie there, every muscle tensed, anticipating someone knocking down the door. Minutes? Hours? Time has lost all meaning. At some point, the sound of the helicopter grows faint, the rhythmic beating retreating into the distance until I can no longer discern the helicopter blades from the ceiling fan swirling above us.

But sleep doesn't come. I lie there in the darkness, holding Valerie, listening to her breathe, and wondering what tomorrow will bring.

APRIL 13TH

An hour or two later, I hear men talking in Caribbean accents directly outside our window. I jump up and peer through the blinds, heart hammering. It's just the grounds crew starting their day. The movement wakes Valerie. There's no going back to sleep now anyway. It's time to get ready and figure out how to face this situation.

We have time to kill before meeting Oliver, so we head down to the hotel restaurant near the beach for breakfast. The moment we step into the dining area, I feel exposed. The space is bright and airy, open to the ocean breeze that carries the smell of salt water and sunscreen. Everyone seems to be staring at us—two felons on the run. We find a table, order, and wait in silence.

When the waitress sets our plates in front of us, we both stare at the food. Steam rises from my eggs, the butter melting into golden pools on the toast. My stomach turns.

"I can't eat," Valerie says quietly.

"Me neither."

The sound of waves crashing against the shore, families laughing and playing in the sand, the clink of silverware against plates at nearby tables—sounds that just a week ago we'd dreamed of hearing—now make us nauseated. The waitress returns, noticing our untouched plates, her expression puzzled.

"We're not feeling well," I tell her. "Just a couple of coffees to go."

Just before eleven, Reuben wheels his car behind a modern white building into an empty parking lot. He parks under the only tree providing any shade from the hot Caribbean sun. The temperature inside the car starts climbing immediately. As we sit there, engine ticking as it cools, sweat beginning to prickle on the back of my neck, Reuben questions why we're looking to meet with a different attorney. I try my best to politely explain that we don't have confidence in Nashwood Forbes, carefully leaving out the part about his suspiciously long pinky nails. Reuben tries again to endorse Nash, but I'm barely listening. My attention locks on a car pulling up on the other side of the building.

I glance at the clock in Reuben's dashboard—eleven on the nose.

"I think that's them," I say to Valerie.

We both hop out and shake Reuben's hand. He tells us to call when we're finished, and he'll come pick us up.

Inside Oliver's office, we're greeted by a tall, striking woman with a short, stylish haircut. She introduces herself in a soft Caribbean accent as Kimone Tennent, Oliver's junior attorney. Oliver emerges from behind her and shakes our hands. His grip is firm, businesslike. He's a short man who walks with an air of quiet confidence. I thank him for meeting us, but he doesn't offer much of a response. He turns toward his conference room and tells us to have a seat.

The conference room is cool, almost cold after the heat outside. The air conditioning hums steadily in the background. At first, I think Oliver might be annoyed about the late-night phone call that forced him to work over the weekend. I'll later learn this is just his personality.

Valerie and I spend the first twenty minutes trying to convince him that we're good people—the kind of people who would never fathom or deserve to be in such a situation. Oliver seems to grow impatient and cuts in. "Why did they arrest both of you?"

Valerie jumps in, explaining how we placed her makeup bag and other items in the duffel to accommodate two bottles of wine we didn't want to leave behind.

"But that is your bag and your bullets?" Oliver turns his eyes to me.

"Yes, sir."

"And you told them it was your bag and your bullets?"

"Yes, sir," I confirm, trying to sound confident.

Oliver pulls out the sheet of paper, Sgt. Charles and Markland had given us, then immediately pulls his phone from his pocket and starts dialing. After a friendly greeting—as if he's calling an old buddy from high school—and a couple of minutes of exchanging pleasantries, Oliver's tone shifts.

"Look, friend, I'm working with the husband and wife who were arrested at the airport yesterday. I'm trying to figure out why you arrested the wife."

He pauses, listening. I can tell from his expression he doesn't approve of whatever reasoning he's hearing.

"Look, the husband admitted to the bag and bullets being his. There's no reason to arrest his wife."

He ends the call abruptly.

"You think they'll let Valerie go?" I ask.

He squints one side of his face. "They should, but I can't say for sure. I still don't understand why they arrested her in the first place. Is there something you're not telling me?"

I shake my head. "I mean, she had items in the bag and was standing there when the security officer started searching it, but I admitted the bullets were mine after they were found."

Oliver leans in. "Let me explain how this works. My goal is to get them to let Valerie go home. They'll then arrest you. When you go to jail, we start working on getting you out on bail. Your case will go to the magistrate's court first—this is just a formality because the magistrate's court can't actually hear your case, so they'll deny your bail. We then apply for bail through the Supreme Court. They should approve it, especially if you have a local willing to put up surety for you."

I'm barely following along. Between his soft tone and the ringing in my ears from my nerves being pegged at an all-time high, I can only nod unsurely, eyes wide.

"So... is there any chance they'll just let me go home on Monday with Valerie?"

He cocks his head, seemingly annoyed that I'm hung up ten steps behind his instruction. "No. They're going to charge someone. They take this too seriously—they aren't just going to turn and look the other way."

"So you think I'll go to prison?"

"Yes," Oliver says matter-of-factly. "They recently changed the laws here, making it a mandatory twelve-year prison sentence."

"But I read about your previous cases. Most of those people just paid a fine."

"Those cases were before the law changed. Everything is different now. We don't know how they'll handle these cases. I'm working on another case for a guy from Pennsylvania who's stuck here—his case is almost identical to yours. The new law has some constitutional flaws, which I'm going to argue. Depending on how the judge responds to my arguments in Bryan's case, it will determine how I structure yours. But this is going to be a long process."

"How long of a process are we talking?"

Oliver shrugs. "Months."

"Months? I'm going to be in jail for months before my case is ever heard?"

"No, I'm going to try and get you out on bail."

"If I get bail, can I go home until my case is heard? I have a family waiting for me. I have work."

"Highly doubtful. I've only ever had one client allowed to return to the U.S., and he had cancer. Ultimately, they just didn't want the bad PR associated with an American dying over here."

My mind is reeling. "How would any of this be good PR for the island? They're trying to put people in prison for a simple oversight."

"Look, the government had to do something because there are so many murders on the island. They wanted to take an aggressive stance on firearms offenses to make the island feel safe."

"If their goal was to make the island safer, they should've arrested me on the way *into* the country. They aren't even scanning bags upon entry. I was leaving!"

"I get it," Oliver says, a hint of exasperation in his voice. "Our government is more concerned with sending a message than doing something to actually keep us safe. An American tourist with forgotten ammunition in their bag isn't the cause of violence on this island."

I try my best to stay engaged in the meeting, but my head is spinning from an overwhelming amount of anxiety and anger. I'm caught in a proverbial undertow, quickly being swept out into an endless dark ocean. I'm drifting further and further from the life I knew, the life I built, frantically looking for anything to latch onto to keep my head above water.

The "bad PR" comment Oliver made earlier keeps echoing in my head, getting louder.

"What if we went to the press?" I blurt out, interrupting him mid-sentence.

Oliver stops and looks up at me. "I don't disagree—the world should know the government is handling these cases in a draconian fashion compared to the rest of the world. But for this to legitimately have any kind of impact, we're talking international headlines. Not just some Joe Bob tweeting about it."

Challenge accepted, I think to myself.

Oliver must see the look of panic in my eyes shift to determination. "Look, you have to understand this is more likely to blow up in your face and cause the island to want to retaliate. You must promise you won't do anything until Valerie is off the island. I think there's a really good chance they let her go, and I can't have you guys mess that up by trying to go to the media."

He's right. The most important thing is getting Valerie home to our kids.

Oliver lays out the plan. We'll return to the police station on Monday, per the demands of the police bail. At the interrogation, I'm to agree to go on camera and tell them it was my bag and my bullets. Valerie is to say she has no knowledge of the ammunition—the bag belongs to Ryan, who just put some of her items in the duffel to make room for a bottle of wine in her checked luggage.

The catch: Oliver and Kimone won't be able to attend our interrogations. They'll both be in a murder trial in Grand Turk. Turks and Caicos is a country made up of a chain of small islands, and despite being one of the smallest islands in the chain, Grand Turk hosts the prison as well as the port where all major cruise ships enter.

"Do you feel like you can manage this on your own?" Oliver asks.

"Basically, I have to go get myself thrown in jail. Yeah, I think I can handle that."

My dark humor doesn't appeal to anyone else, especially Valerie.

"It's very important that you only say: 'my bag, my bullets.' Don't get dragged into saying anything else. You seem like sharp people, but it's important you don't get emotional and say too much."

I can tell Valerie is nervous about being in there alone. She's one of the purest, most genuine people I've ever met. I'm concerned that if the interrogating officer starts twisting her words to make her feel like she's not being honest, she might cave and agree with whatever version they're pushing.

Oliver must sense her nerves, too, because he looks at Valerie and says, "I'll do my best to be back in time to be there with you if you need me, but I don't want to delay them too much and risk you winding up in jail."

Valerie nods. "I can do it."

What Oliver lacks in sympathy, he more than makes up for in his deep understanding of this law and his clear ability to network and pull strings. He just dialed up Sgt. Charles and basically demanded that Valerie be released. We need to secure him as our attorney.

"We want to go with you," I say, with Valerie nodding insistently beside me.

"You don't even know what my rate is," Oliver says dismissively.

"There's too much on the line. I'm not going to let money stand in the way."

I realize immediately that I've just lost any bargaining leverage. I'm now at Oliver's mercy in more ways than one.

After a short sidebar between Oliver and Kimone, Oliver returns to the conference room. "For me to represent you, it will be forty-five thousand dollars. If they arrest Valerie and I have to represent you both, I'll need seventy-five thousand."

I knew I'd already laid my cards on the table, but hearing the number still hits like a punch to the gut. My mouth goes dry. It seems like an insane amount of money, but the fact is, I have less than forty-eight hours to figure this out. I have no time to bargain shop, and I need the best attorney who stands a chance of getting us home.

"That's a lot of money, but we'll figure out a way to pay you," I say, my voice trembling. I can feel Valerie's hand find mine under the table, her fingers cold and shaking.

I might be able to get Valerie home to our kids, but will they be able to afford to live while we drain our bank account in legal fees? I haven't even begun to process just how much this vacation is going to cost our family.

"There's one more thing we need to get figured out before Monday," Oliver says. "We need to secure surety for you. Once you're in jail, you'll have to get bail through the Supreme Court. That bail is going to require a larger asset than what Reuben can provide with his car."

I'm irritated to hear this word again. How in the world can a country expect tourists to find TCI locals willing and able to put up assets for complete strangers? They're clearly trying to stack the deck.

Valerie chimes in. "We have some friends back home that know some-one with a property here. Maybe they'd be willing to help?"

It's worth a shot. We dial up this complete stranger to ask that he put up assets for two American criminals abroad on the basis that we have a mutual friendship. The man on the other end of the line is kind—luckily, our friends back home prepped him that we might call. It must be the panic and desperation in our voices, because I can't imagine we persuaded him with any logical explanation. He sounds empathetic and wants to help, but there's an issue: he's not on the island, nor does he have TCI citizenship.

Oliver helps explain what could serve as surety and who's "qualified" to help. The man pauses, then says, "Let me call my buddy Dale. He's a local restaurant owner. I think he'd be willing to help if I asked."

It seems like a long shot, but we need any help we can get. I'm starting to realize I'm about to ask a very long list of people for help.

Before we finish our meeting with Oliver, we receive a text. Dale, the local restaurant owner, is likely willing to help but wants to meet us first. I try to imagine what it would be like to receive that call out of the blue. "Hey, there are two tourists in a heap of legal trouble for illegally possess-ing ammunition in your country. Would you be willing to put up your assets for them to get bail?" I can only imagine how quickly I would've hung up if I'd received that call. I'm not sure what character trait one must possess to even consider such an act—empathy, trust, altruism? Whatever it is, Dale seems to possess a lot of it, and I couldn't be more grateful.

Later that afternoon, I get a text from Trey. It's a screenshot of a message he received from an old fraternity brother of ours, someone I'd lost contact with. The message is extremely cryptic:

"We know someone who might be able to help Ryan out. My parents know a lady down there who goes by 'the Warden.' She's expecting a text from a 405

area code. Once she receives the text, she'll call that number back, but DO NOT mention any names!"

A lady who goes by "the Warden" will only respond to messages from a certain area code, and we can't mention any names. This seems too made-up to be made-up. My curiosity is piqued, and I'm desperate enough that I have to try. The only issue is that neither Valerie nor I has a 405—Oklahoma City—area code. We've had our phone numbers since we lived in Texas, both with 817 area codes.

I call my mother, who has a 405 area code.

"Mom, I know this sounds crazy, but I need you to text someone for me."

"Who?"

"I'm not sure. I just know she goes by 'the Warden.'"

"The warden?"

"Yes. I have no idea who she is, but I received a message from an old friend saying this lady could help us out."

"Like the warden of a prison? Is she the Warden of the TCI prison?"

"Maybe. I don't know. She's just expecting a text from a 405 area code, and you're the only one I could think of off hand."

"What do I say?"

"Just say I'm your son, and we were told she could help us. Tell her I don't have a 405 area code, so you're texting from yours to provide her mine. After she receives it, she's supposed to call you back."

"This sounds like a scam, Ryan."

"It very well could be, but I can't leave any stone unturned. Mom, just text her! Please!"

"Okay, okay. I'll text her now."

I hang up and immediately start to panic. My mom is one of the sharpest people I know, but she can't operate her phone to save her life. Now my life is the one that needs saving, and it could be riding on her answering this phone call.

The day passes with no response from the Warden.

8:30pm

"Babe, my dad and Lori are calling us," Valerie yells from the living room.

Valerie's dad, Chris, and stepmother, Lori, have only been kept apprised via text message thus far. It's time to speak with them on the phone and update them on everything we know. As I head to the living area, I start to feel anxious. My heart is pounding so hard I can feel it in my throat. I can only imagine the disappointment a father would feel toward the man he entrusted to love and protect his daughter, when that person fails on such epic proportions.

I sit down next to Valerie, sheepish. "Hey, guys."

Chris and Lori seem concerned but not necessarily revealing any anger. I let Valerie do most of the talking as I stare at my feet in shame, absently picking at a loose thread on the couch cushion. Hearing her speak of our situation out loud makes everything seem that much more real. I can tell they're trying to find words to give us some sort of peace, but they, too, are overwhelmed with disbelief.

As Valerie finishes detailing everything we know, I start to speak. "I'm so sorry we're in this situation. I know this is my fault. I promise you I'm going to do anything and everything to ensure Valerie makes it home."

Chris takes a breath and clears his throat. "Guys, we need to share something with you." He pauses, and I can hear him shifting the phone. "When we learned of your situation, we sent a text to all our family members here in Texas, asking for their prayers. Your cousin Ash was at a training in a fire station in North Fort Worth when he received the message."

Another pause. I can feel Valerie tense beside me.

"He apparently read the message out loud, and one of the other trainees—someone he didn't even know, just happened to be sitting nearby—heard him." Chris's voice drops, almost reverent. "Ryan, Valerie... it turns out that this trainee, this complete stranger, has a best friend named Michael Grim."

The name hangs in the air.

"Michael Grim was arrested for the exact same thing in Turks and Caicos. He ended up serving six months in prison there." Chris pauses again, letting it sink in. "And he just got out."

Valerie and I look at each other, wide-eyed, mouths open. My skin prickles with goosebumps despite the warmth of the room. This is the same Michael Grim we'd read about in Oliver's previous court cases. The same Michael Grim whose story we'd been desperately searching for online just hours ago.

"Wait," I manage to say. "Out of all the fire stations in North Texas, Ash happened to be at that one? Out of all the people in that training, this guy happened to be sitting close enough to hear? And this guy's best friend is—"

"Michael Grim," Chris confirms. "The one and only."

Valerie grabs my arm, her nails digging in. She mouths to me, "What!?" Her eyes are filling with tears.

Chris continues, his voice thick with emotion now. "Ash got Michael's phone number for us. I actually called him and spoke to him tonight. He's a super nice guy with a ton of knowledge about what you're facing. He wants to help you guys. He specifically asked me to tell you to call him. I really think you should."

I'm still trying to process the impossibility of it all. What are the odds? Millions of people in Texas. Thousands of fire stations. Hundreds of training sessions happening every day. And somehow, someway, the message about our arrest traveled through our family network to land in the ears of the one person connected to the one man who'd been through this exact nightmare. God clearly is at work here.

Chris clears his throat again. This time, when he starts to speak, I can hear the fear creeping into his voice, the reality of what this divine intervention actually means. "I also have to tell you—we spoke about his time in prison. It's hard to hear, but I think you need to hear it. He has a lot of information that could be useful, especially to you, Ryan."

The momentary wonder at this obvious miracle evaporates, replaced by the cold reality it confirms: I'm going to prison.

APRIL 14TH

Valerie and I bounce around in the back seat as Reuben's car putters up the steep, winding road. Each pothole sends a jolt through my spine. We're on our way to meet Dale, the owner of the restaurant, who might just be willing to put up the surety needed for my bail. The restaurant sits on top of a steep hill overlooking the airport—not only convenient for Dale, but perfect timing and location for us. My parents left our kids with Valerie's father, Chris, and stepmom Lori, and are flying to the island to try and help us, or just be there to support Valerie when I go to jail.

The pothole-riddled parking lot is busy with locals working on the adjacent building. As Reuben pulls to the side of the building, he points to the walkway that leads to the restaurant. He leaves us to have our conversation with Dale in private while he heads to the airport to pick up my parents.

A mix of reggae music and loud conversation grows louder as we make our way down the path. The air smells like grilled fish and cigarette smoke. By the time we step through the entrance of the patio, every eye in the restaurant is staring directly at us. The music and conversation seem to halt mid-beat.

Are they staring because we're two white tourists stumbling into a locals' establishment? Or because word has gotten out about the two worst international arms dealers being on the island? Either way, we're sticking out like a sore thumb.

I flinch as a jet engine roars overhead, the plane taking off from the runway just a few hundred yards below the restaurant. The sound is deafening, rattling the glasses on the bar. At this point, we might as well be wearing t-shirts that say "scared out-of-place tourists."

The locals snicker and turn back to their beers.

We walk up to the bar and tell the young lady behind it that we're here to meet Dale. She looks puzzled that we're asking for the owner by name, cocks her head, and says, "He isn't here yet."

We grab stools and order a couple of waters while we wait. The longer we sit, the more curious the locals get. One extremely tough-looking man makes eye contact with us and waves us over. Valerie and I exchange glances—do we go?—then make our way over and sit next to him.

He offers to buy us food and drinks. Neither of us has eaten since our arrest. Even though eating seems impossible with our stomachs in such knots from anxiety, we finally accept his offer to avoid coming across as rude.

The waitress brings out a plate of their specialty: conch fritters. Which shouldn't be any surprise, considering the island is covered in conch shells, and they've adopted the slimy little mollusk as an essential part of their diet. We do our best to eat what we can in between answering questions from our new curious friend. The fritters are hot and crispy on the outside, chewy on the inside. I force them down.

Despite his drunken state, he can tell we look scared. He says, "I'm not usually a friendly guy, but for some reason, God laid it on my heart to show you some kindness. You seem like good people."

I look over to see Valerie's eyes welling up with tears.

"We're in a bit of trouble," Valerie says, her voice barely above a whisper.

He leans in toward us. "I hope you're believers, because God has a plan for you." He pauses for a minute, tears forming in his own eyes, then leans back in his stool. "I was supposed to be home an hour ago, but God kept me in this stool. He kept me here so I could meet you, kindhearted people. He sent me to remind you—and myself—that He has a plan, so we must believe in Him."

I can feel my anxiety lifting, my shoulders dropping from where they've been hunched near my ears. Not only do I no longer have to fear that we're going to get assaulted or robbed by the local drunkards, but God is also using the most unlikely messenger to assure us that He does have a plan for us.

Not long after, I feel a tap on my shoulder. I turn to see a short, well-dressed local in a bright red polo shirt.

"Dale?" I say as we stand to shake his hand and make a formal introduction.

About that time, another jet engine screams as it approaches the airport below. The noise is overwhelming.

"Follow me so we can talk somewhere quiet," Dale says in a soft tone, as if he's no longer fazed by the deafening sounds of the airport his restaurant overlooks.

We make our way into a locked room on the side of the restaurant. The space is full of slot machines and poker tables, the air thick with the stale cigarette smoke from the previous night. The air conditioner hums in exhaustion, working overtime. The room is freezing cold, the temperature shift jarring after the humid heat outside. He flips the lights on as we sit down. I try my best not to let my teeth chatter from shivering as we speak.

"I just can't thank you enough for meeting us and even considering helping us out," I say.

He nods while tightening his face. It's obvious he hasn't made up his mind whether he should be—or would be—helping us.

I tell him what happened two days ago at the airport. "I never knew those bullets were in that bag," I say, still in disbelief, my voice thick with emotion.

"The island takes its firearms laws very seriously because the island has gotten so dangerous. This seems like an innocent mistake they should have taken into consideration. But then again, some of the police here can't seem to use much reason." Dale pauses before continuing. "I, too, have been charged with a firearms offense."

My attention sharpens.

"A number of years ago, I was in a bar and had words with some other drunk guys, it quickly escalated. Their friends joined in, and the next thing I knew, they had surrounded me. I carried a blade in my back pocket, so I reached back to pull it out. They all drew weapons and told me to get on the ground with my hands on my head." He shakes his head at the memory. "Turns out they were all off-duty police officers. They arrested me and charged me with impersonating possession of a firearm."

I interject. "Wait, they charged you with *impersonating* possession of a firearm? That's not even a thing... is it?"

"It is here. They said the way in which I reached for my blade was acting as if I was going for a firearm."

"Did you go to jail for that?" Valerie asks, leaning forward.

"I did, for a while, until I could get surety."

"What ended up happening? Did you get the charges dropped?" Valerie continues, a note of hope creeping into her voice.

"I did. It took over a year in court." Dale keeps going after a slight pause. "I actually hired Oliver to represent me. He's the best on the island. If there's anyone who can help you out, it's him!"

The endorsement is reassuring, but I'm still hung up on the fact that this nightmare is most definitely going to last longer than I'm willing to accept. I take a deep breath to get my mind back to the task at hand: finding my surety.

"Dale, I wish they would allow us to just pay the bail, but Oliver is quite certain I'll need surety to get out. I'm willing to pay you for putting up surety. How much do you feel is appropriate?"

He twists back and forth in his chair for a bit before saying, "Greg says you guys are good people, and anyone who's friends with Greg is a friend of mine. I think they'll allow me to put up my wife's car or one of my restaurants. We should be able to get it figured out."

Taken aback by his generosity, I start to stammer. "Thank you. Thank you. Thank you! Are you sure we can't pay you? I'd like to show you my appreciation somehow."

Dale shakes his head no.

I stand to shake his hand. Valerie beats me to it and goes in for a hug.

Dale looks at me. "Make sure Oliver tells me when and where to be."

We wrap up the meeting with repeated thank-yous and hugs, then make our way back out to the parking lot. My hands are still shaking—from the cold, from relief, from everything.

In the parking lot, we spot Reuben's black Chevy Suburban idling in a shaded area. Within seconds, the passenger door flies open, and my mom jumps out, sprinting over to us. She hugs us and begins to cry, her shoulders shaking.

I ask her to try her best to hold on to her emotions until we're out of the public eye.

As we make the trek back to the hotel, I ask Mom if she's heard back from the "Warden."

She shakes her head. "Nothing. I've texted her several times and sent her your number. I'm not sure how much I would trust this lady, Ryan."

She's not wrong. I have serious doubts that this person is as important as they're perceived to be, much less that she even truly exists. However, last night I received a screenshot from that old fraternity brother of mine—a message they'd received from this mysterious woman that included details from the arrest record. Details that no one could have known about our arrest, details that wouldn't be accessible without some serious connection. It was enough to lend a strong thread of credibility to this lady.

Mom relentlessly tries to get Valerie and me to order something from the menu of the hotel restaurant. As we reluctantly look through the menu to find something we can choke down on top of stomachs full of anxiety, my phone starts to vibrate.

I look down—a local TCI number.

I jump up and start to jog away from the noise of the restaurant, weaving between tables. I answer the call and hear a woman's voice on the other end, cutting in and out.

This has to be the Warden.

"Hello? Hello? I'm sorry, I don't have great service. Can you give me a second to get somewhere with better reception?" I say as I sprint through the hotel property, past the pool, past startled guests.

The line is cutting in and out so badly that I can't make out the woman's response on the other end.

My desperation causes me to shout, "I'm going to call you right back from our room. Please answer."

I disconnect the line and race back to the room, taking the stairs two at a time. My lungs burn. I unlock the door and throw it open, snatching the phone off the desk at the entrance. With the door still wide open, I dial the number, my fingers trembling as I punch in the digits.

A woman answers.

"This is Brenda Branzeno."

"Brenda, this is Ryan Watson. I apologize, I couldn't hear a thing you were saying."

"It's okay, but I don't have long. I'm getting ready to board a flight."

"My wife and I were arrested on Friday for having ammunition in our bag."

"They arrested you for that? I'm surprised they didn't just confiscate it and send you home."

"No. I wish they did. They're saying they're going to put us in prison for twelve years."

"I doubt they truly send you to prison... at least not both of you. If they do release your wife, she needs to get off the island immediately."

"Why?"

"If I were her, I wouldn't hang around."

My stomach drops. "We have to go in tomorrow for a recorded interrogation."

"Your attorney thinks that's a good idea?"

"I don't really have a choice. I have to take the blame so they don't try to charge Valerie too."

"Well, once they decide not to charge her, she needs to get on a plane and get back to the U.S. before they change their mind. I'll try to keep tabs on you. My plane is boarding. Once I land in the U.S., I'll be utilizing a different number."

"I can take down the number."

"I'll call you. You guys stay safe. Remember, tell your wife to leave the island."

The phone line goes dead.

I stand there, staring at the phone in my hand. This call—which was supposed to help me establish a lifeline and give me peace of mind—seems to do anything but that. Did she even have a grasp of what was going on? Her surprise that we were even arrested makes me doubt she knows much about the island at all. Her insistence on Valerie getting off the island makes it clear she doesn't trust the island.

When I make it back to the table where my parents and Valerie are having dinner, I think they can tell I look even more defeated. My face must be pale.

"Was that the Warden? What did she say?" Mom asks.

"Not much. She just said that if they drop the charges for Valerie tomorrow, she needs to immediately get on a flight back to the U.S."

The table falls silent. Forks rest against plates. The background chatter of the restaurant seems to fade.

It's confirmation that we're dealing with an island that can't be trusted.

APRIL 15TH

We push open the doors to the crowded Chalk Sound police station. The air inside is stale and humid, thick with the smell of sweat. The space is packed with locals—a long line of islanders waiting to file reports with the lone police officer behind a scuffed plexiglass window.

When we finally reach the window to identify ourselves, the officer looks up at us with one finger raised. "Just a minute."

She disappears into a back room for several minutes before reappearing. "The officers in charge of your case are not here. You need to have a seat and wait for them to arrive."

I glance over at the only two plastic chairs, both occupied by locals who still look drunk from the night before. We find a place to lean against the wall and wait.

We stand for hours, listening to locals report traffic accidents. The officer behind the counter charges them thirty dollars cash to write down the details of the incident in a college-ruled notebook. If we had any doubts that we were dealing with a third-world police force, those doubts have now been put to bed.

All morning, the people who come through are locals. Then, after we've been there for a few hours, a tall white guy in his late thirties comes through the line. I catch him repeatedly glancing at us from the corner of his eye. I try my best to avoid any eye contact. I'm embarrassed. Full of shame. Before he leaves, he looks back in my direction once more. I can tell he's tempted to ask what we're doing there, but as I hang my head to avoid eye contact again, he turns and walks out of the building.

I turn to Valerie. "How crazy would it be if that was the guy from Pennsylvania?"

She lets out a dismissive "chuh" to acknowledge my comment, but also to let me know she's not in the right frame of mind to play what-if.

We stand there for so long I seem to forget what I'm waiting for. I'm not sure how impatient one needs to be to get impatient when waiting to go to jail, but I'm clearly that impatient. I'm annoyed. We're on awkward display to all the locals, and Sgt. Charles and Markland are in no hurry to address our matter. I'm ready to get it over with and get Valerie freed from this mess.

My frustration is interrupted by the sound of slamming doors and chains jingling across the floor. The door swings open, and an officer marches a group of prisoners shackled together through the lobby and out the front door. It looks like the first time they've seen the sun in days. They all squint and shield their eyes with their cuffed hands, the metal glinting in the harsh sunlight. They sit on a curb in the parking lot while some of them smoke cigarettes with the officer standing guard.

Mom has seen enough. She starts to break down in tears, coming over to drape herself around me while she cries. We all know that at some point later today, I'm going to be shackled to that chain gang, waiting to be taken for a walk like a dog.

2:50 p.m.

After waiting for nearly five hours, the lady behind the counter looks up at me and motions toward the window with her head. Officer Markland and

Sgt. Charles have finally arrived, walking through the door like they have all the time in the world.

I take a deep breath and tell myself, *Let's get this over with.*

They approach us and explain they're taking us back to the special crimes building—where they took us for questioning on Friday. I'm again confused and annoyed. My parents are now going to have to make arrangements with Reuben to get to the building so they can be with Valerie if she's released.

They load Valerie and me back into their car and transport us to the special crimes building. They sit Valerie at one of their desks, paying no mind that they're seating a person of interest at a desk with evidence bags and police reports strewn about. They tell me they're going to start with my interrogation first and lead me back to the interrogation room.

3:05 p.m.

Sgt. Charles fumbles loading a disc into his computer, then drops it to the floor. It clatters across the linoleum. I bend over, pick it up, and hand it to him.

At the surface, he seems more nervous than I am. He's mumbling to himself, trying to get his equipment set up to start my interview. His phone begins to ring. He silences the call.

His phone rings again. This time, he accepts it, making sure his frustration is known with a snippy "Yeah?!"

The voice on the other end of the line says, "We got ya another one!"

He suddenly turns from his computer to his phone, which he left lying on the table.

Before he can grab the phone and take it off speaker, the voice comes through again, crackling with excitement. "We got you another one with two live rounds in her carry-on. Young white girl in her twenties. You want to come snag her?"

Charles struggles to get out of his chair, his fat belly pinned under the desk. Finally, he frees himself, takes his phone off speaker, and bolts out the door.

Did I really just hear what I think I heard? The voice on the other line seemed excited to share the news. It's now clear to me that something bigger is going on.

My interrogation takes about thirty minutes. Charles and Markland are amateurs at best. There are so many times they're clearly trying to get me to incriminate myself or Valerie, to which I never take the bait. Markland, at one point, gets so frustrated she buries her head in her arms, which are crossed on the desk.

Finally, they ask if I take sole responsibility for traveling with the ammunition.

"The bag is mine, and the bullets that were inadvertently left in the bag also belong to me," I reply.

Markland rolls her eyes and concludes the interview.

When they walk me out of the room, Valerie catches my eyes with hers. Her eyes widen as if to say, Look.

Just then, I see them dragging a young Caucasian girl down the hall. She seems to be in her twenties, but I don't get a great look at her face—her sandy blonde hair and hands cover her face as she cries hysterically. The two officers pull her into a room, towing her carry-on suitcase in one hand

and an evidence bag containing a small shiny brass object in the other, gripping her arm with unnecessary force.

Watching them drag this young girl into the same nightmare I'm living makes my heart ache for her.

They have me sit at the desk where Valerie sat while they conduct her interview. They lead Valerie into the interrogation room, which is about twenty feet in front of where I'm sitting. Once they shut the door, I try my best to peer into the room where they dragged the young "Jane Doe", but the blinds are closed, and I can only see occasional movement through the slats.

I close my eyes to try to focus and listen for any noise coming from either room, but I can't make out anything over the rattling air-conditioning unit.

The next thing I hear is a door swinging open and footsteps coming quickly down the hallway. It's Oliver. I can tell he's been rushing to get here in time for Valerie's interrogation. We make eye contact as he comes down the hallway, and I point him toward the door. He quickly disappears into the interrogation room.

One of the officers emerges from the room where they're holding Jane Doe. He begins speaking, and I think it's directed toward me, so I stand up to address him. That's when I realize, on the other end of the office lobby, separated by a partition, there's a young dark-haired man seated in a chair. He apparently had been traveling with Jane Doe.

I can only make out certain parts of their conversation. The thing I hear him say most clearly is, "I am French-American." He repeats this a number of times to the officer questioning him, almost as if he's pleading with him. I can only assume this means he has dual citizenship.

I feel like they've seen me standing, so I sit back down and try my best to eavesdrop, but their conversation ends abruptly when the officer returns to the room. I try to get the young man's attention by standing back up and staring in his direction, but he's sitting slumped over with his head in his hands.

The door to the interrogation room opens slowly, and Oliver leads Valerie over to where I'm standing. Her face is pale, unreadable.

I lean toward Oliver. "They arrested another girl for ammo in her luggage. I heard the call from the customs agent, and I saw them take her into the room over there." I point to the room to the left.

Oliver doesn't say anything. Just shrugs his shoulders as if to say, *That ain't my problem yet.*

Markland emerges from the interrogation room, looks at Oliver, and just shakes her head.

The look on Oliver's face makes his disappointment known. Markland looks down at the ground and walks back into the interrogation room, shutting the door behind her.

Oliver turns back to us. "They haven't made up their minds yet if they're going to drop the charges on Valerie."

"THEY WHAT?!" I fire back.

Oliver immediately gives me a stern "Shhh," followed by, "I think they will. I just don't want to push them too hard to make a decision and have them do something stupid in return."

I interrupt him. "We have kids, man. They're starting to wonder where their parents are. I mean, I just gave a recorded admission of guilt."

Oliver, showing little compassion, says, "I know you want her to get back to your children, but we have to play this at their speed. They said they'll for sure have their minds made up by Monday."

"A week?!" I say in a whispered shout, shaking my head and turning to Valerie.

She's staring blankly at the floor.

I hug her because I know she's trying to process not only that she's having to stay an additional week, but that she's still very much at risk of being hauled off to prison with me.

Oliver gives us strict instructions not to speak to any officers from this point forward. They bring out the paperwork that extends our bail until the 22nd. Even though I'm instructed not to speak to them, I'm hell-bent on letting them know exactly how I feel. I glare a hole right through both of their faces, not breaking my stare even while signing my bail. The pen digs into the paper with each stroke.

When we get out to the parking lot, I stop my mom, Terry, and Valerie.

"There is something bigger going on. I do not want us talking about any of this in front of anyone, even Reuben."

Everyone nods in agreement as we make our way to Reuben's car, waiting for us.

I sit in the front seat and try to be as vague as possible in answering Reuben's questions. It hurts my heart to be short with Reuben. It seems like he has a heart of gold and is genuinely concerned, but I'm not sure who we can trust.

That's when Valerie slips her phone to me between my seat and the door jamb. It's a message from the principal at her school. It reads: *"Just want you to know that we discovered something strange when we contacted Senator Mullins' office... They said the Embassy had not been notified of your arrest and detainment UNTIL Senator Mullins' office reached out to them."*

This confirms Sgt. Charles' claim that "the Embassy was already notified and knew exactly where we sat" was a lie.

I turn to hand the phone back to her. "I think it's time to call Michael Grim."

My mom, Valerie, Terry, and I all huddle around my cell phone on speaker in the center of a table. When the line connects, we can hear the clank of glassware and casual conversation in the background—the sounds of a normal life, a world away from where we are.

I quickly introduce myself and ask whether there is a better time for us to speak.

I can hear him stand up and head out of the restaurant as he says, "No, Ryan, my family knows how dire this situation is. They told me to take your call and they'll get my meal to go."

It's reassuring to know he wants to help, but also haunting to hear him refer to our situation as *dire*.

"Michael, can you help us understand what this is all about? Money? It has to be money. Who profits the most out of all of this?"

"It's more complicated than just a low-level bribery scheme. This is going to take some time for you to fully grasp, but I'll try to break it down for you."

I grab a pen and start scribbling notes.

"The Turks and Caicos have a long history of corruption, and given that they only allow the original families to vote, it makes it easy for them to keep up the corruption. Put it this way—you're on an island of fifty thousand people, and less than five thousand of them get to vote. If you've paid any attention, you'll have noticed almost all the locals seem to have the same last names. They're either a Forbes or a Misick. Next time you're driving down the road, look around, and you'll notice many of the businesses are affiliated with those families."

I pause from scribbling down notes. He's right. Our original attorney was Nashwood *Forbes*. Our driver is Reuben *Misick*—both last names we've seen on billboards and buildings all over the island.

I flash back to us being in the car with Reuben during the time of our actual vacation. He spoke about being related to practically everyone on the island and boasted about being a cousin of the island's Premier. (The Turks and Caicos Premier is equivalent to the Presidency in the U.S.) Reuben seemed to be related to so many people that we joked about how hard it must have been for him to date, considering he was related to *everyone* on the island.

Michael continues. "The colonial rule and American development have caused a huge disdain for the Brits and Americans alike. When they sentenced me, the locals celebrated—the local paper read, *American Exceptionalism Ends Today*. Premier Misick saw this and immediately went to the appellate court to make this a 12-year sentence. Ryan, you're a political chess piece now, and they're going to send you to prison for twelve years to get votes."

The words hit like a punch. "Well then, who can help us in this situation? We've been in contact with the Embassy, but can they not help us?"

Grim begins to laugh in disgust. "No. When we hang up, I'm going to send you an email that the Chargé d'Affaires, Usha Pitts, sent to my family when I was in prison, telling my family to lose her email. They have no interest in helping you. In fact, you're probably going to find out they'll go out of their way to silence you."

My mom interjects, her voice shaking. "Michael, this is Susan, Ryan's mother. You mentioned your time in prison. Can you tell us a little bit about what that's like? I'm worried about my baby boy."

Michael clears his throat. "It's not going to be easy, but we can talk about ways to get him through it. You'll be the only white person in there. They're going to assume you have money, and they'll try everything they can to extort you. You must avoid using a cell phone at all costs."

"Cell phones?" I ask.

"Yes. You have limited communication with the outside world. You only get two five-minute phone calls a month. They know you'll be desperate to call home, so they'll offer to let you use a cell phone they've smuggled in. Once you do, you owe them a favor. If you don't deliver the favor, they'll threaten you and your family. Since you called your family from their phone, they'll have your family's number, and they'll relentlessly try to extort your family for money to prevent them from murdering you. It's bad, man. Again, avoid cell phones at all costs!"

"Do they feed you?" Mom asks, her voice barely above a whisper.

"They do feed you. You're going to experience a new level of hunger before you get to a point where you can eat it, though. I'm not going to lie— the conditions are rough. The UN actually condemned that prison a little over a year ago. There's no running water or electricity. There are only bars on the windows, so you get eaten alive by bugs. Bacterial infections and blood-borne illnesses are everywhere. You just have to be super careful."

I've found myself at the bottom of a well, unaware of the depth or severity of the situation. The more Michael speaks, the deeper I realize I am. I want to hang up the phone and pretend this isn't my reality, but I can't. Valerie is also at risk of going to prison. I must figure out a way to ensure she makes it home to our kids.

I shake off the self-pity and focus my attention on the call.

"Michael, I know you don't feel like there's anyone who can help us in this situation. What if we went to the media?"

Michael takes a deep breath. "It's... it's a huge gamble, man. Tourism is like ninety percent of their GDP, and that island will do anything it can to protect its image to the outside world. Going to the media will likely make things much worse for you in prison. Besides, there's another guy there from Pennsylvania in the same situation you're in. You'd likely make it worse for both of you."

The phone goes quiet. I look up to see the fear and shock in Valerie's eyes. I try to imagine how I would be able to be a husband and a father, only speaking ten minutes a month on the phone. I feel my face getting hot, and I shiver from the anger filling my body.

"If they're going to destroy my life over something so stupid, I'm going to go down swinging."

Mom buries her face in her hands, shaking her head in disbelief. I can't imagine what she's going through—trying to grasp the reality of your child becoming a political prisoner in a foreign country, and watching that child contemplate lighting a match to try to take it all down with him.

"What would you have done differently in your situation?" I ask.

He pauses. "Well, I guess it would be going to the media. But in my case, I wasn't facing this twelve-year mandatory minimum sentencing. We thought I was going home with a fine until I was sentenced. But if I was you, I guess I would have to consider it. You just have to know that it's a huge risk. They may kill you in prison for it. You also have to consider Bryan in this situation."

I look at Valerie and nod as if to say, *Let's do this.*

Michael says, "I want you to call Bryan before you do anything. He is the one who was arrested in February. He needs to be a part of the decision, and quite frankly, he's down there by himself on bail. He needs someone."

The conversation with Michael pretty much solidifies our plan of action. It's going to be a risky move, but it's clear I have nothing to lose. If I'm going to go down, I want to go down swinging. But we know Michael is right. We need to get Bryan on board.

Earlier that day, Valerie received a text from Melody Mendez. Melody is an NBC news anchor out of Boston who's married to one of my childhood friends, Ricky. The text was simple but powerful: *"I've been praying for you guys. If you think going public would help, I'm here. I can help you tell your story."*

We stare at the message for a long moment. This could be it—the lifeline we need, or the match that burns everything down.

I call her back, my hands shaking as I dial. When she answers, her voice is warm but professional. I can hear the concern underneath.

"Mel, thank you for reaching out. I don't even know where to start."

"Start at the beginning, Ryan. Tell me everything."

So, we do. Valerie and I take turns recounting every detail—the discovery at the airport, the interrogation, Oliver's warnings, the twelve-year mandatory minimum, Michael Grim's stories about the prison. The words pour out of us in a torrent we can't control. At some point, I realize I'm pacing the room, my free hand gesturing wildly as if she can see me.

When we finish, there's silence on the other end of the line. Then Mel lets out a long breath.

"This is... Ryan, this is insane. This is clearly corruption. Like, textbook corruption." Her voice shifts into reporter mode. "This story is bigger than just you guys. People need to know this is happening."

"Do you really think people will care?" I ask, hating how desperate I sound.

"Are you kidding? An American family trapped on a Caribbean island, facing twelve years in prison for accidentally packing hunting ammunition? The government trying to make an example out of tourists? Yeah, Ryan. People will care."

Valerie leans closer to the phone. "What do we need to do?"

"Okay, so here's the thing," Mel says. "This story has legs, but it needs the right person to tell it. I work local news in Boston, but this needs someone who does deep investigative work. Someone who can really dig into the corruption angle. I'm thinking Leslie Gaydos—she's an investigative reporter, and she's excellent. She'll take this seriously."

"Can you connect us with her?" I ask.

"Already texting her as we speak," Mel says. I can hear the clicking of her keyboard in the background. "I need you to understand something, though. I can guarantee this will run on NBC Boston. We'll make sure it gets attention. But whether the national desk picks it up—whether this goes viral—I can't promise that. It depends on the news cycle, what else is happening that day. A lot of things have to align."

My heart sinks a little. "So it might not be enough."

"Or," Mel counters, "it could explode. It could be everywhere. The point is, you're doing the right thing. You're shining a light on something that deserves to be exposed. That matters regardless of how far it reaches."

Valerie squeezes my hand. I can feel tears threatening but push them back.

"Mel, I have to ask—if we do this, are we putting ourselves in more danger? Michael Grim said going public could make things worse in prison."

Mel's voice softens. "I can't lie to you, Ryan. There's risk. But from what you've just told me, you're already in danger. At least this way, the world is watching. That's a form of protection too."

I look at Valerie. She nods.

"Okay," I say. "Let's do it. Connect us with Leslie."

"I'll have her reach out tomorrow," Mel says. "And Ryan? Valerie? I'm praying for you guys. Ricky's whole family is. You're not alone in this."

When we hang up, the room feels different. Charged. Like we've just made a decision we can't take back.

"Are we really doing this?" Valerie whispers.

"I think we have to," I say. "For us. For that girl at the police station. For anyone else who might end up here."

She leans her head against my shoulder. "Then let's go down swinging."

APRIL 16TH

I sit in the front seat as Reuben's car bounces through the rough streets of Five Cays, potholes jarring my spine with each impact. This is an area we'd been warned to avoid due to the violent gang activity that plagues it. Graffiti covers the crumbling walls. Groups of men stand on street corners, watching us pass with hard stares.

"You have friends who are staying in Five Cays?" Reuben asks, his tone suggesting surprise.

"Yes, it's an old family friend who's here for work. I guess his company was looking for a cheap place to keep him while he's here."

I hated lying to Reuben. He's been so kind to us, but we made a group decision that anything regarding our situation or plan can't be discussed in front of any locals.

As soon as we pull up to a security gate at the address Bryan sent, I jump out to greet him before Reuben can follow. I can't be introducing myself to Bryan in front of Reuben after telling him Bryan's a family friend.

I peer over the gate and see the tall white guy from the Chalk Sound police station yesterday. As he comes through the gate, there isn't much introduction needed. Not only do we know exactly what the other is going through—we're about to join arms in the fight of our lives.

We're brothers.

We skip the handshake and go straight for the bro-hug, gripping each other's shoulders tight.

"Dude, I thought that was you guys yesterday! I wanted so bad to ask if that was you," Bryan says, leaning back from our embrace.

"I know, man. I was convinced it was you, too, but the car you were in threw me off. It looked like a company car, not a rental."

"Aww yeah, it's my landlord's car. She let me borrow it."

"Makes sense. Hey man, our driver Reuben thinks you're an old family friend. Let's not discuss anything in front of him."

"Yeah, man. Not a word."

Valerie sets her Bible on the coffee table as we come walking through the door. I can see her face struggle to process the mixture of excitement and sorrow. It provides a bit of strange solace to meet someone in the same scenario, but you feel guilty that the comfort comes by way of someone else's trauma.

Bryan's eyes look hollow and tired from the torment of being alone for nearly sixty days on this island, trying to make sense of a nonsensical situation. The fluorescent light overhead makes the dark circles under his eyes even more pronounced.

Valerie hugs him and starts to cry. "I'm so sorry you've been going through this, but I'm so glad to meet you."

I notice Bryan holding back his emotions as he tries to respond, his jaw clenching. Just as Bryan clears his eyes and his throat, my mom and Terry come through the door and wrap him in hugs. He stiffens for a moment—

probably not used to physical affection after sixty days of isolation—then melts into it.

I grab Bryan a drink as I start to cook dinner for us. The sizzle of meat hitting the hot pan fills the kitchen, and for a moment, things feel almost normal.

I joke, "The theme for dinner tonight is felons and fajitas."

We all laugh too hard. Not that it's a great joke by any measure, but something about the company makes us all feel like we can finally laugh at how ridiculous that statement seems. A fifth-grade math teacher, a nursing home executive, and a medical sales executive with only a couple of speeding tickets between us—the most unassuming group of felons you've ever seen.

We catch up over dinner and get to hear about Bryan's family back home in Pennsylvania. His voice softens when he talks about his wife, his kids. I can see the longing in his eyes, the ache of separation. As dinner wraps up and my mom starts clearing the table, the clatter of dishes a comforting domestic sound, we begin sharing notes on what we know about our current scenario.

Bryan has seemingly memorized every detail of every similar court case involving American citizens in TCI. He rattles off dates, names, and sentences with the precision of someone who's had nothing but time to study. Even though these cases are nearly identical to ours, they seem to pose no relevance to our cases, as they all predate the law making it a twelve-year mandatory minimum.

We talk in most detail about Michael Grim's case, debating whether we might receive a similar sentence. His case took place prior to the new law, but it was the most recent involving an American. Could we potentially have a similar outcome?

The somber look returns to Bryan's face. "When I spoke to Michael, he told me that Oliver made a comment that makes me feel like that won't be the case."

We all lean in.

"After Michael was sentenced, Oliver apparently told him, 'Look, I know you think six months is bad, but they're looking to drop the hammer on you Americans. Yes, you got your tail clipped, but the next American in line is going to get it REAL bad.'"

The words hang in the air like smoke. No one speaks. The weight of it settles over us—we're the next Americans in line.

Trying to ignore the gravity of the comment, I push up from the table. "Let's go sit in the living area and have a drink."

When we settle into the living room, I look over to Valerie. She gives me a nod. The look on Bryan's face makes it apparent he knows we have something to tell him. He sets his drink down on the coffee table, leaning forward with his elbows on his knees.

I lean in. "We have a plan to go to the media."

Bryan starts shaking his head before I even finish the sentence. "I've been told that's a death sentence."

"We've been told that too. But ask yourself—why would there be such a backlash for us going to the media?"

"Because they're trying to protect their tourism," Bryan shoots back.

"Exactly. Tourism is ninety percent of their GDP! This country survives on American tourism. They are legitimately biting the hand that's feeding them." I pause, letting that sink in. "Would you have come here if you knew they were so hell-bent on teaching Americans a lesson?"

"Absolutely not," Bryan says.

"They're trying to tear our families apart to make some political stance."

"Oliver made it very clear to me that going to the media was a terrible idea," Bryan says, making it clear he hasn't swayed. His arms are crossed now, defensive.

I turn to look at Valerie, then back toward Bryan. "I get that it's a risky play, but they're not just threatening me—they're threatening to put my wife in prison as well. I want to hit them where it hurts. I want to wage economic war on this island."

Bryan pauses, staring at his drink. The ice clinks against the glass as he swirls it. "Okay, say we did contact the media. How do we know they'd actually run with it?"

Bryan was right. It was the question no one could

answer with any certainty. Of course, we're outraged by the situation, but would the rest of the world be? We live in a hyper-polarized society, and it needs to be acknowledged that a good portion of the world would likely show us no mercy. Especially considering the fact that we're gun-owning Americans.

Valerie leans in and folds her hands. Her voice is steady, measured. "We've been in contact with a friend who works at the NBC Boston network. They're extremely interested in running our story and feel like the National NBC network will pick it up, but they can't guarantee it will make it past the local desk."

I can see the wheels turning in Bryan's head. His eyes dart between Valerie and me, calculating, weighing. I start to feel a huge weight on my heart. I'm asking Bryan to take a giant leap of faith with us and ignore everyone's warnings. If this plan fails, it means we're not only going to prison for twelve years, but we're also putting our lives at risk.

My voice drops. "Bryan, would you pray with us?"

He looks up, surprised, then nods.

We all join hands in that living room—Valerie's hand in mine, my mom's on the other side, Terry, Bryan completing the circle. I close my eyes and feel the warmth of their hands, the weight of the moment.

"God, we need clarity. We need wisdom. We need protection. Show us the right path, and if this is it, give us the courage to walk it. Keep our families safe. Keep us safe. We trust that you have a plan even when we can't see it. Amen."

A chorus of "Amen" echoes softly.

After we release hands, I have one final thought. The room is quiet except for the gentle hum of the air conditioner.

"I'm in no way willing to put my wife in any additional danger, but we need to look at the optics of this." I glance at Valerie, making sure she's okay with what I'm about to say. "The world is more likely to pay attention if they see that a mother of two young children is caught up in this. Let's get in front of the media now. I was told we can impose an embargo on our story, restricting the media from releasing it until we say the word go. If we record the interviews now, Valerie can lift the embargo as soon as she boards a plane."

I look over to Valerie for acceptance, searching her face for any hesitation.

She nods. "I'm good with that."

We both turn to Bryan. He takes another drink, finishing it, then sets the empty glass down with a decisive clink.

"I'm in."

The three of us place our hands in the center of the coffee table, one on top of the other. The gesture feels both serious and absurd—like kids making a pact before something they can't take back.

"We're doing this," I say.

"We're doing this," Valerie echoes.

"We're doing this," Bryan confirms.

For better or worse, we've just declared war.

APRIL 17TH

We all gathered in the living room with notepads, the coffee table now covered with scribbled lists. We're compiling every person we know who either has influence or knows someone who does. In order for our plan to work, we're going to need people to share it. Views, comments, shares, likes—all of it will determine whether the media continues to cover our story.

As our list continues to grow, we start to feel more confident that this might actually work. The names pile up: friends, family, old colleagues, distant acquaintances who work in media, people we haven't spoken to in years but who might care enough to hit "share."

Becoming intoxicated with optimism, our voices grow louder as we conspire. The energy in the room shifts from desperate to almost giddy.

"This island doesn't even know what's coming!" I say, raising my hand for a high-five from Bryan.

He's about to slap my hand when I freeze mid-air.

A man of Caribbean descent is standing outside, peering into one of the windows from the side of the condo. His face is pressed close to the glass, watching us. Our eyes lock for a split second.

The shock on my face stops everyone else in their tracks. The room goes silent.

"What?" Bryan asks, following my gaze.

They all turn to look at the window, seeing the Peeping Tom. He doesn't move. Just keeps watching.

I walk over, my heart pounding in my ears, and yank the shade down. The fabric snaps against the window frame. I move to another window to check if we're clear, and my stomach drops.

Three other men are outside. One of them holds a garden tool—a rake or hoe—but he's not doing anything with it. Just standing there, leaning on it like a prop. They're all watching the condo.

"Are they the grounds maintenance crew?" Valerie asks, her voice tight.

"They aren't dressed like it," Bryan responds, standing now. "And they're all just kind of... loitering."

I stare out at them through the slats of the blinds. "I don't trust them. You saw that guy—he was clearly watching us through the window. I'm going out there."

"Ryan—" Valerie starts, but I'm already moving toward the door.

"I need to see what they're doing."

I walk out the front door and into the humid air, squinting against the bright sunlight. I stare at them with the same level of curiosity they're showing us. My pulse is racing, but I force myself to appear calm, unbothered.

I walk to the side of the house and make direct eye contact with the peeping tom. He quickly breaks eye contact and begins acting like he's checking a sprinkler head, bending down and fiddling with it in an exaggerated way that screams performance.

He turns and walks back to the others who are assembling next to a white pickup truck. They're talking in low voices, glancing back at me occasionally. I stand there with my arms crossed, not moving, just watching them. Making it clear I see them. That I'm not afraid.

After several minutes—maybe five, maybe ten, time feels elastic—they all load back into the truck. The engine roars to life, kicking up dust, and they speed off down the street faster than necessary.

When I walk back inside, I notice Valerie and Bryan watching me from the window, their faces pressed against the glass like worried parents waiting for a teenager to come home.

"Did they say anything?" Valerie asks as soon as I close the door.

I shake my head. "No. They just... left."

"That was sketchy," Valerie says, wrapping her arms around herself.

Bryan nods in agreement. "Whether that was a coincidence or not, we have to act like people are watching and listening to us."

The room feels different now. Smaller. The walls seem thinner. I glance at the windows, now all covered, and wonder how long that man had been standing there. What did he hear? How much had we said?

"We need to be ultra careful moving forward," I say, lowering my voice even though we're alone now. "If anyone on the island figures out we're devising a plan to go to the media—that we're trying to put economic pressure on them—we're all going down."

Everyone nods solemnly.

"From now on," Bryan says, his voice barely above a whisper, "we only communicate in private settings or through encrypted apps. WhatsApp, Signal, something they can't intercept."

"You really think they're sophisticated enough to monitor our communication?" my mom asks, skepticism in her voice.

"I don't know," I admit. "But we can't risk not taking every measure imaginable."

Valerie moves around the room, double-checking that all the blinds are fully closed, that there are no gaps where someone could peer in. The paranoia is setting in now, crawling under our skin.

"We're not in America anymore," Bryan says quietly. "Different rules. Different game."

I look down at our list of names on the coffee table—all these people we're counting on, this plan we've just committed to. It felt so hopeful five minutes ago.

Now it feels dangerous.

"We keep going," I say, more to convince myself than anyone else. "But we keep our heads down. No more loud celebrating. No more talking freely. We assume someone is always listening."

Everyone agrees in silence, the weight of surveillance pressing down on us like the humid Caribbean air outside.

This island is watching. And now, we're watching back.

APRIL 18TH

Valerie and I set up the laptop we're borrowing from my stepfather, Terry, carefully positioning it on the kitchen table. The screen glows in the dim room as we angle it just right for our interview. We move methodically around the space, removing all the pictures and artwork from the walls, leaving behind rectangular shadows and nail holes. Nothing can be recognizable in the camera angle. Nothing that could identify where we are.

When we checked into the Airbnb the day before, the property manager was immediately suspicious about us booking a condo for two weeks on the same day we arrived. My mom, who booked it, did her best to make an excuse—something about a last-minute work trip—but it didn't seem to appease the landlord. The woman's eyes narrowed, her arms crossed.

Then the property manager said she'd "heard through WhatsApp that there was a husband and wife arrested for possession of ammunition."

The air left the room.

My mom got emotional and begged her to let us stay. I could hear the desperation in her voice through the door, the kind of pleading that strips away all pride.

The landlord paused, considering. Finally, she agreed to let us stay— but only if we agreed not to draw any attention. She didn't want the local community to know she was in any way affiliated with "the Americans." The way she said it, like we were a disease.

We needed the location of our interview to be discreet to ensure our safety and, at the very least, avoid being evicted from our accommodations. One wrong move and we'd be homeless on an island that wants us in prison.

The line connects, and Leslie Gaydos appears on the screen. She's in what looks like a home office, professional but warm. Her eyes are kind.

"Ryan, Valerie, thank you so much for speaking with me," she says. "I can't imagine what you're going through."

She expresses genuine sympathy and concern for our situation. But I'm still guarded.

I lean toward the camera. "Leslie, I need to express my concerns about Valerie's safety. We're asking for an embargo on this story until April 22nd. It's critical that nothing airs before then."

Leslie nods seriously. "I want you to know that any reputable media outlet takes embargo requests very seriously, especially when someone's safety is at stake. You have my word—nothing will air until you give us the green light."

The tension in my shoulders eases slightly. Once this is settled, we start the interview.

Leslie asks us to walk through everything from the beginning—the discovery at the airport, the interrogation, the threats of twelve years in prison. Valerie and I take turns recounting the details, our voices sometimes overlapping, sometimes breaking. Throughout most of the interview, I'm doing my best to get a read on Leslie. Is she legitimately on our side? We've been warned to be wary of reporters—they'll seem nice to get you to say something, then use what you said against you to tell their version of events.

About halfway through the interview, Leslie's voice softens. "What have you told your kids?"

The question hits like a physical blow.

Valerie and I both get emotional. My throat tightens. I can feel the tears coming, but I try to hold them back.

Valerie begins to speak, her voice wavering. "We told them that... that storms delayed our flights. That we'd be home soon." She pauses, wiping her eyes. "They're nine and seven. They keep asking when we're coming home, and we keep lying to them, and I don't know how much longer—"

Her voice breaks completely.

I glance at the screen and notice that Leslie is also crying. Tears stream down her face as she listens to Valerie. She's not even trying to hide it. She's a mother, too, and it's clear she's showing empathy that only another mother could.

Any skepticism I had about speaking with Leslie immediately fades. I know from that moment that she's in our corner. This isn't just a story to her. These are real lives. Real children waiting for their parents.

As we end the recording, Leslie leans closer to her camera. "When you're ready—when Valerie is safely out—I will do anything in my power to help get you out of there. Anything."

I believe her.

"Leslie, there's something else," I say. "We saw another American being arrested. A young woman in her twenties. They dragged her into the police station, and she was hysterical. I've emailed and called Lance Peterson at the Embassy multiple times, but they keep telling me they have no record of another American being arrested."

Leslie's expression shifts. Reporter mode kicks in. "What did she look like?"

"Sandy blonde hair. Early twenties. They had her carry-on and an evidence bag with ammunition. She wasn't alone—there was a young man with her, dark hair. He kept saying he was French-American, like he was trying to claim dual citizenship or something."

Leslie jots down notes. "I'll see what I can find. If she's out there, I'll find her."

"Thank you," I say, and I mean it.

When we disconnect, the room feels different. Lighter, somehow. Like we've just gained an ally in a war we thought we were fighting alone.

Valerie looks at me. "Do you think this is really going to work?"

"I don't know," I admit. "But at least we're fighting back."

Later that afternoon, I get in contact with an old friend from high school named Jonathan. We haven't spoken in over twenty years, but he heard about our situation through the grapevine. Jonathan moved to Washington, D.C., to work in politics and has developed a strong network of politicians across both sides of the aisle over his career.

When he calls, his voice is urgent. "Ryan, I've been following what's happening to you. This is insane. I want to help."

"Jonathan, man, I don't even know what to say. We're just trying to get the word out."

"I can help with that," he says. "I have a strong relationship with Kris Van Cleave at CBS News. He's national. If you can get CBS to cover this in addition to NBC, you're looking at massive exposure."

My heart rate picks up. "You think he'd be interested?"

"I already reached out to him. He's potentially interested. But Ryan, you need to be careful. You can only pursue reporters and media outlets with personal connections. You can't risk tipping off anyone who might disregard your embargo before the 22nd."

"I know," I say. "We're being extremely careful."

"Good. Let me pass on Kris's contact information. Reach out to him directly."

Jonathan texts me the number moments later. I stare at it on my screen, feeling the weight of what this could mean. NBC Boston was a start, but CBS national coverage? That changes everything.

I text Kris immediately, introducing myself and briefly explaining the situation. He responds within the hour—he's interested, but his schedule is tight. After working through some logistical challenges, we secure a time on April 21st to record our interview.

Two national media outlets. Two interviews. Two chances to make the world care.

I look at Valerie, who's been watching me text. "We're really doing this."

She nods. "We're really doing this."

The pieces are falling into place. Now we just need to survive long enough to see it through.

APRIL 19TH

Word back home of our situation was spreading quickly—too quickly. Valerie receives a call from her principal, who tells her that news outlets are calling the school, saying they've heard reports of a fifth-grade math teacher stuck in a foreign country.

As much as it means to us that people are rallying to help, it's equally concerning. We need to ensure our story doesn't get out yet. This is critical for two main reasons.

First: we can't allow the kids to hear the rumor that their parents are locked up abroad. I can't imagine how terrifying that would be for them—hearing it from a classmate or overhearing adults whispering. The thought makes my chest tight.

Second: we need the story to have the biggest impact possible. The timing needs to be perfect for it to go viral. One premature leak could kill the momentum before it even starts.

We try to wrangle this as best we can by disseminating information only to a handful of trusted friends and family. They know how sensitive the information is, so anytime they share it, it's always prefaced with a strong disclaimer: this information cannot be shared until they're given the green light. But it's like trying to hold back a flood with sandbags. The secret is getting too big.

Another friend working behind the scenes for us back home is our dear friend Holly. Holly just retired from a highly decorated career, and she's a go-getter who immediately sought a way to help. My mom reached out to her to see if she—or someone she knows—could assist with managing the media if Valerie and I both go to jail.

Holly immediately gets to work scouring the internet for professional resources. She comes across Jonathan Franks' profile. Jonathan is a crisis consultant who's worked on a number of high-profile cases involving wrongfully detained Americans abroad.

Holly calls my mom. "Susan, I think I might have the perfect guy for the job. I have him on the other line. Is it okay for me to patch you into the call?"

Mom agrees and immediately starts vetting Jonathan, asking rapid-fire questions I can hear from the other room.

Before long, Mom starts calling for us from the kitchen. "Ryan, Valerie, could you get in here, please? There's someone I need to introduce you to."

When we walk into the kitchen, Mom quickly spins her laptop around, pointing the screen in our direction. "Okay, Jonathan, I have the kids here."

A rosy, baby-faced man smiles and waves at us through Zoom. "Hi Ryan! Hi Valerie!"

I hesitantly wave back, then look at my mom with a confused expression that says, *Who am I talking to here?*

Mom jumps in. "This is Jonathan Franks. He's a crisis consultant and has worked on many cases like yours. He also has contacts with Global Reach."

I nod, though I'm still caught off guard and processing whether I should be feeling skepticism or optimism.

Jonathan begins by recounting his experience dealing with wrongfully detained Americans. Politicians, media personalities, government officials—the names fly by so fast it's hard to keep up. I can't determine how seriously we should take this guy.

However, if he truly knows half the people he's referencing, it could be helpful.

I try to act engaged as I pull my phone out under the table and begin searching his name on the internet. I find a story where ABC did an exclusive on him, which lends him some credibility. But the story keeps referencing the non-profit Global Reach, and I'm not clear on the connection.

I jump back into the conversation. "Jonathan, can you explain what Global Reach is? Do you work for them?"

Jonathan leans forward, his energy ramping up. "Global Reach is a non-profit organization founded by the late Governor of New Mexico, Bill Richardson. Their mission is to provide resources to Americans wrongfully detained abroad. You probably heard about them in the recent high-profile case of WNBA player Brittney Griner—they were instrumental in bringing her home."

I suddenly get more interested in what Jonathan's selling. Brittney Griner. That was huge news. That was real.

"And you work for this Global Reach?" I ask.

"It's more like my company works in conjunction with them. We have a long history of working together. I can patch them into this call if you'd like?"

"Sure!" I shoot back, sitting up straighter.

The call goes on brief hold. Muzak plays for thirty seconds. Then the line reconnects with two members from Global Reach—their voices professional, measured, experienced.

Jonathan makes quick introductions, and before we know it, they're investigating extradition treaties and talking logistics like we're a case they've handled a hundred times before. It seems that Global Reach has an interest in our case, but it becomes evident they won't truly commit to taking it on until I'm detained. They need to see if this is real, if this is worth their resources.

As the conversation with Global Reach starts wrapping up, Jonathan asks, "Okay, guys, if you'd like to hire me to assist you, I need to start looking at flights and accommodations. I'd ideally like to be there before Ryan goes to jail."

The words hang in the air. *Before Ryan goes to jail.* Said so casually, like we're planning a business trip.

I clear my throat. "Can we have some time to discuss this as a family? We'll get back to you ASAP."

"Of course," Jonathan says, nodding enthusiastically. "Take your time."

When the call disconnects, I look up at Mom and Valerie. "I don't know, guys. I'm conflicted. Is this guy just another person who is claiming he can help? People know we are desperate and likely willing to throw money at any potential solution. I do have to admit though- he's seemingly experienced and has connections."

Mom responds immediately, her voice firm. "Son, you need to stop being so critical. This guy seems to have real connections. If something happens to both of you, I'm going to need as much help as I can get. I barely even know how to make a post on Facebook." She pauses, her voice softening. "Besides, his pull with the Global Reach program is reason enough for us to hire him."

Mom's not wrong. Global Reach does seem like it would be beneficial when the inevitability of my going to prison happens. But I can't get my head around how Valerie and I can afford it. We're already burning through our savings with attorney fees, food, lodging. The numbers are staggering. When Valerie makes it back to the kids, she's going to need anything we have left to raise them on her teacher's salary. I also can't stand the thought that my parents would have to bear any of the financial burden. They've already done so much.

My mom can see I'm getting overwhelmed, trying to figure out how to make this work. My leg is bouncing under the table, my jaw clenched.

"Son." Her voice cuts through my spiraling thoughts. "Terry and I want to contribute. We'll cover the cost of Jonathan's flight and hotel here. I think it's an investment worth making to ensure you have the best shot."

"Mom, I can't ask you to—"

"You're not asking. We're offering."

After some back and forth, I drop my guard and agree to hire him. But I make one request: I want his flight to arrive *after* I go to jail on Monday morning. I'm worried that he and our attorney, Oliver, will clash. Oliver doesn't like it when his clients ask questions or when outsiders get involved. I can only assume that if Jonathan shows up trying to inject himself into the process, Oliver might drop me as a client. And I can't afford to lose the best attorney on the island, not now.

My sister Jessica was desperate to help in any way she could. She knew we were already spending an insane amount of money on legal fees, accommodations, and food. Not to mention, if—when—I go to prison, Valerie will in no way be able to afford to raise our two kids and pay the mortgage on her salary alone.

Jessica calls, her voice urgent. "Ryan, let me set up a GoFundMe page for you guys."

The suggestion hits me like a gut punch. A GoFundMe. For us. Like we're charity cases.

"Jess, I don't know if I can—"

"Ryan, stop." Her voice is sharp, cutting through my pride. "This isn't about you. This is about Valerie. This is about your kids. You can't let your pride get in the way of them being able to live."

She's right. I hate that she's right, but she is.

It's a hard pill to swallow, but my sister's hitting the nail on the head. I can't let my pride—my stubborn refusal to accept help—get in the way of Valerie being able to provide a shred of normalcy back home. Our kids need food, clothes, stability. They need their mom not to be drowning in debt while their dad sits in a foreign prison.

"Okay," I say quietly. "Set it up."

Jessica gets to work researching and setting up the page. The plan is for it not to be published until we lift the embargo—the same moment the media stories drop. Everything has to happen at once. Maximum impact. Maximum pressure.

I stare at the wall after we hang up, feeling the weight of it all. My family is rallying around us, throwing money and resources and time at this problem. Strangers will soon be asked to contribute to keep my family afloat.

And all of it is because of a freak accident.

Valerie puts her hand on mine. "We're going to get through this."

I want to believe her. I'm trying to believe her.

But right now, it feels like we're building a house of cards in a hurricane, hoping it holds long enough for the world to notice before it all comes crashing down.

APRIL 20TH

We tried to wrap up most of our phone calls by 8 p.m. so we could Face-Time with the kids before they get tucked into bed. This was the best way we knew how to help them believe our story—that we're only trying to correct an issue with our passports. Keep it light. Keep it normal. Keep them from being scared.

Right at 8p.m., we sat next to each other on the edge of the couch and Face-timed the kids. Doing our best to put on a front and act as if everything is completely normal. I can see our living room in the background of the call—the couch where we read bedtime stories, the toys scattered across the floor. It feels like looking at someone else's life.

It's clear that the excitement and distraction of spending unexpected time with their out-of-town grandparents has started to fade. They're missing us. I can see it in their eyes, hear it in the way they keep asking when we're coming home.

Our daughter Ellie's face crumples. Her bottom lip quivers. Then she starts to cry.

"Mommy, are you ever coming home to me?"

The question shatters something inside me. I watch Valerie's face—the way she forces a smile that doesn't reach her eyes, the way her voice goes artificially bright.

"Oh, Ellie bug, we miss you so much, and we'll be home before you know it! You better say your prayers and get to bed now, okay, sweetie?"

But Ellie is still crying as the line disconnects. The screen goes black, replaced by our own reflections staring back at us.

Valerie drops the phone like it's burned her hand. She bolts for the back bedroom, her footsteps heavy and frantic. The door slams behind her with a force that shakes the walls.

Then the wailing starts.

The sound of it quickly fills the entire condo—raw, guttural, unrestrained. You can hear the pain in her voice from having to lie to our children. It's not crying. It's something deeper, something primal. It's the sound of a mother being torn away from her babies.

Bryan, Mom, Terry, and I all sit frozen in the living room, tears streaming down our faces in silence, listening to her fall apart. No one speaks. No one moves. We just sit there, bearing witness to her agony because there's nothing else we can do.

As badly as I want to run through that door and hold her and tell her it's going to be okay, I know she needs a moment of space to cry out completely unrestrained. She doesn't need to hold it together for anyone—not for the kids, not for me, not for anyone.

After a few minutes that feel like hours, I can't take it anymore. I stand and walk to the bedroom door, opening it slowly.

She's lying in a fetal position on the bed, her body shaking with sobs. Her hair is plastered to her tear-stained face. She looks small, broken, like all the strength she's been forcing herself to have has finally collapsed.

There are no words left to offer. If I tell her, "It's all going to be okay," I'd be making the same empty promise we just made to our kids. I can't lie to her too.

Instead, I climb onto the bed and pick her up like I would pick up one of our children—gently, carefully, like she's something precious and fragile. I cradle her against my chest, feeling her body wracked with sobs, her tears soaking through my shirt.

And then I begin to pray out loud.

No formal beginning. No "Dear Heavenly Father." I just start talking to God, telling Him about the pain, the confusion, the desperation I'm feeling. The words pour out of me, raw and unfiltered.

"God, I don't understand this. I don't understand why we're here or what you're doing, but I'm begging you—*please*—don't let her go to prison. Please get her home to our babies. They need her. I need her. I can't do this without knowing she's safe. Please, God, *please*."

My voice cracks. The tears come now, hot and heavy, and I don't try to stop them.

It's the first time I let Valerie see or hear me be truly vulnerable. I've been trying to be strong for her, to be the protector, to have the answers. But I don't have answers. I'm just as terrified as she is.

She needs to know that my heart is in a similar place, and prayer is the most honest way I can show her.

We lie there together in the dark, holding each other, crying together, praying together. Outside, I can hear the faint sounds of the ocean, the distant hum of traffic, the world continuing on like nothing is wrong.

But in this room, everything is wrong.

And all we can do is hold on to each other and hope that somehow, someway, God is listening.

APRIL 21ST

We repeat the process of stripping the condo of any identifiable objects to prepare for our next interview with Kris Van Cleave of CBS News. The walls are bare again, anonymous. We angle the laptop just right, making sure nothing in the frame could give away our location.

When the line connects over Zoom, I recognize Kris's face immediately—I've seen him on the news before. In the background of his office is a wall full of Emmy trophies, their gold surfaces catching the light. Usually, this would intimidate me. But these details are all signs that our story will be shared on a national scale. Real reach.

I don't have time to be nervous. It's time to plead for our lives.

Kris is professional throughout the interview, asking thoughtful questions and showing genuine compassion as we recount our story once again. The words are becoming practiced now, worn smooth from repetition, but the emotion behind them is still raw.

Near the end of the interview, Kris leans slightly forward. "What do you have to say to those who say, 'You broke the law, you have to face the consequences'?"

The question hangs in the air.

I knew it would come. I prepared for it. But somehow it still catches me off guard, hitting like a punch I should have seen coming. Thoughts of all my would-be critics start flooding my mind—the comment sections, the Twitter threads, the people who will say we deserve this. The gun control advocates who will have no sympathy. The law-and-order crowd who will say rules are rules.

I take a deep breath, trying to find the right words.

"I can only pray that they could find the compassion to understand that this was an honest mistake that never endangered anyone. And I can't see how a twelve-year prison sentence is a fair punishment for what amounts to an oversight."

Kris nods, makes a few more remarks, and then we're wrapping up. Thanking each other. The professional pleasantries.

But I'm not really there anymore.

The question and my response are playing on repeat in my head a thousand times over. *Was this an adequate response? Would it truly satisfy the haters we will undoubtedly face?* Whether it was intentional or not, I did break their law. That's the part that keeps nagging at me. The part I can't argue away.

When the call disconnects, I sit staring at the black screen for a long moment.

"You did good," Valerie says quietly, reading my mind.

I want to believe her.

~❖~

Later that evening, I let Mom, Terry, and Bryan know that Valerie and I are going to eat at a restaurant alone. This is possibly the last night we'll spend together, and I want to take her on a date. A real date. One last normal thing before everything falls apart.

We dig out our nice clothes that we'd brought for our vacation—clothes that feel like they belong to different people now, people who were carefree and happy. I put on the shirt Valerie likes, the one she always says makes my eyes look blue. She puts on the sundress she'd been planning to wear to a nice dinner on the beach.

We get cleaned up for each other, taking our time. She does her make-up. I actually shave. For a moment, standing side by side at the bathroom mirror, we almost look like ourselves again.

We walk to a nice restaurant located not far from our condo. The evening air is warm, humid, carrying the smell of salt water and grilled fish from nearby kitchens. Our hands find each other instinctively, fingers intertwining. Neither of us speaks. There's too much to say and no way to say it.

We get a table on the patio, the kind with a view of the water. String lights are hung overhead, casting a soft glow. We order drinks—something tropical and sweet that tastes nothing like the beer and wine we'd normally order. But nothing about this is normal.

Strangely, the nerves I feel on what could be our last date are similar to the nerves I felt on our first date. *What do we talk about? Does she know everything she needs to know about me? Is there anything left unsaid?*

Our small talk is careful, tentative. We're both dancing around the elephant in the room—or maybe the elephant is the only thing in the room, and we're trying to pretend it's not crushing us.

Then a local musician starts setting up his equipment nearby to perform. I think to myself, *This is great! We love live music. This is going to set a perfect vibe for our date.*

He strums his guitar, checks the mic, then starts singing.

"Ain't no sunshine when she's gone..."

Oh no.

I glance at Valerie. She's trying her best to ward off tears with a smile as the lyrics sink in. Her bottom lip trembles slightly. She takes a sip of her drink, blinking rapidly.

"And this house just ain't no home, anytime she goes away..."

I reach across the table and squeeze her hand.

Then the next song starts. Another ballad. A sad one about leaving and longing and distance.

Now I start to think, *Man, this isn't starting off like I had hoped.*

That poor singer must have just gone through a brutal breakup because he sings ballads all night long—every single one about loss, separation, heartbreak. Song after devastating song. It would be funny if it weren't so perfectly, cruelly on the nose.

Valerie finally has all she can take. Her smile has become a grimace, tears threatening to spill over.

"Can we just get our food to go?" she whispers.

"Yeah," I say, signaling for the waiter. "Let's get out of here."

We walk back to the condo with styrofoam containers in hand, the music still drifting after us on the breeze. We try our best to laugh at how ironic it was that the performer sang songs about breaking up and leaving all through dinner. We make jokes about the universe having a twisted sense of humor, about whoever's writing our story having no subtlety.

But there's no avoiding what's coming tomorrow.

The laughter fades as we reach the condo steps. Our footsteps slow.

When we get inside, we sit on the couch with our to-go containers, the food getting cold between us. Neither of us is hungry anymore.

"Tomorrow..." Valerie starts, then stops. Her voice breaks.

"I know."

Best-case scenario is saying goodbye. And that goodbye is likely going to last twelve years.

I pull her close, her head resting on my shoulder. We sit like that for a long time, the food forgotten, the world outside continuing its indifferent spin.

Tomorrow, everything changes.

Tonight, all we have is this—this moment, this couch, each other.

So we hold on as tightly as we can, trying to memorize the feeling of being together, knowing that by this time tomorrow, one or both of us will be in chains.

APRIL 22ND

Reuben pulls up to the front of the Chalk Sound police department right before 10 a.m. This time, it feels different. Everyone in the car knows I'm going to jail. The only question left swirling is whether they're going to send Valerie to jail as well.

I get out of the car and grab the two "jail bags" that my mom and Bryan assembled for us the day before. In TCI, you're responsible for providing your own blanket, pillow, toothpaste, soap—the basics. These are all things Bryan went without while he was in jail, and he wanted to make sure we were prepared.

When I shut the back hatch of Reuben's Suburban, I see him standing there waiting. The smile he always wears is replaced with a more serious look of concern. He's about to turn us over to the hands of the Banana Republic he'd previously joked about, and he knows there's nothing any of us can do once it has its grip on us.

Valerie and I both hug his neck and thank him dearly for all he's done. We snap a quick photo with him—evidence that we were here, that someone cared.

I grab Valerie's hand, look her in the eye. "Are you ready?"

She nods and begins to cry as we walk toward the door.

~❖~

When we enter the police station, the officers behind the glass seem to be expecting us. They motion us to stand in the same corner where we waited for hours the week before. The air is thick with tension.

Mom might be the most nervous of us all. I hug her and tell her I'm going to be alright. She squeezes me tight, like she's trying to hold on to something she knows is slipping away.

Not much time passes before I see a police car pull up outside. It's Officer Markland, wearing the same Ray-Ban Wayfarer sunglasses she rarely takes off her face. The other officer is someone new—I haven't seen or dealt with him before. He's tall and has a slightly more professional appearance, his uniform pressed and crisp.

They walk in the door, barely giving us a passing glance, and immediately disappear behind the second set of doors leading to the back of the building.

I turn and grab Valerie, pulling her close. I breathe in the scent of her hair—vanilla and coconut—trying to memorize it.

I'm not sure how much time passes, but it seems like only seconds before the door opens again.

"Mrs. Watson, follow me," Officer Markland says flatly.

Valerie looks at me, terrified. I squeeze her hand once more, then let go.

The door quickly shuts behind them.

I try my best to see where they're taking her or listen to what they're saying, but I can't hear or see anything. The walls are too thick. The door too solid.

Feeling helpless and nauseous, I lean against the nearest wall. My legs feel weak. I plead the word "please" over and over in my head. I guess I feel like I've spoken to God so much in the past ten days that He knows exactly what I'm asking for.

Please let her go home. Please let her see our kids. Please, God, please.

After about five minutes—though it feels like an eternity—the door opens.

Valerie walks out. She's visibly upset but won't look at me. Her eyes are red, puffy, locked on the floor.

I'm confused. Did they charge her? Is she coming to jail with me?

I start to walk in her direction, but before I reach her, Markland calls out, "Mr. Watson, come this way!"

I take another step toward Valerie.

"Mr. Watson," Markland calls again, sharper this time.

I turn and follow her through the doorway and down a hall. I can see the cell doors at the end of the hall, a couple of sets of arms hanging through the cell bars like they're reaching for something they'll never grasp.

Markland opens an office door on the left side of the hall and motions me inside. The other officer is sitting in one of the chairs in front of the desk. They motion me to sit next to him as Markland sits behind the desk.

She pulls out a piece of paper and clears her throat.

"Mr. Watson, you are being charged with possession of ammunition. This is an offense that carries a minimum mandatory custodial sentence of twelve years. You will be taken into custody today." She pauses, looking at me over the paper. "You have the right to remain silent. Anything you may say may be held against you."

I've heard those rights read a thousand times over in the movies. But when they're being directed at you, they somehow sound much different. Like hearing them for the first time ever. The words echo in my head, hollow and heavy.

It makes my entire body numb.

I'm not sure how long I stare off into the ether before Markland speaks again.

"Mr. Watson, do you have anything to say?"

I shake my head.

"Mr. Watson, DO YOU HAVE ANYTHING TO SAY?"

"No. No comment."

Markland scribbles some notes in her file, shuts it with a snap, then looks over to the other officer and gives him a nod.

The male officer stands. "Mr. Watson, please stand up and turn around."

I comply, my movements mechanical. He leans down and puts shackles on my ankles. The metal is cold and heavy, biting into my skin.

"When we walk out of here, you are not to say a word to your family. If you look their direction or speak to them, you are going to make it worse on yourself."

It dawns on me that they must have threatened Valerie the same way. I'm relieved to know she wasn't avoiding me out of disappointment—she was just following orders.

They walk me back through the doorway and through the lobby, where Valerie, Mom, and Terry are standing. I get two steps into the lobby and think to myself, *They're already taking me away from my family. There's no way I'm going to let his threat deter me from telling my wife I love her one last time.*

I stop and turn to Valerie, looking her directly in the eye.

"I love you."

I immediately get shoved from behind, hard enough to stumble forward. I can hear the three of them get emotional—sobs breaking through—as the officers push me out the door and load me into the back of the police car.

As the car pulls away, I watch them through the window until they disappear from view.

"Valerie's going home, right?" I ask, my voice hoarse.

Markland, without turning her head, says, "As soon as she gets her passport, she'll be free to go wherever she wants."

I sink into the backseat and begin thanking God for allowing her to get back to our kids.

The jail at the Chalk Sound police station is apparently over capacity, so they have to transport me across the island to the Grace Bay station. Grace Bay is in the heart of the main tourist area of the island—a busy two-story shopping center flanked by clothing stores and a dog rescue.

When they pull the car to the front of the building, tourists stop and stare as they pull me out of the backseat. A couple takes a photo. A child points. I'm a spectacle now, entertainment for people on vacation.

They hand me the "jail bag" and escort me into the station, my feet shuffling, trying to keep up with them while shackled. The chains rattle with each step.

The station is smaller than Chalk Sound—a tiny lobby with a similar desk behind a glass partition. We pass through a door and down a hallway toward a lone steel jail door at the end.

There's an older officer waiting. He's a bigger man with a bald head and a thick mustache. When I reach him, he takes the bag from me and places it on a counter.

"Do you have anything on you that can poke or stick me?"

"No, sir."

He pats me down, his hands rough and thorough. Then he unlocks the cell door.

They grab my arm to lead me into the cell, but I don't move.

I turn to them. "Can I please have my Bible?"

The three officers look at each other and shrug.

Markland digs it out of my bag, which is still sitting on the counter. She holds it upside down and quickly shuffles through the pages—checking for contraband, I assume—before handing it to me.

They push me into the small 8x8 cell and sit me on a concrete bench that will now be my bed. They take my shackles off, which is a huge relief because they've been digging into my shin bone something fierce. Red marks ring my ankles.

They stand and exit, locking me in the cell.

When the door swings shut, it gets very dark.

There are no lights in the cell. The only light is the hallway light shining through the small 10" x 10" hole in the door. The vertical bars in the door are worn down from the grip of inmates who stood there before me, their hands polishing the metal smooth.

The smell is wretched—a combination of sweat, urine, and something worse. Fecal matter has been used to make Haitian gang markings on the wall, crude symbols I don't understand.

I sit on the concrete bench and close my eyes.

This is real now.

As I sit in the dark, the only thing I can think about is Valerie.

Did she make it to the airport? Was she able to get on a plane? Was she overwhelmed with anxiety going back through that security line? Did she lift the embargo and green-light our friends back home to unleash fury on social media? Or did she succumb to the threats?

These thoughts swirl in my head, one crashing into the next before I can fully process any of them.

I slide from that concrete bunk and go to my knees on the filthy floor. I start praising God for sending Valerie home to our kids. I'd once read that the same part of your brain that processes gratitude also processes anxiety—that you can't feel both at once. Whether the neurophysiology component of this is true or not, it's working. As my head clears, I begin focusing on the next steps.

I ask God for one thing.

"God, I pray that when Valerie lifts the embargo and our story breaks, it falls on the ears it needs to spread like wildfire."

~❖~

I hear the jingle of keys, then the turn of the lock to my cell.

As light floods in, I see the shadowy figures of two men.

"Prisoner Watson, step this way."

As I stand and walk toward them, I recognize one as the jail guard who checked me in. The other is a tall man with a big smile on his face.

"Mr. Watson, I'm with the forensics department. I'm here to conduct your fingerprinting and mugshots. Please, come with me."

I follow him into an office. As he begins fingerprinting me, rolling each of my fingers across the ink pad, he says, "I saw your Bible in your cell. That's good. You need to stay close to God and trust Him in this process. He can help you turn away from the sin that brought you here."

I feel extremely conflicted. I appreciate his spiritual belief, but I don't feel like being completely unaware of bullets falling into the lining of a bag constitutes a sin.

"You do know why I'm in here, don't you?"

The smile starts to fade from his face. "You're here because you broke the law."

I lean forward and plead with him as if he's the judge and jury presiding over my case. "I've never been in any kind of trouble. I had zero intent for those bullets to be in my bag. This was an honest mistake. I'm not a criminal of any kind!"

He gets even more serious and leans his arms on the table, looking me directly in the eye. "Whether you're innocent or not, that's for the courts to decide. And for that, you will need God."

Whether he means for me to pick up on it or not, his lack of faith in the court system is evident.

He finishes taking my mugshots—front, side, holding a number—and leads me back to my cell. He walks me inside and calls for the guard to come and lock it.

As the cell door swings shut, he quotes scripture. "Philippians 4:6-7: 'Do not be anxious about anything, but in every situation, by prayer and petition, with thanksgiving, present your requests to God. And the peace of God, which transcends all understanding, will guard your hearts and minds in Christ Jesus.'"

The door slams. The lock turns.

Darkness again.

I sit back on that concrete bunk and grab my Bible. I start looking up the verse the forensic officer quoted, but I'm interrupted again by the thought of Valerie and the kids.

I flip back to the cover of the Bible. Before I left for jail, I'd discovered that the cover of Valerie's Bible had started to separate from the binding, creating a little secret compartment. I'd stashed a photo of Valerie and the kids there.

I peek through the hole in the door to make sure no one can see me before pulling out the photo.

The image is worn at the edges from where I've been handling it. Valerie's smiling, both kids in her arms, all three of them laughing at something. It was taken last fall — before any of this.

I start talking to that photo as if I'm talking to them in person.

"I'm so sorry," I whisper. "I'm sorry that my oversight might rob you of the joy you have in this photo. But I promise—I promise I'll do anything and everything in my power to make it back to you."

~❖~

It's impossible to know what time of day it is when you're locked in a dark cell. As soon as I begin to wonder what time it is, I'm quickly reminded that time has lost its relevance to me.

It's a dark thought to process. It causes your mind to trudge even deeper into the darkness.

It isn't long before that voice in my head starts to speak. *Just because your time no longer has relevance doesn't mean the same for Valerie and the kids. You need to tell her to leave you and go find someone new who can help her raise the kids.*

The thought is soul-crushing. The people I live for will likely need someone else in order to truly live.

I begin to hate that voice. The anger swells, and it feels like I'm about to vomit.

I need to let it out.

I drop to the floor and start doing push-ups. As I do rep after rep, I swear to that voice in my head that I will prove it wrong. I never count the push-ups—I just do them until my arms give out.

My face falls to the fecal-ridden concrete floor.

After each manic push-up episode, I sit on the edge of my concrete bunk and read my Bible under what little light is peeking through that square hole in the door.

I hear a familiar voice from the front of the jail. "I'm here to see my son, Ryan Watson."

A boy can recognize his mom's voice anywhere.

My eyes start to well up. I quickly rub the tears away, reminding myself that this time, my mom can't save me from the position I'm in. I also
need her to see that I'm not broken, and have confidence I can endure this
process.

I hear the door to the lobby open down the hall. An officer walks her
a little over halfway down the hallway. I stand up and walk to the hole in
the door.

I can see Mom's face melt as she sees her son behind bars for the first
time.

"Mom, I'm okay."

She tries to walk further down the hallway toward me, but the officer
stops her. "Miss, that's far enough."

She fights back tears. "Ryan, Valerie made it on her flight. She should
be in Florida by now and getting ready to board her flight to Houston."

Immediately, a weight is lifted from my heart. I close my eyes and
thank God.

Mom looks at the guard. "Can I call his wife and let him speak to her?"

The officer sternly says, "No," putting his hand over her phone.

A formally dressed officer emerges from one of the offices in the hallway. "Let her make the call."

I can only assume he's a superior officer because the officer blocking
Mom starts inching her closer to my cell, stopping her a few feet from it.

She reaches out to touch me.

"No touching the prisoner."

Mom quickly pulls back her hand and nervously rifles through the contacts on her phone. She dials Valerie.

The phone rings. And rings. And rings.

Then the line connects.

"Hello?" Valerie's sweet voice comes through, and it nearly breaks me.

I choke back tears and clear my throat. "Hey, baby. Did you make it okay?"

Valerie's voice begins to tremble. "I just landed in Florida; I am waiting for my connecting flight to Houston. Your sister is flying to Houston to meet me, and we're going to stay at your cousin Melani's house until I can catch my flight to OKC in the morning."

"That's good, baby. I'm glad you're safe, and I'm so thankful you have family with you. I need you to know that I love you and I'm going to be okay."

The guard steps closer to Mom and places his hand over her phone. "That's enough."

I speak toward the phone, louder now. "I have to go now, babe. I love you. Please kiss the kids for me."

Valerie begins to cry and barely gets the words "I love you too" out before she loses it completely.

Mom looks up at me as the guard starts to shoo her down the hallway. "I love you, son. I'm so proud of you."

Then she's gone.

I sit back on the concrete bunk and pull out my Bible. I flip over to Acts 12—the story of Peter's imprisonment.

I read it over and over again. The more I read it, the more glaring the parallels between Peter's situation and mine become.

In this story, King Herod persecutes James. After killing James, he realizes this act is pleasing to the Jews. So Herod decides he's going to arrest Peter to gain even more favor. He imprisons him, intending to put him on a public trial. But while Peter is in prison, his church is earnestly praying for him. God then sends an angel who appears in the cell with Peter, puts the guards in a deep sleep, and the chains fall away. The angel walks Peter out the front door.

I set my Bible down and stare at the wall in awe.

The local TCI people celebrated Michael Grim's imprisonment, and Premier Misick responded by increasing the penalty to a twelve-year minimum. The mandatory sentence is painfully similar to how King Herod responded to the Jews. Both are men in power looking to increase their power by appeasing their people through political demonstrations.

I can't help but feel like Peter, sitting in that cell surrounded by guards.

I start to talk to God.

"God, I see how merciful You were to Peter by sending him an angel. I believe You did so because he and his church earnestly prayed and trusted You. I pray that my story is heard and that it inspires others to pray and trust in You as I will." I pause, gathering courage. "And Lord, I pray that You too send me an angel."

I can't tell you how long I lay there and pray that prayer. Hours, maybe. Or minutes. Time doesn't work the same way here.

Later that night, I hear my mom's voice out in the lobby. I can't tell what's being said, but it's undoubtedly her.

After several minutes, one of the officers makes his way down the hall.

"Prisoner Watson, someone has brought you food."

I'm confused. Can people just bring me food?

I sit up from the concrete bunk and walk to the door. The officer is holding a pizza box. He holds it sideways and tries mashing it between the bars in the hole in the door.

I kind of chuckle to myself that he actually thinks it will fit.

After several attempts of trying to fit the box—which is clearly too big—through that small hole, he gets frustrated and unlocks the door. He opens it just enough to hand me the box and slams the door back shut.

As he heads back down the hallway, I see Mom standing in the doorway he left open.

"I love you, son. Try your best to get some food in your stomach. I even brought these nice officers some pizza to say thank you."

The officer walks back and shoos her from the doorway as he closes it behind him.

I can't help but sit there and laugh. If anyone would try to butter up the prison guards with pizza, it's going to be my mom.

When I open the box—despite it being mangled from the guard's attempt at smashing it through the hole—it's evident that someone has taken a big bite out of one of the pieces. I'll later find out that the guards made my mom take a bite of any food she brought to ensure she wasn't poisoning me.

I try my best to force down a piece of that pizza, but my stomach is in a knot. I set the box aside and go back to reading the Bible.

A short time later, one of the officers sees me standing at the door using the hallway light to read my Bible. We make eye contact. He smirks and flips off the light.

This angers me to my core. To keep from saying something, I just lie down on that concrete bunk and shut my eyes.

I'm stewing as I lie there, listening to them have a pizza party down the hall.

Several minutes pass, and I hear the thud of boots sprinting down the hall. I shoot up and catch a flash of one of the officers running past my cell door. Then I hear the door to the restroom—just a few feet from my cell— slam against the wall as he flings it open.

The officer begins to puke his guts up.

I laugh to myself a bit as my mind starts to wander. *Did my mom just poison the guards?* I imagine my sweet mom busting down the hallway any minute with a blowtorch in hand to bust me out.

He emerges after about fifteen minutes of fighting for his life.

I stick my face in the hole of the door. "You good?"

It's the same officer who flipped the lights out on me. He must see a glimmer in my eye from the karma he just received because he just scoffs and walks down the hall.

And flips the light back out.

APRIL 23RD

A boot against my cell door jolted me awake. "Prisoner Watson, get up. You have court today. Time for showers." Turns out there are no shower facilities at this jail. I must be transported miles away back to Chalk Sound where there is a shower for prisoners. Chalk Sound jail would have inevitably been my fate, had it not been so far overcapacity at the time of my incarceration.

I peeled myself off the concrete bench, every muscle screaming in protest. Bryan's voice echoed in my head—he'd told me how much he stretched during his time locked up. I started stretching right there in the cell. Snickers drifted past as officers walked by. Let them laugh. I finished my stretches, then returned to my routine: Bible reading, pushups, waiting.

Hours crawled past. No one came.

When an officer finally passed, I called out, "Excuse me—someone said I had court today? That I needed to shower?"

He shrugged. "They'll get you when they get you."

Two more hours evaporated. My anxiety spiked with each passing minute. How could I make it to court on time if they never came for me?

The older officer with the thick mustache appeared at my door. "Watson, you have court in thirty minutes. Have they not taken you to shower yet?"

I shook my head.

"Do you have clothes for court? You need to get dressed."

I pointed across the hall where my bag sat on the counter.

"Let me grab someone to escort you to the bathroom." He disappeared, returning fifteen minutes later with another officer. They opened my cell and walked me down the corridor. One officer dumped my clothes onto a counter and searched every pocket, handing me each item one at a time like I was receiving prison-issued garments. When he pulled out my belt, he held it up like a trophy. "You're not allowed this." As if I'd smuggled in contraband.

The bathroom was filthy. I searched for a clean spot to set my clothes, found none, and started changing anyway. The moment I got my pants off, fists pounded the door.

"Prisoner Watson, your ride to court is here. You need to hurry up. You're going to make yourself late."

Make myself late? I'd been waiting for hours.

I yanked on my suit as the pounding continued. When I opened the door, Officer Markland stood there with the kind Jamaican woman who'd brought Val and me water during interrogation.

Markland turned to the officer. "Shackle him. We need to leave. We're going to be late."

Sunlight stabbed my eyes as we exited the station. I could barely see as they shoved me into the back of the police car. Markland threw the car into drive.

"You think it's a good look to be late to court?" she said.

I bit my lip hard enough to draw blood and stared straight ahead. Said nothing.

The engine whined as Markland flew through town and across the island toward the magistrate's court. When we arrived, several people stood outside the run-down shotgun-style building. We were clearly late.

As Markland pulled me from the car, I spotted my mom outside with Terry, Bryan, and Jonathan Franks. She was fighting back tears, watching her son being dragged around in chains.

Oliver met me in the doorway. "Remember, this is just magistrate's court. They don't have authority to oversee your case—this is pure formality. You don't need to say anything. Just stand when you're told."

They seated me in a partitioned box at the back of the courtroom. The bailiff knocked on the judge's door. "All rise!"

The judge entered, bowed, and began speaking as he took his seat. I couldn't hear a word. He seemed fifty yards away from my glass-enclosed box. I leaned forward, straining to catch anything. Useless.

Minutes later, his gavel slammed. Everyone stood.

Oliver made his way back to me. "Why were you late?"

"They never came to get me. Never let me shower, never let me out of my cell to change until it was time to leave. I was terrified I'd be in trouble."

He shook his head. "At the end of the day, the judge knows you're at the mercy of the officers. Don't worry about it. I need to rush to the Supreme Court to file your case. I'll come see you later."

I felt the car stop as Markland pulled out of the parking lot. I looked up to see my mom as Markland lowered my window.

"I'll give you one minute," she told my mom.

Mom inched toward the car, thanking Markland repeatedly. She placed her hand on my shoulder through the window. "I love you, son. I'm going to be by your side every step of the way."

"Thank you, Mom. I love you guys."

Terry leaned in. "Hang in there, buddy."

Markland put the car in drive. As we pulled away, I watched my mom crying in Terry's arms.

The Jamaican woman turned to Markland. "That's heartbreaking."

Markland stared at the road ahead.

"I don't understand, though," the woman continued. "Why did the judge say he couldn't rule on his case?"

"All firearms offenses go through Supreme Court," Markland said. "The magistrate appearance is just a formality."

"So he has to stay on the island until Supreme Court? How long will that take?"

Markland shrugged.

"I remember his wife saying they have kids. He has to be away from his kids all that time?"

"He's likely looking at twelve years in prison," Markland said.

Silence filled the car.

"Wait—this man is going to prison for twelve years? For an innocent mistake?"

Markland took a deep breath. "That's the new law. Mandatory twelve-year minimum custodial sentence."

The woman's voice cracked. "I think I might cry."

Markland adjusted her rearview mirror until she caught my eyes. "I want you to know, I don't believe in this. You should have been dealt with at customs, paid your fine, and gone home. But they didn't want customs agents handling these cases anymore, so now we are forced to deal with it."

I couldn't hold her gaze. I turned to the window and stared at nothing for the rest of the drive.

Later that day, footsteps approached my cell. I recognized Oliver's voice and stood as the officer unlocked the door. When he pulled out shackles, Oliver patted his shoulder. "That's not necessary, friend."

Oliver motioned me into an office next to my cell and shut the door quickly.

"We have a major problem," he said. "And you need to fix it."

I blinked. "What problem?"

"Did you not hear the judge's comment?"

"No, sir. I couldn't hear anything from where I was sitting."

"Someone sent him an email."

"Who? What did it say?"

"Some American called TCI a banana republic. Said they'd do everything in their power to make sure no one they knew ever visited the island again."

"Well, whoever it was isn't entirely wrong."

"Is this a joke to you? Do you know how bad this is going to be?"

"Oliver, I never asked anyone to send an email on my behalf. I don't even know anyone with access to that judge's contact information."

"His email address is listed on the website."

"Wait—his email is public, and he's upset that random people are voicing opinions? How is this remotely my fault?"

"You're listed in the email. The judge scolded me. Warned me that no threats would be tolerated."

"I never asked anyone to email a judge. I have no idea who sent it, and I have no way of finding out—especially from behind bars."

"I've asked the Supreme Court to conduct your bail hearing tomorrow. You'd better hope your friend didn't email that judge too."

Oliver stormed out. I walked back to my cell before the officer could escort me. He looked genuinely confused that I'd voluntarily returned to my cage.

I sat on my bench and actually chuckled, wondering who sent that email— probably one of my buddies back home with good intentions but poor judgment. One guy canceling his vacation wouldn't influence a judge.

But it meant word had gotten out about my arrest.

Questions cascaded through my mind. Did it make national news? Would media attention help my situation or make things worse? Would the public respond with empathy or condemnation?

Then one question silenced all the others: How were my kids responding?

I tortured myself imagining their reactions to the news that their dad might go to prison for twelve years.

Van and Ellie are only two years apart, but they have completely different personalities. A nine-year-old boy and a seven-year-old girl have different paternal needs—needs that would evolve over twelve years. My heart shattered thinking about Van not having someone to play catch with. About Ellie not having someone to take her to the next daddy-daughter dance. Were they thinking about these missed moments, too? Or were they just scared because I wasn't there to protect them?

I had zero doubt Valerie could step up and fill the voids in my absence. I've always admired her ability to parent with such ease and grace. She was super-mom.

But regardless of how amazing she was, I would still be leaving voids.

The darkest thought crept back in, the one I'd been pushing away: Was it fair to assume she'd wait for me for twelve years?

A lump formed in my throat. I couldn't swallow. Couldn't breathe.

My brain tried to consider if—and when—I should tell Valerie it was okay to move on. To find someone else to be with. To raise our kids with.

But my heart pulled so hard in the other direction that it wouldn't let my brain complete the thought.

This was the darkest thought I wrestled with. Not the idea of prison. Not the threat of being murdered in retaliation for going to the media.

It was trying to accept the idea that there might come a time when I would need to hand my life over to some other man.

APRIL 24TH

wake to the sound of loose ammunition spilling off a table.

At first, I am convinced that I must be having a nightmare about loose ammunition falling from the sky. Then I realize it's just the sounds of the shift change—officers ending their shift cutting up and laughing as they unload their magazines, and the incoming officers loading theirs.

It always seems to take them forever to load and unload their weapons. I really think it's just a way for them to procrastinate getting to work. Everything on this island runs on "island time," and the police are no different.

The only good part of the shift change is that all the lights are left on and the hallway doors are left open. This allows me to see through a sliver of a window in the lobby. I can generally reset my bearings as to what time of day it is—morning light filtering in, golden and warm.

As I get up from that nasty concrete bunk I've been calling a bed, every joint protests. I stretch and get back to my routine of push-ups and Bible reading.

The day before, I talked a guard into giving me an old newspaper he was about to throw away. I had no interest in reading their local news—I rarely have enough light to even read my Bible. I only wanted the newspaper to lie on the disgusting floor so I wouldn't get some nasty infection from the fecal matter or graveyard of cockroaches I've killed while doing push-ups.

This morning, though, I have ample light. As I'm doing my push-ups, I realize there's an article in the newspaper about two locals wanted for murder—one with the last name Misick, the other Forbes.

I think to myself, *Holy crap, everyone on this island truly does come from one of those families.*

The older guard with the mustache comes by my cell. "Prisoner Watson, sounds like you have court again today."

"I do? When?"

"Not sure what time yet, but we need to get you showered up this time, eh?"

"Yeah, that sounds great. Are we going now?"

"Calm down now, eh. You Americans are always in a rush! They'll come get you when they're ready."

I nod and sit back down, thinking to myself, *No, we Americans just think that showing up to places on time is common respect.*

I quickly realize that instead of trying to retool a culture's concept of timeliness, I'd do better to read as much as I can while I still have light shining into my cell.

A couple of hours must have passed as I read. All the commotion from the shift change has long died down, but all the doors are still open. I stare through the sliver of window in the lobby that I can see from my cell. I wonder what Valerie and the kids are doing. Are they up making breakfast? I'd almost bet she made those pancakes—the ones with chocolate chips the kids love.

It takes me a moment to realize that an officer has stepped into my line of sight. He realizes I'm gazing out that window. He quickly slams the door and goes down the hallway, slamming all the doors shut to the little offices on the side.

The light disappears. Back to darkness.

An hour or so of silence passes before I hear officers walking down the hall. I don't want to get my hopes up that someone's actually coming to get me.

To my surprise, though, the lock on my door clanks open, and four officers pull it wide. One is female, the other three are male. The officer in front is only about nineteen years old. I can tell he looks nervous—his eyes dart around, not quite meeting mine.

They give him a little shove to signal him toward me. The shackles in his hands start to jingle from his tremble as he holds them out.

I kind of feel sorry for him. "Would it make it easier for you if I sit down?"

One of the other males in the back orders sharply, "Prisoner, move towards the door for Officer Watson to shackle you!"

"Hey, we have the same last name, bud!" I joke with him, trying to help calm him down.

He cracks a nervous grin as he kneels to shackle my ankles. He fidgets with them forever before he finally ratchets them down on my ankles, digging into my shin bones. I wince.

The officers grab me by the arms and start pushing me down the hall. I try to walk, but my feet can hardly shuffle an inch. The times I had the shackles on before, I could at least walk with a super short stride, but this time I can't hardly move my feet at all.

One of the officers orders, "Let's go! Move your feet!"

"I can't move them, man. Something's wrong with the shackles."

They ignore me and continue dragging me down the hall, my shoes scraping across the linoleum.

I hear the old man with the mustache say, "Hey, man, he's going to need his things," as he holds my bag and follows us down the hall.

When we walk outside, there are quite a few tourists in the shopping area adjacent to the station. They all stop and stare as the officers load me into the SUV at gunpoint and throw my bag in the back.

Those tourists must think I'm guilty of something extremely gruesome to warrant such a detail.

One male officer gets into the driver's seat, the heavy-set female officer sits in the passenger seat, and another male officer sits in the back seat with me.

The officer pulls off through the parking lot a few feet before jerking to a halt. He begins to wrestle with the submachine gun that's harnessed across his chest. It's preventing his arms from being able to turn the steering wheel.

I can't help it—I'm laughing before I even realize I'm laughing.

He shoots me a glare through the rearview mirror as he continues to wrestle the gun and harness off him. I try my best to keep from laughing, but he looks like a little kid trying to pull off a turtleneck two sizes too small.

When he finally gets it off and passes the gun to the female officer in the passenger seat, the barrel of the gun swings by mine and the other officer's faces in the backseat.

We both duck.

"Geez, man, watch where you're pointing that thing!" the officer next to me says.

The female officer jumps in. "Now what do you want me to do with this?" holding the machine gun in the air like it's a snake she doesn't want to touch.

"Just hold it while I drive," the officer says as he puts the car back in drive and pulls out onto the road.

She fumbles with it a bit before deciding she'll just point the barrel out the passenger window.

Oh, great, I think. *This is how I die. Not in prison, not murdered by inmates, but by incompetent police officers who can't handle their own weapons.*

We fly through the little town of Grace Bay on our way to the Chalk Sound police station. We pull up to the intersection to turn left onto Dock Road from Leeward Highway.

I notice a lady pulled up next to us. She has her visor mirror down, putting on makeup at the intersection. She's not paying attention to anything around her—I've seen Valerie do this many times before.

At some point, I guess she's happy with her makeup and turns to look out her window.

She sees the barrel of a submachine gun pointed directly at her.

The lady jumped out of her seat, hitting her head on the roof of her car. I can't hear her, but I can see her mouth scream, "What are you doing?!"

I think to myself, *I'm wondering the same thing, lady! I'm in the custody of the most ragtag police force known to man.*

As we make our way down Dock Road, the female officer says, "Hey, pull in here, man. I'm starving," pointing to a food trailer parked along the road.

The officer driving casually just pulls off the road and puts the car in park.

The female officer gets out and stands in line to order.

"Hey man, don't we have to get to court soon?"

The officer just ignores me and turns up the radio. Some reggae song I don't recognize fills the car.

At least ten minutes tick by before the female officer returns, excited and singing along to the song on the radio. She pulls her food from the sack—the smell of fried fish fills the car.

As the officer driving puts the car back in drive, he turns down the volume. "The American prisoner doesn't think he has time for your lunch."

"Pssh, I work hard, baby. I'm entitled to have a lunch break."

When we pull up to the Chalk Sound police station, the two male officers get out as the female officer sits in the passenger seat, enjoying her lunch.

As they're pulling me out of the car, the officer holding my bag pulls my suit from it and holds it up.

"No racks!"

"No, what?" I ask, confused.

"No racks!" He shouts again, holding up my suit, shaking it in my face.

"Sir, I'm sorry, I have no clue what a rack is."

"No racks!"

About that time, an officer comes out of the Chalk Sound station. "He's talking about your hangers, but don't sweat it, man. He's cool, man, he can't do anything with that rack." The officer says this to the other, like I'm not even there.

The three of them try to escort me into the building, but my feet still can barely shuffle an inch.

"What's wrong with him?" the Chalk Sound officer asks.

One of them replies, "Nothing's wrong with him. He just won't cooperate."

I try to shuffle my feet as fast as I can, but I can't keep up with them, so they just grab my arms and drag me into the station. My shoes scrape across the pavement, then the tile floor.

They drag me through the lobby and down the hall. As we pass the cells to my left, I can see how overcrowded they are. It looks like a dog shelter with a bunch of dogs crammed into one pen. Men pressed against the bars, staring out with hollow eyes.

There's a bathroom just beyond the cells. When we get there, one of the officers kneels down to unshackle my legs.

He starts laughing hysterically as soon as he sees my feet.

"Hey, boys, you've got to come see what the rookie did!"

Several officers enter the bathroom, take a closer look at my shackles, and start busting up laughing.

"Hey, boy, the rookie officer put your shackles on upside down and inside out."

I'm confused, so I lean over to see what they're mocking me for. The shackles the young officer had put on my feet are placed upside down, so that the pieces the chain connects to are on the outside of my legs, not between my legs like they should be.

"Hey, boy, here we were thinking you were being difficult, and it was just that we had you hog-tied with your shackles." He slaps his knee, still laughing. "But hey, I ain't laying down on that floor to take them off of you, so we need you to lie down on your belly and hold your legs up."

Since the keyhole to the shackles is now on the underside, they make me lie face-first on that nasty bathroom floor while they take them off.

As soon as I get down and hold my feet up, one of the officers says, "Wait, wait, wait, I have to get a picture of this."

They all laugh and take pictures of me lying face-first on the bathroom floor, pointing at the misplaced shackles on my feet, before finally taking them off.

I stand, my face burning with humiliation, and start stripping for the shower.

The shower is freezing cold, but it feels good to wash all the grime off me. I keep it quick—I'm not sure how long I have until court.

I tiptoe, dripping wet, across the dirty floor to grab my towel. As soon as I dry my face—

Bang, bang, bang!

"Prisoner Watson, hurry up in there!" One of the guards shouts through the door.

The only time any of these guards is ever concerned about time is when I'm changing.

I hop one-legged all over that bathroom, trying to pull my suit on over my damp body.

"Bang, bang! Prisoner Watson, you're about to make yourself late for court!"

I've only been in here for four minutes tops, and *I'm* the one who's going to make us late?

I quickly throw my socks and shoes on and open the door while still trying to stomp one foot down in my shoe.

"What took you so long?"

I just hand him my bag and hold up my pant legs for him to put my shackles back on.

"I'm not bending down on that floor to put those on. Put them on yourself." The guard hands me the shackles.

I'm over this guy's attitude. I've been nothing but respectful, and he continues to berate me like a rented mule.

I just stare him in the eyes, kneel down, and slap the first shackle on my ankle like I've seen done in the movies.

Damn. I got it way too tight, and it's digging into my shin bone. I don't want to flinch or ask him to loosen it and lose my tough-guy message I'm trying to send. So, I make sure to put the second one on more carefully.

I'm careful not to break my stare as I stand up.

We stand there in the hall playing the don't-blink game for a few moments before he grabs my arm.

TURKS AND CHAOS

"Walk!"

I sit quietly staring at my feet as we make our way to the Supreme Court building. The shackle on my right ankle is definitely cutting into my skin—I can feel something warm, probably blood, trickling down.

I realize the car has started to slow down. I hear the ticking of the turn signal, so I look up and start looking around for the building.

All I can see is a two-story, run-down strip mall.

One of the officers sees my eyes panning around in confusion. "We have to make another stop."

"Don't I need to be at the courthouse? I thought we were in a hurry?"

They all just ignore me as the car pulls in and up to a restaurant at the corner of the strip mall. I can see several other police cars parked at the restaurant.

The officer who's driving gets out and goes into the restaurant. A few minutes later, he comes out with a line of officers following him. I can tell they're laughing about something.

As they approach, the female officer rolls down her window as well as mine in the backseat.

They all crowd around, peeping into my window like I'm an exhibit at a zoo.

"This is the American, huh?"

They all laugh and make jokes. I can't make out most of what they're saying, but I catch "stupid tourist" and something about "twelve years."

The driver answers his phone and quickly shoves it back in his pocket. "Okay, okay, we have to get him to court now."

He jumps back in the car, and we speed off toward the Supreme Court building.

As much as their game of show-and-tell pisses me off, it has to be a sign that word must be spreading.

I carefully climb the stairs to the courthouse one step at a time. I'm pretty sure my right leg is bleeding from the shackle being so tight. It provides a good distraction from the submachine gun that's pointed at my side.

That officer has already made it clear he's a liability trying to pack that gun around, and I feel no better about it being in my side.

As we make it to the top of the stairs, I hear someone shout, "There you are!"

A Black man in a black robe and a blonde powdered wig is running toward me.

"Oliver?"

"We need to discuss your case. The DPP has offered not to contest bail if you agree to be remanded to the island."

"Oliver, why are you dressed up like the Quaker Oats guy?"

"You are not taking this seriously."

"I'm trying to take you seriously, but I'm just a little thrown off by your outfit."

"I'm a part of the King's counsel. This is how you're to dress in a British courtroom."

"So is everyone dressed up like that? Do I need a robe and a wig?"

"No, you don't need a robe. You just need to listen. The DPP is NOT going to contest your bail if you remain remanded to the island. This is a positive first win."

"Man, you said you would at least try to get my passport back, you know, given the nature of my work."

"I'm telling you, they were never going to give your passport back. They knew exactly what would happen if they gave that back to you."

As much as I want to throw up a Hail Mary in an attempt to get my passport and get off the island, I know he's right. They're never going to let me leave, and I do not want to go back to that jail cell.

"Okay. Let's accept those conditions."

Out of the corner of my eye, I notice a local man about twenty yards off to the right. He's trying to be sneaky and snap pictures of me with his cell phone.

I tell Oliver under my breath, "There's a man over there taking photos of us."

Oliver looks up and immediately recognizes him as a local reporter. "You know it's a violation of the crown to take photos here."

The reporter smirks. "It seems to me like your client wants his photo out there. He's doing everything he can to get it out to the world."

"I know you got a little money tucked away. Don't make a member of the King's counsel come and take it—you know I'd gladly do so." Oliver shoots back at him.

They both laugh as the reporter tucks his phone back in his pocket.

Oliver turns to me. "We must get in there."

~❖~

We enter the Supreme Courtroom. It's much different than the magistrate court. Everyone, including the bailiffs, is dressed in robes and wigs. It looks like I'm watching some theatrical remake from a British courtroom in the 1800s.

They place me in a wooden box. It looks like I'm in a wooden birdcage.

Mom, Terry, Bryan, and Jonathan are all seated directly behind me. I turn and give Mom a small smile. Her eyes are red—she's been crying.

The courtroom gets silent. The bailiff marches over to the door to the judge's quarters and gives it three perfectly timed knocks before pivoting and standing at attention.

The door opens, and the judge in her bright red robe and blonde powdered wig steps into the room.

"All hail the King!" the bailiff shouts.

Everyone in attendance repeats, "All hail the King!"

Judge Jackson bows, and everyone else around me bows. Distracted by all the theatrical performance going on around me, I'm a little late with my bow.

When I look up from bowing, I can see the judge scowling and staring a hole through my forehead.

I stand awkwardly as she makes her way to the bench.

She reads aloud, "The King versus Ryan Watson..."

As she continues reading the charges, I keep thinking to myself, *This can't be real life. One oversight, and now it's me versus the royal court? This all has to be the most elaborate prank someone has ever pulled.*

"Mr. Watson, please take your seat."

I snap back to reality and look around. Everyone is staring at me.

It must be obvious to everyone that the combination of shock and trying to sleep on a concrete slab the past couple of nights has left me not tracking at regular speed.

I take my seat and try my best to pay attention to what's being said between Oliver and the DPP. But given they have me seated near the back of the courtroom, coupled with their thick Caribbean accents, I'd need subtitles to follow along.

"And does Mr. Watson have surety?" I finally make out a question the judge has asked.

I nervously pan the seats behind me to make sure Dale has actually shown.

"He does, Your Majesty," Oliver replies.

I never spot Dale, but Oliver answered confidently enough to curb my anxiety.

"The bail will be set at fifteen thousand, to be provided in the form of surety."

Whack! The judge slams the gavel and stands.

"All rise!" the bailiff shouts.

The judge bows, then immediately darts her eyes back in my direction to ensure I bow back to her in a timely manner.

I bow quickly this time.

Once she leaves the courtroom, everyone starts conversing and milling about. I stand up as Oliver makes his way over to the birdcage.

The bailiff shouts, "Mr. Watson, please remain seated until everything gets sorted."

I quickly sit back down.

"I'm going to go downstairs and help get your surety sorted out with Dale," Oliver says as he takes off his blonde wig and robe.

Mom approaches the cage I'm in and asks Oliver, "Is it okay if I hug him?"

"Yeah, man," Oliver says, gesturing in my direction.

Mom, Terry, and Bryan all line up to hug me. It catches me off guard when I feel Terry's body start to shake as I hug him. I realize how lucky I am to not only have a mother who loves and supports me through it all, but to also have a stepparent show up for me in this way.

It brings me to tears.

We're finally given the word that they're finishing up with my paperwork, and we can go downstairs. We follow the bailiff down the stairs into the lobby.

Dale is there, finishing up his portion of the paperwork. I walk up and hug his neck. Not sure he's much of a hugger, but I want him to know I truly appreciate what he's doing.

I ask him again if there's anything I can do to repay his generosity. He declines my offer and makes his way out the door.

Oliver makes his way over and gives me the terms of my bail. The court needs to know my whereabouts at all times, and I'll have to sign in to jail every Tuesday and Thursday. Any violation of these orders will land me right back behind bars.

I sign the order.

Oliver says, "You are officially out on bail."

We walk out of the courthouse, and there are several local reporters in the parking lot taking photos of us.

Mom clenches my hand. "Son, you're probably going to have to get used to people snapping photos of you."

I nod, accepting the challenge. I've always hated being in front of any camera, but this is the potential path off the island I chose.

"I'm starving. Can we go get some food?"

Mom looks up at me. "You bet, but we need to probably eat quickly."

I'm confused. I'm stuck on an island—it seems like I have nothing but time.

"Son, this story has blown up. You have a lot of interviews to get to."

This news stops me in my tracks halfway down the courthouse steps. It's the first confirmation I've heard that our story has gotten out and caught any traction.

I'm joyed and scared all at the same time.

No backing out now.

Mom turns back to me. "Come on, we have a lot to talk about in the car."

We all pile into Reuben's Suburban. Jonathan turns to me. "It's good to finally see you not behind bars or in chains. A lot has taken place in the past seventy-two hours. We need to plan out what the next twenty-four hours look like with media."

I look up to the rearview mirror to see Reuben looking back at us in the backseat. The jovial expression on his face that I've come to expect is replaced with one of concern.

I smile, and he smiles back, but I can still see concern in his eyes.

I look to Jonathan. "I look forward to catching up at the restaurant, but I'd like to call Val first."

Terry hands me my phone from the front seat. He's been holding onto it since before I went to jail—we did this to prevent the TCI police from going through it and seeing all the planning that went into going to the media and waging economic war.

When I unlock my phone, I see there are hundreds of missed calls and text messages. I can barely get to Valerie's contact as there are still messages and calls coming in by the second.

I quickly hit the FaceTime button before another alert comes across my phone.

It rings. And rings.

Finally, she picks up.

"Hey, good-looking," I say as I flash a big grin at her in an attempt to distract her from my chin quivering as I fight back tears.

I can tell she's trying to fight back the same tears of joy and heartache.

"Hey, babe. I love you and miss you."

I can hear the kids in the background ask, "Is Daddy on the phone?"

I take a deep breath and put on a brave face as they run to the phone.

Within seconds, the kids are crawling into Valerie's lap to get a look at me through her phone.

"Hey, guys! It's so good to see you. Daddy loves you and misses you."

"We love you too," they both say in unison.

"Daddy, were you in jail?" Ellie says.

I can't help but chuckle. When you're seven, you want to cut to the chase.

"Yes, honey. Daddy had to go to jail for a bit, but I'm out now, and I'm okay."

"Does that mean you're coming home tomorrow?" she shoots back.

"No, honey. Daddy still has some things I have to work out here."

"So, when are you coming home?"

Valerie can see my heart breaking through the phone, so she jumps in to answer Ellie. "Baby, we don't know when Daddy's going to come home. But he's working very hard to make it home to us as soon as possible."

Van is being quiet, and I can tell he's thinking hard about something.

"Van, how are you, buddy?"

"Good," he says while trying to smile.

I can tell he's hurting.

"Buddy, I'm sorry this is happening. Your dad never meant for us to go through this, but I do know that God has a reason for us in all of this. I'm going to do everything in my power to make it back home to you and to help Mr. Bryan get back home to his family. You know that, right?"

He nods while staring down at his lap.

"But most of all, we're going to serve and glorify God through all of this."

He looks up at me and nods with a look that's beyond the seriousness anyone would expect from a nine-year-old.

"Daddy, you're on the TV," Ellie says.

I laugh. "I am? Do I look handsome?"

Ellie gives me a bashful grin.

"You guys are probably going to see and hear a lot as we go through this. I want you to remember one thing. This was a really unfortunate accident, and sometimes people get in trouble for things that are complete accidents. It doesn't mean they're bad people."

Valerie pulls the phone a little closer to her face. "There's a lot we need to discuss in terms of the media plan. Can you call me later tonight?"

I agree, and we say our goodbyes.

As I look up from the phone and wipe the tears from my eyes, I can tell everyone else in the car is doing the same.

We're all in this together, and we're sharing emotions.

Reuben pulls up to a restaurant, and we all pile out to grab some food. We make our way to a table in the back corner of the restaurant to have some bit of privacy.

As we walk through the restaurant, it feels like every person there is staring.

I lean over to Bryan. "I guess this is something we're going to have to get used to."

"It feels so strange," he says, trying to digest our new reality. "By the way, I ended up moving into the condo with your mom and Terry. Things have been sketchy on the island since the news broke."

I patted Bryan on the back. "I am glad to have you stay with us. We are in this together. We are brothers now."

As we order lunch, Jonathan starts laying out all the interviews we have lined up in the next twenty-four hours. There are a lot of interviews to do, but we have to prioritize them. It's important this story isn't just a flash in the pan. We need to get the public invested and keep them engaged to increase pressure on the TCI government as well as our U.S. elected officials.

The first step to doing this means I need to show the world that I'm just a family man who made a simple oversight while on vacation. We'll then need to quickly redirect the spotlight to Bryan as his court date is up first.

~❖~

After we finish our meal, we all go up to Jonathan's hotel room. He's set up his laptop and moved lamps around his room to create a makeshift studio—something we'll all get pretty efficient at in time.

I do so many interviews back-to-back in such a short span of time that I lose track of who I'm talking to. Local news, national news, podcasts, radio shows—they all start to blur together.

I do my best to end every interview by stating, "We're not the only family being torn apart by this. Bryan Hagerich has been stuck on this island for seventy days, and his trial is looming."

After the first couple of interviews, Jonathan starts getting booking producers asking if he can connect them with Bryan.

This is such a relief to see—they're interested in telling more of the story.

We pause from my interviews and put Bryan in front of the camera—aka laptop. I step out of the room to give him some privacy and keep him from getting nervous or uncomfortable.

When I get outside, Mom hands me her phone. "Someone wants to speak to you."

"Hello?"

"Ryan, this is Mark Wayne Mullin."

"Senator Mullin! It's awesome to hear from you!"

"I want you to know that I'm personally going to take the lead on your situation, and you can call me anytime, day or night, if you need me. You have to just promise me one thing..."

"Anything, buddy! Just name it."

"Promise me that when you get home, you won't take up politics and run against me!"

I bust up in much-needed laughter.

"Seriously, man, I've never gotten so many phone calls and letters on a matter. We had to designate someone to just handle all the calls and messages on your behalf."

"Man, I'm humbled to know that many people are on my side, but I can promise you I have no business in politics."

"But seriously, though, I'm going to do anything and everything I can to get you out of there. My wife Christie is on the phone with Valerie now to offer her some additional support back here at home."

"I greatly appreciate that, and I know Valerie will greatly appreciate that as well. I know God chose us to go through this for a reason, and we're going to lean on Him through all of this."

"Can I pray for you?"

"I would love that!"

I choke back tears as Mark Wayne says the most eloquent prayer—asking God for protection, for justice, for our family to be reunited.

"Buddy, know that Kristi and I are here for you and Val and will continue to fight and pray for you."

"Thanks, buddy!"

As the line disconnects, I think to myself, *Did I just call a sitting U.S. Senator buddy?*

I peer through a sliver between the curtains covering the sliding glass doors to the patio. Bryan is just wrapping up his last interview.

I slide the door open. "How did it go?"

"Good, I think!" Bryan replies.

Jonathan chimes in. "Oh man, you guys did great! This was quite a day of making some serious media impact! We'll have another big day tomorrow. You guys need to go get some rest, and we can start back at it tomorrow morning."

As we walk out to the parking lot, I take a deep breath of the warm Caribbean air.

I'm out of jail. I'm on bail. The story is spreading.

But I'm still trapped on this island, and the fight is just beginning.

APRIL 25TH

wake to the constant dinging of my phone. As I rub my eyes, a wave of anxiety washes over me at the sight of all the unread messages. They're all messages of support, concern, and requests for updates on my well-being.

I feel overwhelmed by the feeling that I owe a response to everyone who's showing me support. The number keeps climbing—fifty, sixty, seventy unread messages.

I stumble into the kitchen to grab a cup of coffee, my bare feet padding across the cool tile floor. Mom is sitting behind the laptop, diligently reading and taking notes, her glasses perched on her nose.

"Hey," I say, my voice still hoarse from sleep.

"Hey, baby. You want me to make you something for breakfast?"

"No thanks. I'm just going to have coffee."

I pour a cup, the steam rising with the familiar smell of dark roast, and sit down next to her. "What are you working on?"

"Just going through all of the articles to see what everyone is saying." She pauses, looking at me over her glasses. "Ryan, you need to know that a large majority of the world is supporting you. But there are people out there saying some pretty awful things about you."

"We knew there would be, Momma. Just ignore those people. All the ignorance and hate they spew in the comments section from their parents' basement will only draw more attention to the matter. Let them stir the pot—it'll only help."

"You don't know what it's like to be a parent and to read someone say such terrible and untrue things about your child." Her voice cracks slightly.

"I get it, but do your best to stay out of the comments sections."

I open my phone back up, the screen bright in the morning light. "I need to get started on trying to respond to all of these messages."

"Don't overwhelm yourself, son. People know you're going through an insanely difficult time and don't expect you to message back right away."

As I open my emails, I notice the most recent one is from my old friend Casey Thompson. The subject line reads: "YOU DID IT."

The email says: "You wanted your story to make a splash. You just got the attention of the entire world. It's time to do something with it! See the attached…"

I open the attachment. It's a chart showing the metrics of our story—reach, engagement, and media outlets covering it. In the top-right corner, a box shows the total number of media impressions.

Confused at what I'm looking at, I rub the remaining sleep from my eyes and look again.

It reads: "Total Media Impressions: 2.9B"

"Bryan, get in here!" I yell, startling Mom, who's still sitting right next to me at the kitchen table.

"What! What is it?" Mom says, her hand on her chest.

As Bryan makes his way into the kitchen, I hold my phone out for them both to see.

"I just received this email from my friend Casey, who's in PR. She's been running metrics on our story to help give us guidance. Look at the total number of media impressions."

They both lean in closer, squinting at the screen.

"Does that say two point nine *billion*?" Bryan asks.

"Yes, it does!"

"Holy crap! That's amazing!"

"No, that's God!" I stand up, adrenaline surging through me. "He's given us the world's attention. Now we have to get to work on exposing this island!"

My mom, Terry, Bryan, and I sit around the table and start making a plan. We need to use the media not only to put economic pressure on the island but also to pressure our government to intervene.

I know we have the support of Senator Mullin, but he'll need the Department of State's involvement. What would actually cause the State Department to get involved?

After several hours of searching online, my mom comes across a document that lists eleven justifications for the State Department to intervene. Out of the eleven, there are two very clear justifications: (1) inhumane prison conditions, (2) U.S. citizens being targeted based upon their citizenship.

The first is going to be easy to prove. There are articles all over the internet about the United Nations condemning Turks and Caicos' "Her

Majesty's Prison." In addition to this, we can use Michael Grim's firsthand account of the prison, if he's willing.

We all very clearly sense that Americans are being targeted, but proving that to the public and the State Department is going to require a lot more than just a feeling.

We need to find the Jane Doe we saw dragged into the station for also having ammo. In my gut, I know there's more to her story, and that could be exactly what we need.

Bryan has a connection: Croc. Croc is a guard at Chalk Sound jail who was actually friendly toward Bryan. It turns out Croc has become friends with and is still in contact with Dave O'Connor. Dave is a New Yorker who got arrested for having ammunition in his bag prior to Michael Grim. He was on the island for a month or so before paying a fine and being allowed to return home. Dave is a successful business owner and helped out Croc financially after he returned home. I'm sure this had an influence on Croc's willingness to help Bryan.

Bryan calls Croc and tells him we're looking to find a blonde girl who was detained at the airport on April 15th for having ammunition in her bag.

Croc says he hasn't heard of any girl aside from Valerie being arrested, but he'll poke around while at the station.

While Bryan's trying Croc, I decide to try Lane at the U.S. Embassy.

When I mention the girl, I notice he pauses and quickly changes his tone. "We are not aware of any other U.S. citizen having been arrested. But even if we had, we cannot discuss or disclose any information regarding their situation."

Bryan looks over at me as I hang up the phone. I shake my head. "He says they don't have any other report of a U.S. citizen being arrested, but also noted he wouldn't be able to disclose any information regarding their case. I could tell it wasn't the first time he was hearing about that girl, though."

I look down at my phone and see the time. It's 3 p.m.

"I have to go sign in to the jail!"

It's my first required day to sign the bail book at the Grace Bay jail, and I've almost forgotten due to the shuffle of media interviews and research. I can't give them any reason to put me back behind bars.

I throw my tennis shoes on and fly out the front door into the blazing afternoon heat.

It's about a mile and a half to the station. If I book it, I should be there in under ten minutes.

As I run, my mind starts to race. The more it races, the faster my feet move. I'm not sure if I'm still trying to make it to the jail on time or if I'm pretending to run away from this place.

I'm strangely comforted by all the discomfort my body is starting to feel—the burning in my lungs, the sweat stinging my eyes, the pounding of my heart. I realize in that moment how numb I've felt up until now. This pain is real. This pain is mine.

When I get to the Grace Bay station, I stand outside trying to catch my breath. My shirt is soaked through with sweat. I look around to see a number of tourists staring at me.

I don't know if they're recognizing me from the news or if they're staring because I've been running in a dead sprint to the police station.

Still trying to catch my breath, I pull open the door and duck into the station. The air conditioning hits me like a wall of cold.

I walk up to the partition window, where one of the officers who saw me just the day before is standing.

"I'm here to sign the bail book," I manage between breaths.

The lady officer stares back at me with a look of disapproval. "I need to see your ID."

"Ma'am, I don't have my ID."

"How do you think you're going to sign the book without a form of ID?"

"Ma'am, you confiscated my passport when you arrested me." I pause, catching my breath. "If you'd like to return my passport to me, I'll gladly show that to you."

I smile. She glares.

Another officer appears from the back. "Just let him sign the book. We all know who the American is at this point."

She takes out the book and shoves it at me through the hole in the glass.

As I sign, I realize the sweat dripping from my hand has caused the ink from all the other signatures to bleed and smudge across the page.

She takes the book back, sees what I've done, and her face hardens.

As I open the door to leave, I shrug. "Sorry, it's hot out there. Y'all have a blessed day!"

I know it's petty, but it feels good to know I'm under their skin.

~❖~

Later that evening, Bryan gets a call from Croc. At first, I see a look of disappointment come across Bryan's face, but in an instant, his expression turns to shock.

He can see I'm in suspense to learn what he's been told.

As he hangs up the phone, he says, "Croc says there's no record of any female being arrested."

"That's crazy! We all saw her!"

"Ryan," he pauses, his voice dropping. "He did find that there was another American male arrested, though. He was coming off a cruise ship in Grand Turk when they found a bullet in his bag."

Mom and Terry spring up from the kitchen table and come to the living room where we're talking.

"They arrested another American?!" Mom says in disbelief.

My mind immediately starts spinning. Could this hurt our situation? Was he knowingly breaking the law? What if he's a questionable guy? There are so many questions stirring, but I know we need to help him.

We need to figure out how to get in touch with him.

Bryan gets his name from Croc. We pass it along to some of our media contacts, knowing they'll likely be able to track his family down.

We're right. We have his wife Jerrianne's contact information in under an hour.

We call his wife, Jerrianne. I can tell by her voice that she's young—probably mid-twenties. She seems like she's in shock and doesn't really have all the pieces to make sense of what's going on.

We try our best to explain to her what we're all facing while also trying not to send her into a panic attack.

She's extremely quiet. It almost seems like she's reluctant to believe us.

She mentions she hasn't spoken to Tyler, as he's still in custody at Her Majesty's Prison, but he's planning on staying there to avoid having to pay for bail.

Bryan and I both try to explain that this is a bad idea. Not only are the prison conditions horrific, but being out on bail is really the only way to help his attorney build a defense.

She tells us that Tyler's dad, Michael, has flown to the island and is staying in Grand Turk. He's the only one in direct communication with Tyler, which is taking place during approved visitations.

We try to reassure her that we'll do anything we can to help Tyler. I'm not sure how much assurance she gets from the two of us—two guys she's never met, calling her out of the blue with horror stories.

As we end the call, she sends Michael's contact.

I immediately dial Michael. When he answers, Bryan and I both introduce ourselves.

He responds, "I've been watching both of your interviews and reading up on your stories."

"Yeah, I know the media is a little crazy, but we've looked at this from just about every angle, and we believe it's our only way off this island."

"I have to be honest, guys. It makes me really nervous. While walking to the prison to visit Tyler today, one of the main guards picked me up in his car. He told me he really didn't appreciate the media attention you two were stirring up."

"I'm not going to sugarcoat it—this is economic warfare, and we're probably going to ruffle a lot of feathers."

"Tyler's a pretty quiet guy, and I can't see him wanting to get in front of a camera. We just think it would be in our best interest to lay low and try to handle this quietly."

"Michael, that's entirely up to you and Tyler, and we'll respect that. I do want you to know that the media already has his name and will most likely be reporting on it by tomorrow morning. I really just wanted to call and offer to help in any way we can." I pause, choosing my words carefully. "Jerrianne mentioned he's planning on staying in prison until his hearing. I really think this is a bad idea. Beyond worrying about his well-being in that prison, I worry he won't be able to find and assemble the best defense."

"I think he's trying to do this mostly to manage the financial impact it'll have on his family."

"His bigger concern should be getting back to his family. If the court allows him to pay a cash bail, I'd be happy to assist with the cost. They'll likely make him find surety, as they did with me. If that's the case, I'll make calls on his behalf to the few locals we know."

There's a pause on the other end of the line. "Really? You'd be willing to do that?"

"Absolutely! Whether he knows it or not, we have a bond now. We're in this together. Talk to Tyler tomorrow. I think it would be best for him to be out on bail."

Bryan chips in. "Michael, this is going to be a much longer process than you think. I've been on this island for over seventy days, and I haven't even gotten to my hearing yet. It really would be best for him to try and get bail."

Michael concedes, his voice heavy with exhaustion. "Okay. I'll go to the prison and talk to him tomorrow. I'll call you tomorrow afternoon."

Bryan and I walk out to the screened-in porch. It's late, and the air is cooler now, the sound of crickets and distant waves filling the silence. It feels like we don't have to worry about being seen or heard out here.

We strategize how we can utilize the fact that there's another American being arrested to avoid being washed out of the news cycle. There's a pattern of Americans being arrested, and we can focus on that. Tyler doesn't necessarily have to get in front of a camera for his arrest to add fuel to the fire.

We begin to fire off messages to every media relation we've acquired to this point. Our phones light up the darkness, fingers flying across screens.

My mom comes outside to bring us drinks—sweet tea in plastic cups, condensation already forming on the outside.

When she sees us with stacks of notes, newspapers, and phones laid out on the table, she jokes, "It looks like you boys are in the war room planning your next mission."

We grin and give each other a cheers, the plastic cups clinking together.

"Welcome to the war room, Mom!"

We've only known each other for a few days, but we're in a workflow state that would normally take teams years to achieve. We finish each other's sentences, anticipate each other's next moves, and divide tasks without discussion.

That porch, from that moment forward, becomes affectionately known as the "war room."

TURKS AND CHAOS

The place where two strangers became brothers.

The place where we declared war on an entire island.

And the place where we refuse to surrender until we're home.

APRIL 26TH

The media is already in an all-out frenzy. As news of Tyler's arrest starts to circulate, it only adds more fuel to the fire—gasoline on an already raging blaze.

Messages from friends start pouring in with screenshots of different politicians and celebrities posting in support of us. My phone buzzes constantly, each notification bringing a new wave of surreal validation.

"Holy crap, Watson! Joe Rogan just tweeted about you." One message from Trey reads.

I stare at the screen. Joe Rogan. The Joe Rogan. Tweeting about me.

These all seem like some sort of victory, but the question gnaws at me: will the noise help us get home, or are we just stirring the hornet's nest?

The local newspapers and social media posts all have the same sentiment: "Americans cry to the media when told they are not above the law."

We assure ourselves that the posts from the Trump family, Rogan, and others have each amassed multiple million times the media impressions that the island newspapers have. The numbers don't lie. We're winning the attention war.

This reinstates our confidence in the plan we're carrying out.

We're riding high that morning, joking that at any minute the call might come in—the island conceding, letting us go home. The atmosphere in the condo is almost giddy. We're laughing, high-fiving, planning what we'll do when we get back.

Then Bryan's phone rings.

The laughter stops. We all look at him as he answers.

I can tell he's nervous. His face goes rigid, his jaw tight.

It's a brief conversation—maybe thirty seconds—but when he ends the call, I can tell he's no longer on my same level of confidence. The light has gone out of his eyes.

"That was Oliver. They set the date for my hearing." He pauses, swallowing hard. "It's May 3rd."

"Okay." I try to sound confident, reassuring. "We have one week to ramp up the media and put the pressure on this island."

"Yeah..." Bryan nods, but his voice is flat. "I'd better go call Ashley."

As he walks somewhat somberly to the porch, I can tell he's questioning what impact our plan will have on his hearing. Is he wondering if we made a mistake? If going to the media will make things worse instead of better?

I start to feel an overwhelming sense of guilt. The question starts pinging in my head like a pinball I can't stop: *Did I just lead him astray?*

I take a deep breath and try to shake off the doubt. The fact is, we started this fight, and there's no turning back now. We're committed. We're all in.

But what if I'm wrong?

APRIL 29TH

The island headlines begin to mirror the locals' sentiment toward "the Americans." Every day, the paper is littered with scathing articles about us. Opinion pieces calling us entitled. Editorials saying we deserve what we get.

We grow increasingly concerned that Bryan will not have a fair hearing. How can he, when the entire island has been whipped into a frenzy against us?

Bryan reaches out to the Embassy consulars multiple times, but they quickly dismiss his concerns. Their responses are curt, almost annoyed.

When he requests a representative of the Embassy be present at the hearing, they state it isn't within their budget to fly someone to the island.

Not within their budget?

Despite this easily being the most public affair concerning American citizens under that Embassy's jurisdiction, they seem more annoyed than anything. Like we're inconveniencing them by being imprisoned.

I'm pissed. Beyond pissed. The anger burns hot in my chest.

I know I need to play our next card and force them to get more involved.

So I call Michael Grim.

"Hey, Michael. I need to ask your permission for something. I know you've wanted to avoid any of the media due to implications with your career. But we need a favor."

There's a pause on the other end. I can hear him breathing, thinking.

"Okay. What do you have in mind?"

"I want to leak the email that Usha Pitts sent your mom."

Silence.

I press on. "The one where she told your mom to lose her email address. Where she basically said it isn't her responsibility to know about the well-being of her son."

He pauses briefly before responding. When he speaks, his voice is hard, determined.

"Screw it! That lady deserves to be exposed. Let's do it!"

I immediately call Leslie Gaydos. She was the first reporter who took an interest in us, and I know she has the brass to actually run with it. If anyone will go after the State Department, it's her.

"Leslie, I think it's time we dig a little deeper into this story."

"I'm listening."

"I'm going to send you an email that Usha Pitts, Chargé d'Affaires of the U.S. Embassy, sent to Michael Grim's mother when he was in prison. Telling her to lose her email, saying it isn't her responsibility to know about the well-being of her son."

There's a beat of silence on the other end. Then: "Okay. Send it over. I'll get to work."

I hold my breath, waiting for her to call me crazy, to tell me this is too risky, that going after the State Department is career suicide for all of us.

Instead, she says, "It'll take a number of days because we have to give the State Department a chance to respond prior to running the story. But yeah, this is a story."

As much as I've come to trust Leslie, I'm still surprised she doesn't hesitate. She doesn't tell me to back down. She doesn't warn me about consequences.

She just says, "Send it."

I forward her the email and establish communication between Michael and Leslie.

As I hang up, I lean back in my chair and stare at the ceiling.

We just declared war on the U.S. State Department.

Not just the island anymore. Our own government.

Bryan walks in from the porch. "What did you do?"

"I leaked the Usha Pitts email."

His eyes widen. "You did what?"

"We need them scared. We need them engaged. If they won't help us out of the goodness of their hearts, maybe they'll help us to avoid a PR nightmare."

Bryan sits down across from me, processing. "So, we're not just fighting Turks and Caicos anymore."

"No," I say. "We're fighting everyone who failed us. The island. The Embassy. Anyone who thinks we're disposable."

He nods slowly. "Okay. Then let's make sure we win."

That night, I lie in bed unable to sleep. My mind races through scenarios—what happens when the story breaks? Will the State Department retaliate? Will they help us or bury us?

I think about Bryan's hearing in four days. About Tyler in that prison cell. About Valerie and the kids back home, watching this unfold on the news.

I think about the email from Usha Pitts, the cold dismissal of Michael's mother, the bureaucratic indifference to American citizens suffering abroad.

And I think about how, in just two weeks, we've gone from two unknown guys in a nightmare to the center of an international incident.

Two point nine billion media impressions.

Joe Rogan tweeting about us.

The Trump family posting in support.

And now, the U.S. State Department about to be exposed for abandoning Americans in crisis.

I grab my phone and text Bryan, even though he's just in the other room.

"No turning back now."

Three dots appear. Then his response:

"Never was."

I set the phone down and close my eyes.

The war is escalating.

And we're just getting started.

We receive confirmation that ABC is flying a crew to the island for Bryan's hearing. By giving them exclusive interviews, they've also agreed to fly his wife, Ashley, to the island.

This feels like a huge victory. We figure having media crews on the island will increase the pressure—make it harder for the courts to railroad Bryan in the shadows.

I also get a call from my good buddy Seth Faurot—Holly's husband. He wants to fly out on Thursday, May 2nd, to provide me with some emotional support. The timing will be perfect because Bryan will be staying with Ashley in a hotel, giving up the other twin bed in the room we've been sharing.

Having Ashley, Seth, and the media crew come to the island gives Bryan and me both such a boost in confidence and morale. We're not alone. The cavalry is coming.

MAY 1ST

The morning of May 1st, Bryan leaves early to rent a car so he can pick up Ashley from the airport and get to and from the hotel. I've just gotten back from my run, still sweating through my shirt, when I hear the screen door on the porch slam.

I look over to see Bryan and Ashley walking into the condo.

We hadn't planned on meeting up until later that afternoon.

"I couldn't wait to meet you," Ashley says, her voice quivering as she walks through the doorway with open arms. "I made Bryan bring me here straight from the airport."

We give each other the longest hug. I can feel her trembling slightly, whether from exhaustion or emotion, I'm not sure. Probably both.

I'm so relieved. I've been so worried that she'd be upset with us for taking this gamble with the media—for putting Bryan at risk with our plan.

"You know you're my sister now, right?" I say, my eyes welling up. "Whatever happens in all of this, we're all in it together."

The bond I feel with the Hagerichs truly is nothing short of familial. We've known each other for just over a week, but we've lived a lifetime together in that time.

Shortly after, my mom and Terry arrive back from the grocery store, their arms full of bags. I watch as they have a nearly identical reaction to Ashley—immediate embrace, tears, whispered reassurances.

Within minutes, Ashley is calling my mom "Mom."

I know in that moment that one of God's purposes for my mom on this island is to be a mom to everyone involved. She takes up that role without missing a beat—cooking meals, offering hugs, staying up late to talk through fears.

I'm honestly so grateful she can be there to serve that role.

MAY 2ND

May 2nd is a busy day of filming interviews with the ABC crew. The condo is a chaos of cameras, lights, boom mics, and producers. Cables snake across the floor. The air conditioning struggles against the heat from all the equipment.

Terry goes with Reuben to pick Seth up from the airport. I hate not being able to go, but I know it's probably best that I not be seen near that airport. The last thing I need is to give them an excuse to revoke my bail.

I'm in the middle of talking with one of the producers about Bryan's case when Seth pulls up outside. I immediately break the conversation mid-sentence and rush out to greet him with a hug.

I try not to be overly emotional, but his being here means the world. For him to break his busy schedule and fly to an island to visit TCI's public enemy #1 is a sacrifice and a risk. He could've just sent a text or made a phone call, but he showed up.

I can tell he's somewhat overwhelmed with all of the cameras and lights crammed into that tiny condo. He barely has a place to set his bag that isn't in some camera angle.

I feel bad that after flying all that way, he has to sit for the rest of the day and watch us do interviews. Take after take. The same story told slightly different ways for different outlets.

After we wrap up later that afternoon, I know he needs something to eat. We walk to lunch—just the two of us, no cameras, no media, no strategy sessions.

It's good to be distracted as he updates me on all of our mutual friends back home. Normal life continuing without me. Weddings being planned. Kids starting baseball season. Someone bought a new truck.

His being here is a big comfort. A taste of home.

Shortly after getting our checks, I get a text from Leslie.

"US State Department piece is airing tonight."

My heart jumps. I show Seth the message.

"We need to get back," I say, already standing. "Now."

We rush back to the condo to make sure we can get access to the live feed on Terry's laptop.

"Hey, Leslie's piece is airing after the commercial break!" Terry yells from the kitchen.

We all gather around the laptop anxiously. Bryan and Ashley are at their hotel watching on their own, but everyone else is here—Mom, Terry, Seth, and me, all crowded around the small screen.

As it starts, we all sit in silence. The only sound is the laptop speakers and our breathing.

In my periphery, I can see everyone's jaws start to drop as Leslie tears into the Usha Pitts email. She doesn't pull punches. She reads it verbatim, lets the cold bureaucratic language speak for itself.

Then she shows clips of Michael Grim's mom discussing the State Department lying about delivering care packages to Michael. The complete abandonment that took place while he was in prison. A mother begging for help and being told to lose the email address.

As Leslie wraps, she shows a public apology issued by the State Department for the mishandling and inappropriate nature of Usha Pitts' email.

A *public apology.*

The State Department doesn't apologize. Not publicly. Not unless they're terrified.

I'm in shock, staring at the screen even after the segment ends.

Seth grabs me by the shoulders. "Bro! This has to be HUGE! The State Department HAS to get involved now!"

The reality hits me. We just forced the U.S. government to publicly admit wrongdoing. We just made them blink.

The four of us erupt in cheers. I'm sure the neighboring condos must think our team just scored a last-second goal. We're jumping, hugging, yelling like we've won the Super Bowl.

I try to calm my excitement so I can start composing messages. We have groups of friends from all over that we send news stories to, who then delegate to everyone in their networks. It's our version of a Rube Goldberg machine to tip the most dominoes possible.

And it seems like it's working.

As I'm texting, I get a message from Bryan, who's watching from his hotel room.

"DUDE! Did you see Leslie's piece?! That is HUGE!"

I respond: *"State Dept just apologized publicly. Game changer."*

"This has to help tomorrow, right?"

And there it is. The reminder that crashes back down on us like a wave.

Tomorrow is Bryan's hearing.

All this media, all this pressure, all this noise—it all comes down to one moment. One judge. One decision.

We're riding so high right now that for a moment, we'd forgotten what's actually at stake.

Bryan could be sentenced to twelve years tomorrow.

The celebration in the room dies down as the same realization hits everyone else.

Mom looks at me. "Do you think it'll be enough?"

I want to say yes. I want to tell her that, of course, it'll be enough that the media pressure and the State Department's involvement will force the judge to be lenient.

But the truth is, I have no idea.

"I hope so," I say quietly. "I really hope so."

That night, I lie in bed staring at the ceiling. Seth is in the other twin bed, already asleep—or pretending to be.

My mind won't shut off. I keep replaying Leslie's piece. The State Department's apology. The media frenzy.

But then I think about Bryan sitting in that courtroom tomorrow. About Oliver in his wig and robe. About Judge Jackson staring down from the bench.

About how we've done everything we can, and it still might not be enough.

I grab my phone and text Bryan, even though it's late.

"You good?"

Three dots appear immediately. He's awake too.

"Nervous. But ready."

"You're going to be okay. We've got the world watching now."

"Yeah. But it only takes one judge to not care."

He's right. And that's what terrifies me.

"Get some sleep. Tomorrow we show them they can't do this to Americans."

"Thanks for everything, brother."

I set the phone down and close my eyes, but sleep doesn't come easily.

Tomorrow, we find out if any of this was worth it.

Tomorrow, we find out if the war we started can actually be won.

MAY 3RD: BRYAN'S HEARING

We all shuffle into the Supreme Court room a bit early, around 9:30 a.m. We're traveling with a pretty big entourage at this point—Mom, Terry, Seth, Ashley, the ABC crew, Jonathan—and we want to make sure everyone has a place to sit.

Bryan's face starts to get white and expressionless. His nerves are taking over. Hell, I'm nervous too. His case is going to be pivotal in mine and Tyler's case. If Bryan gets twelve years, we all do.

Ashley's hands begin to tremble as she strokes Bryan's arm in an attempt to comfort him. But I can see her own fear radiating through her touch.

The silent whispers and slow tick of the ceiling fan overhead only fuel the fire of nerves spreading across the courtroom. The sound is maddening—*tick, tick, tick*—each second stretching into an eternity.

I know I need to do something. But the search for the right thing to say becomes frantic, and my heart rate continues to climb. My mouth is dry. My palms are sweating.

I start to pray for the right words to comfort Bryan and Ashley.

As I pray, I feel like God is asking me, *"Ryan, if you're trying to overcome the silence, why are you praying in silence?"*

The truth is, praying out loud in front of others is something I've always struggled with. Many times in Sunday school, I would sit and stare at my feet in shame, trying to avoid being called on to pray out loud for someone. The fear of saying the wrong thing, of not being eloquent enough, of disappointing God in front of people.

My heart continues to race. My throat begins to swell as I try to think of the words.

I try to shake it off and ignore what I know God is asking me to do, but it only amplifies the noise in my head.

Then, suddenly, my thoughts screech to a halt when I hear a voice say, "Can I pray?"

As I look up, I feel everyone's eyes fix on me.

Wait. Was that *me* who just said that?

Ashley looks at me with tears in her eyes. "Would you please?"

I nod slowly and stand to my feet as I try to figure out what just happened. Did I really volunteer to do this?

I pan across the gallery. "We're going to have a prayer. I'd like to invite everyone to join in."

Surely someone else in the room will step up and deliver a prayer with a higher level of eloquence than me. Someone more qualified. Someone who actually knows what they're doing.

But everyone in the room—with the exception of the local reporters and the bailiffs—circles around and joins hands. Mom on one side, Ashley on the other. Bryan, Seth, Terry, the ABC producers.

As we bow our heads, silence falls again.

I know then—it's me.

I hear a whisper from God: *"I got you."*

My voice shakes as I start to pray. Not one word is processed before it's spoken. I just begin pouring my heart out, raw and unfiltered.

"God, we need You. We can't do this without You. Bryan and Ashley need You. Their kids need their daddy home. We're asking You to move in that courtroom today. We're asking You to give Judge Jackson wisdom and compassion. We're asking You to protect Bryan. To protect all of us. We know You're sovereign. We know You have a plan. Help us trust You, even when we're scared."

Certain bits of scripture that have been tucked away in my heart start finding their way out—verses I didn't even know I'd memorized.

My voice grows louder as I realize I'm no longer trying to find the most eloquent word or assemble them in dramatic fashion. I'm just talking to God as if He's standing in the center of that circle.

Because we all know He *is* in the center of that circle. And He's the only one who can see us out of that courtroom.

We're unified in desperate dependence.

As I finish the prayer, I look up to see tears streaming down everyone's faces. Even the looks on the faces of the local reporters seem to change from disapproval to a semblance of sympathy.

Before I can process what just happened, Ashley nearly tackles me with a hug. As she squeezes tighter, I feel Bryan's long arms wrap around us both.

"Thank you for that," Ashley says into my shoulder.

"I'm not sure how much of that was me, to be completely honest. But God—God has this."

With Bryan locked in the wooden birdcage, the court begins its traditional procession—powdered wig entrances, bows, and introductions.

"All hail the Queen!" the bailiff shouts.

We all bow. The theater begins.

I can barely hear Oliver as he begins his arguments. His soft-toned Caribbean accent is difficult enough to make out, but the prosecutor, Clement Joseph, leans forward and coughs into his microphone every time Oliver says something pertinent.

Cough.

The cough is obviously fake—just some immature tactic to disrupt and distract.

Cough.

This goes on for quite some time before Judge Jackson gets fed up. She leans forward, her red robe rustling.

"Mr. Joseph, your persistent coughing is disruptive to these proceedings. If you are ill, perhaps you should seek medical attention rather than contaminating my courtroom."

He blames it on a cold, putting his hand to his chest dramatically.

She's clearly annoyed by his distractions and BS excuse. "Proceed, Mr. Smith."

Oliver continues with his arguments, citing piles and piles of case law. He's extremely buttoned up and making a really good argument for the unconstitutionality of the recent twelve-year mandatory minimum sentencing.

Judge Jackson, on several occasions, breaks her usual phlegmatic stare to raise an eyebrow and nod in agreement with Oliver.

With every head nod, nerves are replaced by confidence. If Oliver can get Jackson to bite and rule on the unconstitutional nature and path that was taken to bring this sentence to life, it means a greater chance we all have to make it home.

Oliver then leans into Bryan's character. He has a squeaky-clean record. A working father who regularly contributes to his community. Volunteers at his kids' school. Coaches Little League.

It's clear that Bryan is different than 99% of the defendants who have been locked in the birdcage before him.

Oliver then dives into the bullets that were in Bryan's luggage. He reads an expert witness statement that does a deep dive into the caliber.

"The sole intention of the 6.5 PRC cartridge is for hunting large game animals. The FBI database shows no record of this caliber ever being utilized in a violent crime. The only weapon capable of firing such a cartridge is a long rifle chambered to fire the 6.5 PRC caliber. It cannot be fired from just any gun, such as a handgun."

'*No duh*,' I think to myself, but as I watch Judge Jackson's facial expression, I realize this is news to her.

It reminds me just how naive these people are about guns. To them, any gun can fire any bullet, and they're both equally dangerous, independent of each other. They don't understand that a hunting rifle cartridge is nothing like a handgun round.

Oliver sits down. He's done his job. Now we wait.

They allow us a quick recess before the prosecution makes their case.

As I get up from my chair, I nod at Oliver and whisper, "Great job!"

I can't tell how much he likes me, and I want to take the opportunity to stroke his ego a bit.

He nods and quickly moves on about his business, already reviewing his notes for rebuttal.

A short fifteen minutes later, we're all finding our way back to our seats. The air in the courtroom feels heavier now, charged with anticipation.

Clement Joseph starts his arguments while slouched in his chair with his powdered wig falling off one side of his head. He looks like he just rolled out of bed.

Judge Jackson interrupts him before he can even get started. "Members of the King's Counsel usually *stand* when they are addressing the court, Mr. Joseph."

"Your Ladyship, I am not only suffering from a cough, but a bad injury as well. May you grant me permission to sit for my arguments?"

"Granted," she says, her tone clipped.

I'm not close enough to see it for sure, but it seems like Judge Jackson gives him a pretty big eye roll.

His arguments are just nonsensical. Everyone in the courtroom is looking at each other, trying to make sense of his ramblings. He's all over the place—jumping from point to point without any coherent thread.

The more he goes on, the angrier he gets. His face reddens. His voice rises.

"These Americans think they can come to our island and do whatever they want! These Americans believe they are above our laws! These Americans—"

It's obvious his arguments aren't aimed at just Bryan. He's prosecuting all Americans. All of us.

After shuffling through some papers—making a show of it—he holds up his finger and stands from his seat as if he's just uncovered the lynchpin in his case against Bryan.

"My learned friend just spent much of the court's time discussing the firearm safety training Mr. Hagerich has conducted. But I would like the courts to acknowledge the 2009 mass shooting in Fort Hood. This was carried out by a military person who had received *much greater* safety training than that of Mr. Hagerich."

My cheeks feel like they're on fire.

Is this guy really trying to associate Bryan with a terrorist? A mass shooter?

Why isn't Oliver objecting? Why isn't he demanding that these accusations be struck from the record?

Ashley's leg bounces like a sewing machine as she rocks back and forth. I can feel her unraveling next to me.

It's maddening to listen to this slob stop at nothing to ensure we're going to be locked away for every bit of twelve years. He's not interested in justice. He's interested in making an example of us. In proving a point.

After Clement finally ends his rambling, Judge Jackson slowly gathers all of the papers on her bench. The courtroom is silent, waiting.

"In light of the question of constitutionality brought forth by the defense, I will need to allow myself plenty of time to review the following."

She pauses, looking down at her notes. "We will schedule the sentencing for May 24th."

She smacks her gavel.

Whack.

"NO," Ashley says, her voice breaking as she starts to cry. "I need him home. Our kids need him home."

I hug her quickly, trying to console her and keep her from getting reprimanded for speaking out.

"We're in this together," I whisper. "God's timing isn't always going to make sense to us."

I turn to Oliver, who's talking to Bryan through the bars of the birdcage.

"Oliver, is that a normal amount of time for it to take for sentencing?"

"No," he says, wiping his brow. "But I think it might be a good sign. If she's going to rule on the constitutionality of the law, then she's going to need time to justify her ruling. She can't just throw out a twelve-year mandatory minimum without extensive legal reasoning."

"See," I say, turning to Ashley and Bryan. "There might be something bigger He's working on."

Ashley nods but doesn't look convinced. Bryan just stares through the bars, his face unreadable.

We all slowly file out of the courtroom, not sure of exactly what just took place.

It feels like Oliver put together a much better defense. Judge Jackson seemed genuinely interested in the constitutional arguments. But we're all wildly uncomfortable that the prosecution was left unbridled to paint all Americans as potential terrorists.

As we step out into the sunlight, the ABC crew surrounds us, cameras rolling.

"How are you feeling about the hearing?" one of the producers asks.

Bryan looks at Ashley, then at me. "I don't know. I thought it went well, but now we have to wait three more weeks."

Three more weeks. Twenty-one more days. Five hundred and four more hours.

MAY 5TH

Ashley flew out earlier that morning, so Bryan just moved back into the condo with us.

We're discussing the hearing, and we're all still stewing on Clement Joseph's remarks. The anger hasn't cooled. If anything, it's gotten hotter with time to think about it.

"Dude, I can't believe that scumbag tried to compare you to the Fort Hood shooter!" I say, my voice rising. "How did that not get struck down by Judge Jackson?"

"I know, man. If only someone from the Embassy had actually shown up, they would've been able to witness the disdain they have for Americans."

"I'm going to ping Senator Mullin. Maybe he can get them to actually do something."

I pull out my phone and message Senator Mullin a link to Leslie's piece on Usha Pitts and the State Department, adding: *"The State Department got exposed for doing nothing, yet they still refused to send someone to Bryan's hearing where the prosecutor made countless 'these Americans' comments."*

Almost immediately, my phone starts ringing. Mullin's name flashes on the screen.

"Hey, guys, it's Mullin." I answer on speakerphone so we can all account for what we witnessed.

After we recount the comments and tone of the hearing—Clement's anti-American rhetoric, his comparison to Fort Hood, Judge Jackson's failure to intervene—Mullin's voice comes through tight, controlled.

"I need the names of the people at the Embassy you've been in contact with. Just so I'm clear—they have never visited you?"

Bryan leans in toward the phone. "Senator Mullin, I've been here for eighty-two days, and they've never visited me. We've only spoken to them twice, and the second time was to request them to be at my hearing due to our concerns. To which they responded, it wasn't in their budget."

I can hear Mullin take a deep breath on the other end, the sound of barely contained fury.

"I will make some calls. I assure you guys I'm also working this from multiple other angles here in D.C. I have a number of meetings revolving around you guys tomorrow. I'll keep you posted. You two keep the faith!"

There's a pause, then: "Have you heard anything from the other guy... What's his name... Tyler?"

"Yes, he actually got bail on Friday. His dad texted me and said they got him moved into their condo in Grand Turk."

"Can he move to your part of the island? I think it would be in his best interest if he were close to you guys."

"I think his attorney would have to file a request. Due to the terms of his bail, he's having to check in at the prison."

"You two need to encourage him to have his attorney file the request. I'll contact you tomorrow with an update."

The line goes dead.

We all sit in silence for a moment, processing.

"He's pissed," Bryan says.

"Good," I reply. "He should be."

MAY 6TH

'm drinking a cup of coffee out on the front porch—the war room—watching the sun as it begins to peek over one of the nearby hotels. The sky is painted in shades of orange and pink, the kind of beautiful morning that feels wrong given everything we're going through.

I hear the sounds of someone else rummaging through the kitchen, likely looking for a clean coffee mug—the clatter of dishes, the opening and closing of cabinets.

As the door creaks, I look up to see Bryan rubbing his eyes and taking a sip of his coffee, which is clearly still too hot to drink.

He plops down in the chair, spilling coffee in his lap, and immediately springs forward. "Shoot, that's hot!"

"You're pretty good at making my peaceful morning not so peaceful."

"Brother, there isn't a thing about this place that's peaceful."

"True," I say as we both laugh and turn back to our coffee.

Bryan pulls out his phone and begins scrolling. I watch as something catches his attention—his eyebrows raise, his body stiffens. He sets his coffee mug down and leans forward.

"Dude, did you hear that the airport got shut down from a bomb threat yesterday?"

"The TCI airport?"

"Yeah, apparently so!"

My stomach drops. "Wait, Ashley was at the airport yesterday. Did she make it out okay?"

"Yeah, she made it home safe and sound. It must have happened after."

We both sit with that for a moment—how close she came to being caught in whatever that was.

"You don't think it has anything to do with us, do you?" I ask.

"It was probably one of your redneck friends back in Oklahoma!" Bryan grins.

We both laugh. We know that none of our friends would do such a thing, but it's funny to think about. Truth be told, the thought of anything disrupting this island brings us some thread of amusement.

As the pot of coffee starts to run dry, Bryan hollers at me from inside the kitchen.

Initially, I think he just wants me to start another pot. He's good at a lot of things, but making coffee isn't one of them.

As I open the screen door, Bryan says, "Guess who finally wants to meet?"

"Who?"

"The Embassy. I guess ol' Mullin must have lit a fire."

A surge of satisfaction runs through me. "Lane?"

"No, it's some lady named Karen. Seems like she's above Lane."

"Okay. Okay. So what's the plan?"

"She says she's flying in tomorrow. Wants to meet us at some deli near the airport. It's called Top O' the Cove Deli."

I can't help but roll my eyes. "Oh! Well, glad we can make things convenient for *her*."

"Right? Eighty-two days and now suddenly she can find a flight."

Later that afternoon, I get a text from Valerie. She's been talking with governor of Oklahoma, Kevin Stitt, and his staff. He's going to conduct a call with President Biden's staff and needs to ensure he has all the facts straight.

My heart rate picks up. The President. This is really happening.

I let Valerie know I've already done all of the interviews for the day and can talk with him anytime.

Shortly thereafter, my phone rings.

"Hello?"

"Ryan, it's Kevin Stitt. How are you holding up, bud?"

"I'm hanging in there, Governor. Thank you for reaching out."

"You bet! This situation is ridiculous, and we're doing everything we can on our end. I know Senator Mullin is working diligently on this, too. I conducted a call earlier with Governor Dileeni of the island." He pauses. "That was pretty much useless. I have a call scheduled with Biden's staff here in about an hour. I just want to make sure I have all of my facts straight."

We talk for the better part of thirty minutes. I do my best to update him on everyone's situation as well as how everything is being handled—the hearing, Clement's remarks, the Embassy's absence, Bryan's eighty-two days, and Tyler's six days in that prison.

He listens intently, asking clarifying questions, taking notes. I can hear the frustration building in his voice.

"I'm not sure exactly if Biden will help, but I feel like he should if he knows the story."

"I appreciate that, Governor. We're just trying to get home to our families."

"I know you are, bud. I know you are."

When I get off the call and update Bryan, I find myself feeling sad for him.

Both Oklahoma senators and the governor are reaching out, trying to do everything in their power to help us. Bryan can't get a response from any of his senators or the governor of Pennsylvania. He only has one congressman in his corner—Congressman Guy Reschenthaler.

It's not fair. We're in this together, but my state is rallying while his is silent.

"From now on, you're going to be an honorary Okie," I tell him.

He smiles. "I'm a redneck now! I consider it an honor."

"Damn right you are."

My phone rings later that evening. It's Governor Stitt again.

I answer immediately. "Governor?"

"Ryan, I just got off the call with President Biden's staff."

I hold my breath, waiting.

"They essentially stated they're aware of your case but have no plans to intervene."

The words land like a punch to the gut. I'm not surprised, but I'm still disappointed. I had little faith that President Biden would involve himself, but some small part of me had hoped.

"I appreciate you trying, Governor."

"Hey, I'm not giving up." His voice is firm, determined. "I'm going to be writing a letter and taking every media opportunity I can. I need your blessing to turn up the heat."

I don't hesitate. "Crank it up, buddy!"

"That's what I wanted to hear. These people need to know Americans are watching. That we take care of our own."

When I hang up, I walk out to the porch where Bryan is sitting in the dark.

"Biden's not going to help," I say, sitting down next to him.

"Didn't think he would."

"Stitt's going to keep pushing, though. Going to the media, writing letters."

Bryan nods. "Good."

We sit in silence for a while, listening to the waves crash in the distance. The sound that used to bring peace now just reminds us we're trapped.

"You know what the worst part is?" Bryan says finally.

"What?"

"We did everything right. We went to the media. We got the world's attention. We exposed the State Department. We got senators and governors involved. We did everything we were supposed to do." He pauses. "And we're still here."

I don't have a response to that. Because he's right.

"We keep fighting," I say finally. "What else can we do?"

"Yeah," Bryan says quietly. "What else can we do?"

MAY 7TH

Bryan's little rental car putters down the highway as we try to follow the GPS navigation. The air conditioning barely works, and we're both sweating in the midday heat.

"I think that was it!" Bryan says, whipping a U-turn on Leeward Highway.

The tires squeal. I grab the door handle. "Dude!"

"Sorry. GPS is worthless here."

The parking lot is tiny, and there's only one spot available. Bryan pulls in, and I immediately notice the problem.

"Dude, there's a giant puddle on my side!" I say, opening the passenger door to see murky water covering half the space.

"Tough stuff, sister! There isn't a parking space on this island without a pothole filled with water."

"You could have at least been a gentleman and gotten the door for me," I joke back after giving my best attempt to hurdle the puddle. My shoe still catches the edge, soaking my sock. We finally get to meet face-to-face with someone from the U.S. Embassy, and now I am squishing through the parking lot.

The razzing continues as we make our way to the restaurant, both of us trying to keep things light before what we know will be a tense meeting.

When we arrive at the restaurant's door, I recognize a familiar face.

It's Reuben.

He looks surprised to see me—genuinely caught off guard.

"Hey, Reuben!"

That's when the lady he's talking to turns to face me.

It's Officer Markland.

My stomach drops. I can tell by the looks on their faces they're just as surprised as I am to be bumping into them. What are the odds?

Markland looks back at the table and quickly places her hand over a notebook, sliding it closer to her chest. The movement is protective, secretive.

"You found the best sandwich spot on the island!" Reuben says, trying to force his usual jovial spirit. But his smile doesn't reach his eyes.

"Good to hear! I'll let y'all get back to it," I say as I open the door to the deli.

The moment the door shuts behind us, Bryan looks over at me. "Isn't that the officer who arrested you? What is Reuben doing meeting with her?"

"No clue. Do you think we should tell Karen we need to change the meeting spot?"

"Maybe. It looks like they're packing up, though, so maybe not." He pauses, watching through the window as they stand. "Definitely weird that your driver is having a meeting with the lady who arrested you, though."

A moment later, the bell above the door chimes as a taller blonde woman pulls the door open. She smiles as she takes off her sunglasses and walks toward us.

"Bryan? Ryan?"

"Yes, ma'am!" we say in unison.

"Hi! I'm Karen. Have y'all had lunch yet? I'm starving!"

"I could definitely eat some lunch," I say, though my appetite has disappeared.

After ordering our food, Karen pulls out a pen and notebook from her bag. She flips to an empty page, then carefully arranges them in front of her with a precision that feels rehearsed.

"Okay... Well."

Bryan and I stare blankly across the table at her, fidgeting in our chairs. The silence stretches.

She awkwardly begins to laugh. "Okay... I'm just going to say it. Everyone in the department wants to know—why don't you two just jump on a boat and make everyone's lives easier?"

She continues to laugh, like it's the funniest thing in the world.

I glance at Bryan, then look back at her. "Karen, are you saying that is an option?"

"Well, no. But it's just kind of become the running joke."

I tilt my head, maintaining eye contact. My jaw tightens. "This situation is a joke to you? Our lives have become the burnt offering of a corrupt government trying to secure its next election cycle."

Her smile fades. "No government is perfect, but I'm not sure you could say they were targeting you. They have laws, and you two broke them."

The words hang in the air like an accusation.

"Karen, We sent Lane an email about a girl my entire family witnessed being taken into custody for possession of ammunition on April 15th at 3 p.m. She's nowhere to be found. No record of her arrest."

"Yes, I heard about your concerns about this mystery girl. But we looked into it. The police department states there was no American taken into custody on that day."

"So, she wasn't American, and she was presumably released?"

"I don't know what happened to her. Turks has no obligation to update us on any non-American."

I lean forward. "So, if she was released for the same offense, at the same time frame, that four Americans were arrested for—that isn't a pattern to you?"

"Well, your wife was released. That's something you should be thankful for."

The casual dismissal, the implication that I should be grateful they didn't railroad Valerie too—it makes my blood boil.

Bryan can see I'm about to blow my lid, so he taps into the conversation. "Karen, we've looked into it. There are a number of reasons that give cause for the State Department's intervention. One is Americans being targeted."

Karen tries to interject. "You can't—"

Bryan continues, his voice firm. "The other is inhumane prison conditions. That prison was deemed inhumane by the United Nations last year."

"We've been told they've made improvements. As soon as I'm done meeting with you two, I'm jumping a flight over to Grand Turk. I'm planning to meet with Tyler and tour the prison."

"Okay, so what happens if the United Nations assessment is correct and it is deemed inhumane?"

"I'll pass my report on to D.C." She shrugs. "I can't say what, if anything, changes for you guys, though. Especially with you, Bryan. Your sentencing is in what—twelve days?"

Bryan gets quiet and closes his eyes. I can tell he's trying his hardest not to accept the defeat Karen seems insistent he accept. His jaw clenches. His hands ball into fists under the table.

I take a deep breath and try to maintain my composure. The sandwich in front of me sits untouched, growing cold.

"Look, Karen, we need to be on the same team here. It really feels like at this moment in time, you're spending more time trying to defend this island than help us."

"We are on the same team. You guys just have some crazy expectation of what you think I should be doing. You aren't going to be satisfied until SEAL Team 6 comes busting in to take you home."

"I'm not going to be satisfied until you start doing your job!" My voice rises. Other diners turn to look. "Your boss, Usha Pitts, tried to ignore Michael Grim. Don't be the next public apology the State Department has to make!"

"It was just a poorly worded email to his mom." Her voice hardens. "We knew it was you who leaked that email. I know you think the world is behind you, but Ryan, have you read the comments section?"

I pull a family photo from my pocket—the one I've been carrying since jail, the one that's worn at the edges—and slam it on the table in front of Karen.

She glances down at it, then back up at me.

"Look at it," I say, my voice low and dangerous. "You think some troll in his basement, hurling insults in the comments section, is going to keep me from getting home to them? I will stop at nothing."

Silence falls on the table. Karen chews her lip, staring at the photo. Valerie smiling. Van and Ellie laughing. A moment frozen in time before all of this.

Finally, she speaks, her voice quieter now. "Look, guys, the reason for this meeting was a welfare check. You both look healthy. Are there any medications you're in need of that you don't have access to?"

"Nope. Healthy as can be," I say, the sarcasm thick in my voice.

"Well, that's good. I'm going to go ahead and head to the airport to catch the next flight over to Grand Turk. I'll touch base with you both tomorrow to give you an update on my findings of the prison situation." She pauses, gathering her things. "I would encourage you both to make any necessary arrangements back home... just in case it isn't the outcome you're hoping for."

Bryan and I sit in silence as she collects her things and walks away from the table. The bells above the door chime as she leaves.

Neither of us touches our food.

After a long moment, Bryan finally speaks. "Make necessary arrangements back home. Did she really just tell us to prepare for twelve years?"

"Yeah. She did."

"And the welfare check—that's it? That's what the Embassy does after eighty-three days?"

"Apparently so."

We sit in silence, staring at our cold sandwiches. The lunch rush continues around us—tourists laughing, locals chatting, the normal rhythm of life on a beautiful island.

And here we are, drowning.

"The photo," Bryan says. "That was heavy."

I pick it up from where Karen left it on the table, fold it carefully, and put it back in my pocket. "It's the only thing that matters. Getting home to them. Nothing else."

"Yeah."

We finally stand to leave, our sandwiches barely touched. As we walk out, I glance back at the table where Reuben and Markland had been sitting.

What were they discussing? Why the secrecy? Why the surprise when they saw us?

The questions pile up, unanswered.

Just like everything else on this island.

MAY 9TH

We receive word that more bomb threats have shut down the airport. Again.

Reuben forwards a picture of one of the supposed emails through WhatsApp. My hands shake slightly as I open it.

The second paragraph of the email reads: *"You need to release Ryan Watson, Bryan Hagerich, and Tyler Wenrich or else..."*

I show Bryan my phone. "This doesn't look good, man."

"No. No, it doesn't at all." He pauses, scrolling. "Did you notice the comments in that WhatsApp thread?"

"No, I didn't look past the pic of the email."

"Someone says, '*You know it's the Americans doing this.*' Another person says, '*Someone needs to do something about it.*'" He hands me my phone back.

I read through the thread. The anger is palpable, building with each comment.

"This ain't good," I say.

Bryan gets on his phone and starts scouring articles from the local news sources. Public officials are insinuating it's us making the bomb threats. The comments sections attached to the articles are flooded with locals blaming us.

We start to freak out. Whoever is doing this is only making our situation worse. They think they're helping, but they're painting targets on our backs.

I need to clear my head, and I also need to check in at the jail. So, I change my clothes to do my daily run over to the Salt Mill Plaza.

Music blares through my AirPods as I run along the curb of Bonaventure Crescent. The rhythm steadies me, the lyrics pulling me into memories of home. Of Valerie. Of the kids.

I break stride as I come up on some road construction—a small section of the street closed off with orange cones and equipment scattered across the pavement. I dodge between the cones and construction equipment, making my way back up on the curb.

I'm back in stride for about three hundred yards when something catches my right periphery.

A flash.

Without thought, my reflexes cause me to dive to my left.

As I'm in the air, I feel something brush my heel—hard—and spin me. When I land, I'm looking in the opposite direction, disoriented. My palms scrape against the pavement.

I look back over my shoulder to see an older, small four-door sedan idling in the road. The engine rumbles, a low, threatening sound.

I hear the shift in transmission. See the reverse lights glow dimly.

The car is backing up. Coming back for me.

I scramble to my feet, still not fully comprehending what just happened. All I know is I need to get out of there. Now.

I look to my left—there's a fence overgrown with shrubs. I try to scurry up it, but the fence is dilapidated, held together only by the vegetation that's grown through it. It can't support my weight. The wood cracks and bends beneath my hands.

Realizing that I have limited options, I turn back to the car and begin to approach it. My hands ball into fists. My heart pounds in my ears.

It's time to fight.

I hear the transmission shift again. The engine revs.

The car speeds off, tires squealing.

Confused, I turn and notice that a second car has pulled onto the street.

I stand on the side of the road, breathing hard, watching my assailant disappear around the corner. No license plate I can make out. No clear view of the driver.

I slowly pat myself down, checking for injuries. I'm amazed that with the exception of a few tiny scrapes on my right elbow and left shin, I'm relatively unscathed.

Did that really just happen?

I search for my AirPods that fell out during the dive. I find one next to the curb, the white plastic scratched but still working. As I kneel to pick it up, I notice the black tire mark on the curb—fresh rubber burned into the concrete right where I'd been running.

I think in that moment it would be easier to accept that I'm going crazy than to come to terms with the fact that I'm now being hunted.

Evening falls on the island, and there's still no word from Karen. We're anxiously awaiting her report on the prison. Bryan is losing patience.

"I'm texting her!" he announces.

I know that her not calling is everything we need to know.

Shortly after texting her, his phone begins to vibrate. He points the screen in my direction, eyebrows raised.

"Well, well, well."

He answers and places the call on speaker. I motion to him not to mention I'm on the call. After our clash at lunch, I know I'm the last person she wants to deal with.

"Hey, Karen. I was hoping to hear what you found at the prison."

"Yeah, sorry for my delay in getting with you. We've had a busy day here in Nassau." Her voice is casual, light. "Well, I did get to meet Tyler yesterday and tour the prison. Tyler is doing well. It's really great that his dad can be with him..."

Bryan knows she's stalling. "So, tell me about the prison."

There's a pause on the other end. When she speaks again, her voice has changed—more careful, more measured.

"Look, it's not great. Many countries lack the resources we have in the U.S. They have made some improvements to one of the wings, though, and I really think I could help to place you guys in one of those."

Bryan's head falls into his hands. He apparently still had some shred of hope she was going to act on our behalf. That she'd see the UN report was right, that the conditions were inhumane.

He finally breaks the silence. "So, you're saying you disagree with the UN report and feel as if it is safe?"

"I can't say that the conditions pose an immediate threat."

"Open-air prison. No running water. No electricity."

"There is electricity in one area of the prison."

Bryan tosses the phone on the coffee table and sits back in his chair, shaking his head. His jaw clenches. His hands grip the armrests.

"Hello? Bryan, did I lose you?"

Bryan never responds. He just stares at the phone lying on the table like it's something toxic.

"Well, if you can still hear me, can you please update Ryan on our conversation? Also, let me know if there are any medications you need. Good luck."

The line goes dead.

We sit in silence for a long moment. The only sound is the ceiling fan overhead, slowly turning.

"Good luck," Bryan finally says, his voice hollow. "She said good luck."

"Yeah."

"Like I'm going to need luck. Not help. Not intervention. Just luck."

MAY 10TH

Valerie is updating me on all that's going back at home. Her voice fills the empty space in my chest, even if just for a moment.

Between interviews, she's returned to work, trying to maintain some sense of normalcy for our kids. The routine of school drop-offs, homework, and dinner. The pretending that everything is okay when their dad is trapped on an island facing twelve years in prison.

There are some days the only time I get to see her is on joint interviews we're doing through Zoom—both of us performing for the camera, telling our story again and again, trying to keep the world's attention. So, the days we get to spend time on the phone together, just talking, are cherished.

In the midst of her telling me about one of the kids' activities—something about Van's baseball practice—I have a call beep in.

I glance at the screen. Senator Mullin.

"Crap, babe, I hate to jump off of here, but it's Senator Mullin."

"Take it, babe! Just call me later and update me." No hesitation. She knows the hierarchy of calls now.

"I love you."

"I love you too."

I click over to the other line. "What's up, buddy?"

"Hey, buddy. I just wanted to give you an update." His voice sounds energized, purposeful. "We've put together a letter that's being sent to the TCI government on y'all's behalf. It's endorsed by a ton of senators."

My heart rate picks up. "That's awesome! Thank you for that."

"I'm not sure what impact it'll have, but it's one of many steps we're taking." He pauses, and I can hear papers shuffling in the background. "I'm also in the process of putting together a CODEL."

"What's a CODEL?"

"It's a Congressional Delegation task force."

"Okay..." I'm not sure what that means, but it sounds official. Important.

"We're looking to put together a task force to fly to the island and sit down with their government. Show them that the United States Congress is paying attention to how they're treating American citizens."

"*Sweet!*" The word barely captures what I'm feeling. Senators. Flying here. Confronting the government that's trying to bury us.

"These things take time to put together, though. There's a lot that has to go our way for this to take place. Coordinating schedules, getting approvals, securing the funding."

"Any chance this could happen before Bryan's sentencing?" I hold my breath, waiting.

"I can't make any promises. Like I said, a lot of pieces have to fall into place."

My hope deflates slightly, but not completely. "Okay. Well, at least I know what specifically to be praying for. I appreciate everything you're doing."

"You got it, buddy. Keep the faith."

The line disconnects.

I sit there for a moment, staring at the phone. A CODEL. A Congressional Delegation. Senators flying to confront TCI.

This is real. This is happening.

A little later that afternoon, I get a text from my friend Jonathan in D.C.

"Did you hear they're forming a CODEL?"

I text back immediately. *"Yeah, I just learned about that from Senator Mullin."*

Three dots appear. Then: *"Ryan, that is HUGE. I've been in D.C. for years, and I think I've only seen one other CODEL formed. This could really be a big deal!"*

I stare at the message. Jonathan knows D.C. He understands how the system works, how rare this is, how significant.

The fact that news of the CODEL is spreading in D.C. indicates this is truly a big deal.

My confidence in Mullin is at an all-time high. I immediately have to give the Lord praise for placing him in our corner. For giving us someone who doesn't just talk but *acts*. Who doesn't just offer prayers but marshals resources.

     TURKS AND CHAOS

Now we just need this CODEL to take place before the 24th.

MAY 12TH (MOTHER'S DAY)

In so many ways, this is a Mother's Day I've been dreading.

It breaks my heart to think of Valerie waking up on Mother's Day without me there. On a day she should be waking up to breakfast in bed, showered with gifts and attention from our kids, she's now faced with a harsh realization: she's likely going to be a single mother for the next twelve years.

Some of my sweetest friends back home rushed around and helped me piece together a few things for her—flowers, a card with the kids' handprints, some gifts I had them buy and wrap. But deep down, I fear they'll be like flower arrangements at a funeral. Never possessing enough beauty to distract you from the reason they were sent.

The other lady I need to celebrate today is my mother.

Without hesitation, she put her life on hold, boarded a plane, and flew to a foreign country to be by my side. Undoubtedly, the biggest of her countless sacrifices. She left her home, her routine, her comfort, to sit with me in this nightmare.

How can I even begin to show her how much I appreciate her?

I decide to take her to church and out for lunch. Being out in public on the island is extremely uncomfortable for me now—the stares, the whispers, the recognition. But it's a small price to pay to show her how much she means to me.

We pull into the parking lot of Harvest Bible Church. Male church leaders are directing traffic and greeting patrons as they get out of their vehicles. The parking lot is tiny, and they're packing cars in like sardines.

After squeezing us into a grass section of the lawn, one of the church members opens our car door. The moment he sees me sitting in the back seat, the smile he's been greeting everyone with vanishes.

His face telegraphs the message: *"What the hell are you doing here?"*

The silence stretches. His hand is still on the door handle, but he's frozen. Just staring.

It's awkward. I want so badly to turn around and go home, crawl back to the condo and hide. But I'm not going to let them deter me from taking my mom to church. Not today.

"Thank you," Mom says, stepping out of the car, breaking the tension.

He nods stiffly and moves to the next car.

Rows of mismatched chairs line the tiny church—plastic folding chairs mixed with old wooden ones, creating an uneven sea of seating. We find a place to sit over in the corner, trying to be inconspicuous.

But we stick out like a sore thumb.

Wide-eyed glances and hushed whispers fill the congregation. I can feel every set of eyes on me. Every head turned slightly in our direction, pretending not to look while absolutely looking.

I'm wildly uncomfortable. My skin crawls. I stare at my feet through most of the service, focusing on the scuffed tile floor beneath my chair.

The preacher talks about motherhood, about sacrifice, about the love that never quits. The irony isn't lost on me—my mom sitting next to me, having sacrificed everything to be here, while the congregation judges us.

At some point in the sermon, I look over my shoulder to see a local reporter named Wilkie staring right at me. His eyes bore into mine, cold and calculating.

No.

How in the world did we pick to attend the same church he's a member of? Of all the churches on this island, we walked into his.

My stomach drops.

When the preacher begins wrapping up, I notice Wilkie stand up and walk out of the congregation. He doesn't leave through the back—he positions himself at the exit, waiting.

The moment the preacher dismisses us, we quickly gather our things and try to slip out the door. But we're not fast enough to beat the crowd that gathers to exit. Bodies press together in the narrow aisle. Everyone shuffling slowly toward the back.

We keep our heads down, moving with the flow. But we can't figure out what's taking everyone so long to file out. The bottleneck at the door is worse than usual.

It's not until we finally get near the doors that we see why.

Wilkie is standing at the exit, handing out his newspapers. One by one. To every person leaving. Making sure no one can pass without taking one.

When we get to him, he looks at me and smiles. It's not a friendly smile. It's something else—triumphant, maybe. Vindictive.

He hands me a newspaper with my mugshot on the front. The headline reads something about "American criminal" and "disrespecting TCI laws." My face stares back at me in grainy black and white, the worst photo they could've chosen.

"No, thank you," I say, my voice tight. I keep my head down and keep moving toward the car.

He doesn't push it. Just keeps smiling. Keeps handing out papers to everyone else, making sure they all see my face, all know who I am.

When we get to the car, we're still blocked in. Cars packed so tightly we can't move.

It feels like we're trapped in a fishbowl.

The entire church stands and stares as we wait for the vehicles in front of us to exit. Some of them hold Wilkie's newspapers now, glancing between the mugshot and me. Confirming the match. Whispering to each other.

Mom sits in the front seat, her hands in her lap, trying to maintain her composure. But I can see her jaw clenched, her eyes fixed straight ahead.

"I'm sorry," I say quietly.

"Don't you dare apologize," she says, her voice fierce. "You have nothing to apologize for."

But I do feel sorry. Sorry she had to endure that. Sorry I brought her into a church only to be humiliated. Sorry this is her Mother's Day.

When we finally get a chance to pull out of the parking lot, Bryan breaks the silence with a weak attempt at humor. "Well, that was awkward."

"No joke," I mutter. "So much for trying to blend in."

Terry, who's been silent the whole time, speaks up from the driver's seat. "That man with the newspapers—that was intentional. He was waiting for you."

"Yeah," I say. "That was Wilkie. He's the one who's been writing all the hit pieces about us in the local papers."

"He ambushed us," Mom says, her anger finally surfacing. "In a church. On Mother's Day."

The car falls silent again as we drive away, Harvest Bible Church disappearing in the rearview mirror.

MAY 13TH

Time has run out on the condo we've been renting. The financial strain of this nightmare is mounting—bail, attorneys, and living expenses on an island where everything costs twice what it should.

Luckily for us, an attorney named Brian from Oklahoma got in touch after seeing our story in the headlines. Brian owns a condo in the Bight district, just a few miles from where we're staying. He very graciously offers to let us use his condo for however long we need.

This is a tremendous relief. One less thing crushing us.

Bryan, Mom, and I all pack up our suitcases to begin moving our things to the new condo. The process feels surreal—we're just moving from one temporary prison to another, reshuffling our lives while trapped.

Bryan and I take the first load over. We dump our suitcases and get a quick tour from the property manager—here's the kitchen, here's the AC controls, here's where the washer is.

As I lock up, Bryan heads out to the car. When I open the door, he's staring at his phone, his face pale.

"Get in! News is breaking!"

"What do you mean? What news?"

"Our favorite local newsman, Wilkie, just tweeted that an American woman was arrested at the airport for possession of ammunition!"

My heart jumps. I hop into the passenger seat of Bryan's rental and pull up social media, hands shaking slightly as I search for Wilkie's post.

"Dude, the way this is written makes it seem like Wilkie witnessed her arrest," I say, scanning the tweet.

"Yeah, that, or one of the airport security officers notified him."

When Bryan says that, I have a flashback to the airport security officer taking selfies with my ammunition at the airport. The smiling faces. The casual cruelty of it. This is a game to them, and I'm sure they're now itching to brag to the local media about their latest catch.

"Can you text Croc? I bet he can get her name."

"Already on it!" Bryan's thumbs are flying across his screen.

I continue to toggle between social media apps, refreshing constantly, looking for any new information. When the page refreshes, I realize Wilkie has a new post.

"Sharrita Lucas! Wilkie just posted her name!"

I immediately begin searching Facebook for Sharrita Lucas, but I can't find anyone with that name. The search comes up empty.

"Maybe try spelling it with one R instead of two."

"Yeah, I did that, and there are a ton of Sharita Lucas's." Pages and pages of results scroll by.

I spend the next couple of hours shuffling through Sharita Lucas profiles. I look through countless posts, photos, stories, mutual friends. I click through vacation photos and family pictures, birthday celebrations and work updates. Trying to find any clues that any of these women are the one we're looking for.

But nothing fits. No recent posts about Turks and Caicos. No indication of travel. No signs of distress.

Was there truly a woman arrested for possession of ammunition, or is Sharita Lucas a red herring? Is Wilkie playing games with us?

Just as we settle into the new condo—suitcases still half-unpacked, our lives in temporary limbo—Bryan receives a text back from Croc.

The woman we're looking for is Sharitta Grier. Apparently, Lucas was a name from a previous marriage.

He also informs us that one of the women Sharitta was traveling with is her daughter, Destiny.

While Bryan has Croc responding to texts, he takes the opportunity to ask where they're holding Sharitta.

While we wait for Croc to respond, I begin rifling through photos and posts of all the Destiny Griers on Facebook. More profiles. More photos. More dead ends.

I start to feel like I'm on a cold trail again. My eyes blur from staring at the screen.

Then, there it is.

A picture of Destiny and Sharitta posing in the crystal-blue waters of Turks and Caicos. Smiling. Happy. Unaware of what's about to happen to them.

"FOUND HER!"

Everyone huddles around my phone to get a look at Sharitta and Destiny. Two women, mother and daughter, beaming at the camera in their vacation best.

I immediately send a friend request to Destiny and attempt to call her through the Facebook app. It rings and rings. No answer.

I call several more times before deciding to send her a message.

I write it several times, deleting and rewriting. Each version makes me sound like a crazy person. *Hi, you don't know me, but I'm trapped on the same island as your mom...*

Then it dawns on me—there's no way not to sound like a crazy person. Just send it.

"Destiny, my name is Ryan Watson, and I am an American citizen remanded to the island. I would like to see how we can help you and your mother in this situation. Can you please call me at xxx-xxx-xxxx?"

I hit send and stare at the screen, willing her to respond.

Several minutes after reaching out to Destiny, Bryan's phone dings.

"It's Croc. They're holding Sharitta at Grace Bay."

The Grace Bay station. Where I was held. Where I sign in every Tuesday and Thursday. Where the officers know my face, know my name, know to hate me.

Bryan and I jump to our feet and start putting on our shoes. We have to go. We have to see if we can help.

We look up to see Mom also lacing up her tennis shoes and putting on a ball cap, pulling it low over her eyes.

We watch her in confusion.

She looks up at us. "You two boys are public enemy number one and two on this island. Do you really think they're going to let you in there? I'm going with you!"

Bryan looks at me and shrugs his shoulders. "I mean, she has a point."

It's hard to admit, but I know she's right. The officers would recognize us immediately. They'd never let us back to see Sharitta. But Mom? They might let her through.

"Okay. Let's go."

We drive to the Salt Mill shopping center, where the Grace Bay station is located. The same shopping center where tourists mill about, buying souvenirs and sunscreen, completely unaware of the horror happening inside the police station.

We make sure to park around the corner so none of the officers will recognize Bryan's rental car or see us sitting in it.

As Mom gets out of the car and disappears around the corner, I find myself starting to get nervous. My palms sweat. My leg bounces.

The longer we sit in that hot car, the more worried I get. The sun beats down through the windshield. The air grows stale and thick despite the AC running.

"She's been in there for over thirty minutes now," I say, checking my watch again. "You don't think anything happened in there, do you?"

"Surely not... Right?" Bryan's voice lacks conviction.

I can tell he's concerned as well. He's really grown an affinity for my mom and Terry, seeing them as his own family now.

"I think I should go in there." I unbuckle my seatbelt. "Many of those officers saw my mom while I was in there. I'm sure someone recognized her."

When I reach for the door handle, I hear Bryan say, "There she is!"

I look up to see my mom walking from around the corner, wiping tears from her eyes. Her shoulders are shaking slightly.

She gets in the car and collects herself before she starts to speak. The silence in the car is heavy, waiting.

"It took some convincing, but they finally let me back to see Sharitta." Mom's voice cracks. "She is very scared and confused. She knew nothing about you guys. Says she never watches the news and never researched the island because the trip was a last-minute surprise trip from her daughter. All of her family that she was here with flew back to Florida."

My stomach drops. She's alone. Completely alone.

"Does she have an attorney?"

"She does have a publicly appointed attorney, but she couldn't remember their name."

"Are they working on getting her bail?"

"She did say the attorney mentioned they would try to get bail, but she was worried about the cost." Mom squints her eyes shut as tears start to roll again down her cheeks. "Guys, we have to help her get out of there."

She pauses, composing herself.

"They had her in the office, handcuffed to a chair by her ankle."

The words hang in the air like a bomb.

"She is *what*?" I can't process what I'm hearing.

Mom nods her head, fighting back tears. "They have her handcuffed by her ankle to a chair. There was a mat next to her that she's been sleeping on while handcuffed to the chair. She was so worried because she has a history of blood clots, and she hasn't had access to her medication. She said she was cold and hungry."

I feel rage building in my chest, hot and violent.

"So, I promised her we would go get her some clothes, blankets, and food."

Bryan immediately puts the car in gear and starts driving to the closest store. He doesn't ask where. He just drives, his jaw set, his hands gripping the wheel.

I feel my blood boil as we drive. These idiots are going to kill this poor woman. Everything about the conditions they're putting her in is a contraindication for someone who has a history of blood clots. Handcuffed to a chair. Unable to move. No medication. Cold.

They're torturing her.

Mom pulls out her phone and composes an urgent email to the Embassy.

"*An American citizen is being held in inhumane conditions at Grace Bay station. She is handcuffed to a chair, denied medication for a life-threatening condition, and at serious risk. Someone needs to intervene immediately.*"

"Someone from the Embassy better get their ass over to the island and fix this," I say out loud after Mom hits send.

But I already know they won't. They didn't help Michael Grim. They didn't help Bryan. They didn't help me. They won't help Sharitta either.

We're on our own.

A couple of hours later, we return to the station with a bag full of bedding, clothes, and food. Blankets to keep her warm. Comfortable clothes. Snacks and water.

This time, Mom is only in the station for a few minutes.

When she gets back in the car, her face is hard. "They didn't let me back to see her again, but they did say they would get everything to her."

"Did they?" I ask. "Did you see them take it back?"

"They said they would."

We all know what that means. We have no idea if she'll actually receive any of it.

"Did you get to try a bite of her food?" Bryan jokes as we pull away from the station.

It's dark humor. Gallows humor. But we all laugh anyway, because what else can we do?

I'd always heard that soldiers in war often develop a darker sense of humor. I now better understand why that might be. Sharitta's conditions are no joking matter, but we're so far detached from reality at this point.

We're providing aid to a woman we don't know in a foreign country in the absence of our own Embassy. Not one ounce of this seems real.

Humor seems to be a way for us to ensure that none of this *should* seem real.

MAY 15TH

Bryan and I are itching to see Sharitta. I need to check in at the station to sign the bail book anyway, and we convince ourselves there isn't anything the police can do to us for asking to visit her.

What are they going to do—arrest us again?

Bryan drives us over to Grace Bay. The same route I've run dozens of times. The same parking lot where tourists shop, oblivious. The same station where I spent days in a cell.

When we walk into the station, I recognize the young officer behind the desk immediately.

It's Officer Watson. The nineteen-year-old who put my shackles on upside down and inside out. The one they all mocked. The one whose hands trembled when he approached me.

"Hey, cousin!" I say with a grin.

He looks at me with wide eyes that clearly say, Don't say that. Don't acknowledge we have the same last name. Don't make this weird.

"I need to sign the bail book."

He flips to the open page without a word. As I sign, I lean in slightly. "Hey, man, we were also hoping to see Miss Sharitta. Can you let us back there for a minute?"

He nervously looks over his shoulder, scanning the empty hallway. "I'm the only one here."

"Buddy, you know I'm harmless. I just want her to know that I'm praying for her."

He shifts his weight, considering. I can see the internal debate playing out on his young face—following the rules versus doing what feels right.

He nods, trying to reassure himself as much as us. "Okay. But just for a few minutes."

"Thank you so much!"

He walks around the desk, unlocks the door, and leads us down the hallway. The same hallway I was dragged down in shackles.

He opens the door to a small office.

And there she is.

Sharitta sits in a chair, wrapped in one of the blankets we brought. The blanket is pulled tight around her shoulders. The handcuff is still around her ankle, the chain connected to the chair leg—the mat on the floor beside her shows where she's been sleeping.

"Sharitta?" I say softly. "I'm Ryan."

She looks up, and her eyes immediately fill with tears as she realizes who I am.

"You're Miss Susan's boy?"

"Yes, ma'am."

"I swear your mother is an angel. She is my angel."

Her voice breaks, and I can see the weight of what she's been carrying alone.

"Yes, she is," I say, smiling despite the lump in my throat.

"You don't understand." She leans forward, earnest. "I was locked in this room praying to God to show me He was real, when I heard your mama's voice asking for me by name. I'm here alone. No one could have known my name. She must be an angel."

The words hit me hard. Mom showing up, asking for Sharitta by name, at the exact moment she was praying for a sign. God's timing.

"A lot of people know your name now, Sharitta. We're going to help you get out of here." I pause. "Is there anything you need now?"

She starts to shake her head no, but then I notice she suddenly looked nervous. Her eyes dart past me.

I look over my shoulder to see Officer Watson standing behind us in the hallway, watching. Listening.

An idea comes to me. Risky. But worth it.

"I'd like to pray for you, Sharitta." I turn to face Officer Watson. "Officer Watson, we're all going to hold hands and pray. Would you pray with us?"

He looks back down the hallway toward the front desk. "There's no one at the front. I'm supposed to be up there."

"You're already back here. I'd like to pray for you, too. I'll make it quick."

He hesitates, caught between duty and something else—curiosity, maybe. Or the simple human desire to be included. To be seen as more than just a uniform.

He reluctantly slides into that small office. The space is cramped with all four of us. We all join hands—my right hand in Sharitta's, my left in Officer Watson's. Bryan completes the circle.

I close my eyes and begin to pray.

"God, we thank You for being here with us right now. We thank You for Sharitta, for her strength, for her faith, even in this terrible situation. We ask You to protect her, to heal her, to bring her home to her family safely. We ask You to give her peace that surpasses understanding. We ask You to work in the hearts of those who have the power to help her."

I feel both Sharitta's and Officer Watson's hands begin to squeeze mine tighter.

"We pray for Officer Watson, for his kindness in letting us visit. We pray that You would guide him and protect him. We pray for all the officers here, that You would soften their hearts and help them see us as human beings, not just cases or problems to solve."

Officer Watson's hand trembles slightly in mine.

"We pray for Bryan and his hearing in nine days. We pray for justice, for mercy, for Your will to be done. We know You have a plan in all of this, even when we can't see it. Help us trust You. Help us have faith. Help us remember that You are good, even when circumstances are hard."

Sharitta's hand squeezes tighter. I can hear her breathing, shaky with emotion.

"We ask all these things in Jesus' name. Amen."

When I open my eyes, I notice both Sharitta and Officer Watson have tears rolling down their cheeks.

Empathy has started to intrude on Officer Watson's preconceived feelings toward us. He can see it now—we're not criminals. We're just three people who are about to spend a good chunk of our lives in prison for an innocent mistake. Three people who pray. Three people who cry. Three people who are scared.

Three people just like him.

He wipes his eyes quickly, embarrassed. "I better get to the front now."

We hug Sharitta—carefully, mindful of the handcuff. She holds on tight, like we're a lifeline.

"We're going to get you out of here," I whisper. "I promise."

"Thank you," she says, her voice thick. "Thank you for seeing me. For remembering me."

MAY 16TH

Senator Mullin has assembled the members of CODEL, and they're racing to make it to the island before Bryan's sentencing. The plan is for them to fly to the island on Sunday, May 19th, and force a sit-down with the government on Monday, May 20th.

Eight days until Bryan's sentencing. Eight days for senators to fly here and change everything.

Bryan and I are both in regular communication with Mullin and his staff. The pieces are falling into place. The momentum is building. It all seems like everything is finally taking shape.

Our hopes are high. Higher than they've been in weeks.

It's later in the afternoon, and I've just gotten back from what is now a five-mile round trip to sign in at the jail. My shirt is soaked through with sweat. My legs ache. But the routine has become almost meditative—the run there, the tense interaction with officers, the run back. Time to think. Time to pray.

My phone rings. It's Mullin.

Excited to get an update, I wipe the sweat from my hands on my shorts and accept the call.

"Hello!"

"Hey, buddy. I want to give you an update."

The sound in his voice lets me know immediately—this is probably not the update I wanted to receive. My stomach drops.

"We hit a little snag."

"Okay..." I sit down slowly on the couch. "What kind of snag?"

"It's Schumer."

"As in Chuck Schumer? What does he have to do with anything?"

"We need the Senate floor to call recess on Monday, and for that to happen, the CODEL needs to be more... well, more bipartisan." He pauses. "But I do have a plan."

"Okay." I'm holding my breath, waiting.

"I have a really good relationship with Senator Fetterman, and given that Bryan is from PA, I think I can talk him into it. The big issue is timing."

"How much time?"

"We need him to agree by tonight, so we can get his security clearance by Friday for us to fly on Sunday. If we don't get it by tonight, it could be several weeks before we have another chance to fly there."

Several weeks. The words echo in my head.

"Bryan doesn't have several weeks!" My voice rises despite myself.

"I know. I know." His voice is steady, determined. "I'm going to try my best to get him to commit. I'll let you both know by tonight."

I don't know if I have the heart to tell Bryan. I feel like I can see the final grains of sand falling from his hourglass. Each second ticking away. Each possibility narrowing.

I try to discreetly open the sliding glass door to the porch, but the track is rusty, causing a ruckus every time it's opened or shut. The screech of metal on metal announces my presence.

Bryan walks into the living room, his face lit with anticipation. Excited to hear the latest news. Expecting good news.

"What did Mullin have to say?"

I take a breath. "Man, there's a snag."

His face falls. "What kind of snag?"

"It sounds like he needs to get a Democrat on board to make the CODEL a bipartisan endeavor."

"Are you kidding me?!" His voice cracks with frustration. "This is about politics now? While I'm sitting here eight days from sentencing?"

"He says he's going to call Fetterman. Since you're from PA, he thinks—"

Bryan takes a deep breath and tries to process the information. I can see him fighting to stay calm, fighting the despair that threatens to overwhelm.

"We just really need to pray that Fetterman agrees. And agrees by tonight."

Bryan looks back up at me with a puzzled look on his face. "Why tonight?"

"Due to the time it takes to get security clearance, if he doesn't commit tonight, it will delay the CODEL several weeks."

"I don't have several weeks!" He stands, pacing. "I have eight days! Eight days until Judge Jackson decides if I spend the next twelve years in prison!"

His voice breaks on the last word. The reality crashing down on him.

"The only thing we can do on our end is pray," I say quietly. "And pray specifically for him to commit tonight."

Bryan stops pacing and looks at me. "So everything—everything—comes down to whether one senator from my own state decides to help me. Tonight."

"Yeah."

"And if he doesn't?"

I don't answer. Because we both know what happens if he doesn't.

We pray repeatedly as the next several hours drag on. Each prayer more desperate than the last. Please, God. Please move Fetterman's heart. Please let him say yes. Please let it be tonight.

We're constantly checking our phones to ensure we don't somehow miss a call or a message. Every buzz, every notification sends our hearts racing. But it's never Mullin. Never the news we're waiting for.

The clock on my phone shows it's after 10 p.m.

I know how unlikely it is to receive good news at this hour. Senators don't commit to international trips at 10 p.m. They've gone home. They're done for the day. The decision isn't happening tonight.

I can sense that Mom and Terry have felt the same. The hope slowly deflating in the room like air from a punctured tire.

They take extra care to be quiet as they put dishes away, communicating with one another through glances and head nods. Not wanting to add to the weight we're already carrying.

I don't want to admit that this is transitioning to a melancholic time of acceptance. That we're moving from hope to grief. From possibility to reality.

Bryan sits on the couch, staring at his phone in his hands. Not scrolling. Not reading. Just staring. Waiting for a notification that isn't coming.

"Maybe tomorrow morning," Mom says softly. "Maybe he'll commit first thing tomorrow."

But we all know that's not how this works. Mullin said tonight. Security clearance needs to process by Friday. Flying Sunday. The timeline is impossibly tight. If it doesn't happen tonight, it doesn't happen in time.

The clock shows 10:15 p.m.

Then my phone lights up with a message notification from Signal.

My heart stops. I stare at it for a moment, afraid to open it. Afraid it's the confirmation of what we all fear to be true.

I slowly slide it open, my hands trembling slightly.

My voice cracks as I read the message aloud:

"Fetterman is in! Working out the rest of the details now."

For a moment, nobody moves. We all just stare at each other, not quite believing what we just heard.

Then the four of us erupt in screams and cheers.

Bryan jumps up from the couch, his hands in the air. "He said yes! Fetterman said yes!"

We hug each other countless times as we celebrate. Mom is crying. Terry is laughing. Bryan is yelling. I'm doing all three at once.

In that moment, hope is restored.

Not just restored—it's resurrected. Brought back from the dead when we'd already started mourning it.

MAY 17TH

I've been in contact with a local business owner named Danny. He owns a popular hot sauce company on the island—a slightly fruity tropical taste reminiscent of the Caribbean. Tourists often bring bottles back to the States, spurring demand abroad.

Danny saw the news while traveling in the States for work and reached out to see if he could help.

Now I need to call in a favor. For Sharitta.

She needs someone to provide surety. I feel uneasy asking someone I've never met to put up the title to a $15,000 asset for a stranger. But it's what the situation calls for. And if I don't ask, who will?

I dial his number, rehearsing what I'll say.

"Danny, I hate to have to ask this. You might have seen on the news that they arrested a woman from Florida earlier this week. They're requiring a local to put up surety for her to get bail. I know this is a huge ask, but she's in a really bad situation. She's been handcuffed to a chair for the past four days, and we need to get her out of jail."

There's a pause on the other end. Then: "They have her shackled to a chair?! I swear this island can't get out of its own way."

"Yeah, man. It isn't good. To make matters worse, she has a history of blood clots. The longer she stays shackled in that chair, off her medication, the higher the chances she throws a clot."

"I'll call my attorney. He can access the title to my boat. Shoot me her attorney's number, and I'll have him take care of it."

Relief floods through me. "Thank you so much, Danny!"

I hang up the phone and send him the contact for Sharitta's attorney. One more piece falling into place. One more person showing up when they didn't have to.

I struggle to breathe the hot, humid air. Each breath feels thick, heavy, like trying to inhale water.

My runs to check into jail have become a daily mental challenge. The increasing intensity of the heat is a brutal reminder that I've been on this island too long. That summer is coming. That time is passing.

My new route from the Bight district to Grace Bay and back is much longer. The piece of island between the two tourist areas is riddled with old, run-down houses, shanties, packs of wild dogs, and herds of goats.

A white tourist running through here stands out like a sore thumb. It would be the perfect spot for someone to try to take another crack at me.

I take my AirPods out so I can stay alert during this desolate stretch. Every car that passes makes me tense. Every person I see makes me wonder—do they recognize me? Do they hate me? Do they want to hurt me?

I take a left off Lower Bight Road onto a small side road. I notice there's a car parked directly in the path ahead of me.

As I get closer, I realize the car has actually crashed into some small trees and shrubs. It had to have just happened because the engine is still sputtering, smoke rising from under the hood.

I peer into the driver's side window. Stereo wires dangle from the dashboard. The steering column is missing.

Stolen. Recently crashed.

I quickly back away from the vehicle. The absolute last place I need to be is near a crime scene. This island is itching for a reason to put me back in jail. I can already see the headline: "American Criminal Found at Scene of Car Theft."

I immediately cross to the other side of the street and sprint out of there. My heart pounds—from running, from fear, from the constant awareness that I'm always one wrong place, one wrong time away from losing everything.

I don't slow down until I reach the well-manicured perimeter walls of the resorts in Grace Bay. The difference is stark—from poverty and crime to luxury and safety in the space of a few blocks.

I start to see tourists up ahead of me. Carefree. Tooling along on their turquoise beach cruisers, smiling, laughing, without a care in the world.

Completely oblivious to all the nefarious activity taking place just on the other side of the resort walls.

Two different islands. Two different realities. And I'm stuck somewhere in between.

~❖~

After I check into the jail—the same bored officer, the same book, the same ritual—I know I have to find a different route back to the condo. I'm not going back anywhere near that crime scene.

I pull out my phone and search for any other option.

Much to my displeasure, the only other option is to run along the beach.

Running on sand is torture in my opinion. But on top of that, my face is on every news station on a daily basis. I fear I'll be recognized running through the crowded beaches. Someone could snap a photo of me and make it seem like I'm out on a leisurely jog, enjoying the beach. Like this is all a vacation for me.

I have no other option, though.

I pull my cap down low and take off down the beach, trying to make myself small, invisible.

Running past all the families laughing and playing causes invidious thoughts to flood my mind. Children building sandcastles. Fathers throwing kids into the waves. Mothers applying sunscreen.

All the things I should be doing with Van and Ellie right now.

I know that the chances of me ever hearing my kids' worry-free laughter again are almost nonexistent. If I get twelve years, Van will be twenty-one when I get out. Ellie will be nineteen. They won't be kids anymore. I'll have missed everything.

I plug my AirPods back in to drown out the noise. I crank up the music to a painful level—loud enough that I can't hear my own thoughts, can't hear the children laughing, can't hear anything but the pounding bass.

And I keep trucking.

When I finally make it back to the condo, I'm drenched in sweat and near hyperventilation. I lean over at the front door, hands on my knees, trying to catch my breath.

I shake my head, trying to clear the echoes of children's laughter that followed me all the way home.

"Stop that," I tell myself as I reach for the door. "Stop thinking about what you're missing. Focus on getting home."

When I open the door, I realize Mom, Terry, and Bryan are all gathered on the couch. As I get further into the entryway, I realize there's another person sitting with them.

They all turn to look in my direction.

"Sharitta?!"

"She got bail!" Mom says excitedly, jumping up from the couch.

I'm stunned. "How did Danny already get the surety set up?"

"He didn't have to. Sharitta's attorney, Sheena, secured it for her."

I run over to Sharitta and give her a hug. She's stiff in my embrace—I can't tell if she's still in shock or if it's the fact that I'm covered in sweat and probably smell terrible. But she's here. She's out.

"We need to celebrate!" I announce. "Let's go out for pizza."

Everyone gets changed, and we make our way back over to Grace Bay, where the best pizza shop on the island is located.

As we wait for a table, a small TV above the bar flashes a news story with all of our photos. A lineup of mugshots and headlines. The accused Americans.

Sharitta sees the news story as we walk through the bar. She places a hand over her face to hide, ducking her head as we make our way to the table.

I reach over and pat her on the shoulder. "It gets less awkward, I promise."

She does her best to flash a smile at me, but I can see the fear in her eyes. The shame. The disbelief that she's become a headline.

I joke with her, trying to lighten the mood. "You didn't pay all that money for a gold tooth just to hide it."

She finally laughs for the first time. A real laugh. The kind that breaks through tension.

My mom chips in, grinning. "Sharitta, those two tease each other constantly like brothers do. You're their sister now, so you'd better get ready to dish it back."

Sharitta smiles and nods. From that point, it's game on.

We all razz each other through the entire dinner. Bryan makes fun of my running form. I make fun of his coffee-making skills. Mom tells embarrassing stories about me as a kid. Terry adds commentary. Sharitta slowly opens up, adding her own jabs, laughing more freely.

It genuinely feels like a family dinner. Like we've all known each other for years instead of days. Like this is normal—strangers bound together by a nightmare, eating pizza and laughing like we don't have a care in the world.

For a moment, we pretend this is just a vacation. Just friends enjoying the island.

For a moment, we forget.

MAY 19TH - THE CODEL COMES TO THE ISLAND

We know the CODEL is supposed to land on the island around 4 p.m. We want to watch that giant military aircraft land on the tiny island runway—a symbol of America finally showing up.

We all load up and head over to Dale's restaurant, which overlooks the airport. It's the perfect spot to watch the plane fly in.

My mom, Bryan, Terry, Sharitta, and I find a table out on the patio with an unobstructed view of the runway. Every time we hear a plane in the distance, we all quickly start panning the sky to see if we can be the first to spot it.

Commercial jetliner. Too small. Wrong colors.

We put our phones away and sit back down. Order another round of drinks. Try to contain our excitement.

Then we hear a distant rumble. It's different from any of the others we've heard up to this point. It sounds more like a thunderstorm rolling in—deep, resonant, powerful.

We keep listening, panning the sky.

As the rumbling gets louder, we all, one by one, get out of our seats and line up along the deck railing. Everyone pulls out their phones, pointing them in the direction the other planes approached.

Suddenly, the giant white plane tears through the clouds, landing gear unfolding from its underbelly like the talons of an eagle.

I'm overwhelmed with patriotism. I start to sing "And I'm proud to be an American" as I film the plane descending, my voice cracking with emotion.

When it touches down, the island shakes. The restaurant's glassware clinks. The building trembles under the weight of it.

This adds to the noise of us cheering and high-fiving one another.

The locals all stare in confusion. They don't understand what this means. What's coming?

We don't care. We're on top of the world.

The cavalry just arrived, and I'm suddenly brimming with confidence that we'll be going home on that jet.

The Dinner

The CODEL is hosting a dinner for us at their hotel that night. The hotel they happen to be staying in is only a few hundred yards from our condo.

We get cleaned up and changed for dinner.

When I come out of the bathroom wearing my cowboy hat, Bryan hollers, "Wooo boy! You're going full redneck tonight!"

"You're dang right! The cavalry is here, so I don't care about standing out anymore."

Though I'm joking, I do feel guilty that I'm breaking a promise I made to Valerie. She'd always said my cowboy hat attracted too much attention, and she didn't want me drawing any more attention to myself in this situation. I promised her I wouldn't wear it until I got home.

But this is the first time I've felt any shred of security since any of this started.

We walk over to the hotel a bit early to meet Tyler and his dad. When we get to the lobby, I notice begin to recognize several people with earpieces carefully observing everyone coming and going. Security. Military. Serious men and women scanning faces, watching exits.

My mind starts to wander—what must the vacationers in this hotel be thinking, seeing all these military-looking characters pacing the lobby?

I hear someone call my name from a small seating area in the corner. It's Tyler and his dad, Michael. We walk over and visit with them for a minute before we're greeted by one of the staffers.

She introduces herself and escorts us to the patio of the hotel. They have one long table set up close to the end of the patio near the beach, surrounded by several smaller tables.

As we approach, I hear Senator Mullin say, "That's my boy from Oklahoma right there!"

I walk up to him, and he gives me a big bear hug. He jokes, "I know some might think you wear that hat because you're a cowboy, but I know it's just to cover that bald head of yours."

His humor is comforting. It's like getting ribbed by an old buddy from back home. Any nervousness I felt about the situation, or meeting a bunch of politicians I've only seen on the news, vanishes.

We continue joking around for several minutes before the staffer comes back over. "We're going to go ahead and have everyone find their seats at the table."

Mullin instructs her to make sure each AMCIT—American Citizen—is seated next to their respective senator or congressman.

I sit across from Senator Mullin, with Oklahoma Congressman Josh Brecheen on my right and the new Chargé d'affaires, who replaced Usha Pitts, to my left. Tyler and Michael sit next to the congressman from Virginia. Bryan sits at the far left end of the table, next to Senator Fetterman and Congressman Guy Reschenthaler of Pennsylvania.

Sharitta wants my mom and Terry to sit next to her and the representatives from Florida and the congressman from Texas. At the far right end of the table are members of the U.K. Embassy and other security advisors.

It's overwhelming, to say the least.

Mullin asks if we can all bow our heads and pray before we get started. I appreciate that he takes the time to give God the praise for opening the doors for the CODEL to assemble and asks for continued guidance and protection.

I can only imagine how easy it would be, in a position of influence, to slip into thinking you did this all yourself. He hasn't.

After he prays, he goes around the table and introduces every member of the CODEL. By the time he's finished, I think we're all convinced it's a well-assembled cast.

Then Mullin asks the AMCITs to introduce ourselves and explain our situations. He asks Tyler to start.

Tyler, being a man of few words, keeps his introduction brief. I'd hoped he'd go guns blazing, but that's just not his personality.

It's Bryan's turn next. He looks over at me and winks before he stands up from his chair.

I know exactly what that means.

It's go time.

Bryan and I have spent hours rehearsing what we'll say given the opportunity. We want to ensure the CODEL is aware of every detail of the island's corrupt history and their political motivations. We're also going to expose how the Embassy has been going out of its way to brush everything under the rug and leave us to rot.

Bryan starts. "My name is Bryan Hagerich. I was arrested on February 13th while traveling back to Pennsylvania after vacationing here on the island with my family."

"So you've been on the island for ninety-six days?" Mullin asks.

"Yes, sir."

"In the ninety-six days you've been on the island, what has the Embassy done to support you or your family?"

"Support?" Bryan's voice carries just the right amount of disbelief. "The Embassy has only returned two phone calls. In those calls, they basically told me I was in the wrong and there was nothing they could do for me. Even when I expressed concerns that I wouldn't receive a fair trial and requested they send someone to attend my hearing, they told me they didn't have the resources to send someone to my hearing."

I can see the Chargé d'affaires and legal counsel from the Embassy roll their eyes before they object. "We did send a local liaison to the hearing, based on the concerns expressed by Mr. Hagerich. Despite firmly believing his concerns were unfounded."

"The liaison you sent got up and walked out of the hearing less than an hour after it started!" I shoot back from my chair, unable to contain myself. "She never even heard the prosecution, where he repeatedly carried on about 'all these Americans,' or the part where he compared Bryan to the terrorist who committed the Fort Hood shooting! It was painfully obvious to everyone in that courtroom that it wasn't just Bryan on trial—it was all Americans."

Mullin leans in intensely, staring at both the Chargé d'affaires and legal counsel. They both stare down at the table to avoid his glare.

Bryan sees the opportunity to drive the point further. "When the Embassy finally decided it was in their budget and sent a consular to meet with us, one of the first things she said to Ryan and me was, 'You guys should just make everyone's lives easier and hop on a boat.'"

"I'm sure she was just trying to lighten the mood," the legal counsel remarks dismissively.

"Lighten the mood?" I can't resist jumping back in. "My life is on the line, and the people I'm supposed to rely upon are more concerned with making jokes about our situation! Later in that same meeting, she looked me dead in the eye and said I wouldn't be satisfied unless they ordered SEAL Team 6 to stage a rescue."

The Chargé d'affaires and the legal counsel woman's eyes both dart around the table. They can tell by everyone's body language that they themselves are now the ones getting put on trial.

The legal counsel woman postures up in her chair and folds her arms. "I think everyone here needs to be reminded as to what the role of the

Embassy is in this scenario. We can only ensure the AMCITs have legal representation and have access to necessities such as food and medication."

"Okay, what about Sharitta then?" Mom interjects from across the table.

Everyone turns their attention to Mom.

"Sharitta was chained to a chair by her ankle for four days! This woman has blood clots. Did she receive her anticoagulation medication? Did she receive food? No! The only aid she received was the aid the boys and I brought her! You never even responded to our emails begging you to intervene!"

There's an audible gasp from every member of the CODEL.

One of the congressmen turns to Sharitta. "I'm so sorry you had to endure that."

Mullin turns to Mom. "Susan, who did you email at the Embassy?"

"Lane and Karen."

Mullin turns to the Chargé d'affaires, his voice hard. "Bring them both over here. Now."

I can see the Chargé d'affaires nervously fumbling with his phone as he texts them to come to the table.

Lane and Karen walk over from one of the smaller tables where they were seated. As they approach, it's clear they know they're about to be grilled.

Mullin asks, "At what point did you learn about Miss Sharitta being handcuffed by her ankle to a chair?"

"Officially?" Karen responds.

"What do you mean, officially?" Mullin's tone sharpens.

"We never received any information about Sharitta's detainment from any official channels."

Mom holds up her phone. "I have a time-stamped email from May 13th where I emailed you!" She hands her phone to Mullin.

Karen continues her defense. "We don't consider an email from the mother of an AMCIT an official channel."

"If you don't have someone here on the island to assess the conditions of the AMCIT, what would you consider an official channel?"

He turns to Sharitta. "Miss Sharitta, were you handcuffed to a chair by your ankle for four days?"

Sharitta nods.

"Did anyone from the Embassy conduct a welfare check or ensure you had access to your blood thinners?"

She shakes her head no.

He looks sternly back at Karen. "Sounds to me like you chose to ignore some pretty sensitive information, putting an American citizen's life on the line, and you're saying this is because you didn't like who sent you the email?"

Karen stands there, refusing to answer.

Congressman Brecheen breaks the awkward silence. "We have members of the U.K. Embassy at the table, do we not?"

A gentleman from the end of the table slowly raises his hand.

"How do you think it would look if this got out to the media? That a grandmother was left handcuffed to a chair for four days in a U.K. territory?"

The gentleman shakes his head and quietly says, "Not good."

Mullin looks at Karen and Lane as if he's scolding two children who just got caught in a lie. "I think you two need to stand there and listen to the testimonies of the AMCITs you've been ignoring. Ryan, can you tell us about you and Valerie's arrest?"

I stand up from my chair and tell everyone about traveling to the island for my 40th birthday—the day of the arrest. How from the moment the airport security officer started taking selfies with the ammunition, we started picking up that it seemed like a game for the island.

The legal counsel woman interrupts me. "There have been a lot of allegations made that the island is anti-American. There's no evidence for such a thing. We cannot say a country doesn't have the right to protect itself. Also, the island relies heavily on American tourism."

I cut her back off. "Can we please stop with the notion that arresting us is in any way protecting the island? Every one of us was arrested leaving the island. If they were truly interested in protecting the island, they'd be scanning bags upon entry. But we know that's not what this is. We're pawns."

I lean forward, gaining momentum. "When their government recognized it was being celebrated by the local families and newspapers for sending Michael Grim to prison, they scrambled to up the ante and make this a twelve-year minimum mandatory sentence."

One of the congressmen asks, "What do you mean by local families?"

"Only the original families of this island get to vote. That's how the Misick family has stayed in power."

He looks over at the Chargé d'affaires, confused.

"Did he not tell you that in 2009, the U.K. had to step in and dismantle the government because Michael Misick—younger brother of current Premier Charles Misick—was involved in massive corruption? Embezzled millions of dollars. But given the fact they're one of the largest families on the island, soon after being handed the reins to govern themselves, the older brother gets voted in." I pause. "Yeah, the island and the family running it have a pretty dark history of corruption."

The Chargé d'affaires responds, "Look, a lot of these Caribbean countries have their challenges, but we cannot say they have any history of being unfair toward our American citizens."

I'm growing tired of everyone from the Embassy trying to dismiss that we're being targeted as Americans.

"Do you have any record of the island arresting and imprisoning a non-American tourist?"

He looks over at me with a smirk on his face. "The fact that it's only Americans caught up in this is more of a black eye for America than it is the island."

"What about the blonde girl?" I press. "My entire family witnessed a blonde female taken into custody for possession of ammunition on April 15th at 3 p.m. I heard the call the officers received from airport security. I saw the ammunition in an evidence bag while they drug her through the station. She was presumably not American. Where is she?"

The Chargé d'affaires turns and looks at Karen and Lane. "Is he talking about the Brazilian girl?"

Mullin slams his hand on the table. "Hold on a minute! We just had a briefing before this dinner, and the four of you told us you were unaware of any other non-American citizens being detained for possessing ammunition. Supposedly had zero knowledge of any girl taken into custody on April 15th, and now suddenly you know her country of origin!"

"The island has no obligation to inform us of any situation pertaining to citizens of other countries. Yes, we hear of situations with non-American citizens, but they don't come through official channels, and therefore they can't be confirmed, nor do we have the authority to validate such happenings."

"We have four American citizens who witnessed one of these events and gave you a detailed report. A report that clearly illustrates Americans are being targeted. But you chose to not only ignore this information but lie to us when we asked you about it? Why?"

The Chargé d'affaires begins to nervously fidget with the silverware in front of him, refusing to look up from the table.

I stand quietly. Speaking now would only give them refuge from the table that's all glaring down on them.

After several long moments of watching them writhe under the disgust and disapproval being shot in their direction, I have to make my final point.

"You know, the last thing I haven't been able to figure out? How is it that, barely a year after the United Nations condemned the prison here on the island, deeming it inhumane, does our Embassy find it's completely habitable for its citizens?"

I turn and look directly at Karen.

She shoots me back a vexed look before loading a half-cocked grin. "The island has been working to make improvements to the prison. I conducted a full tour of the prison when I came and did a welfare check on the AMCITs earlier this month."

I see Tyler perk up across the table. "That's not true. You told me when we met in Grand Turk they didn't allow you past the lobby."

                                        TURKS AND CHAOS

The Virginia congressman sitting next to Tyler leans in. "How exactly can you make a determination on whether a prison is inhabitable for our AMCITs from the lobby?"

Her eyes grow wide. She darts around the table, frantically trying to craft another excuse.

But it's too late.

Everyone's focus leaves Karen and turns to whispers and side conversations. It's apparent the table has already reached its verdict.

Up until that moment, I'd often wondered if I was going crazy by accusing a branch of government of a cover-up. I could even sense that my closest friends were beginning to worry I was.

To be validated in this moment doesn't just help the CODEL understand what we're up against—most importantly, it gives me back my sanity.

Mullin dismisses them from the table and asks that we stay around to debrief before their meeting with the TCI government in the morning.

There's a lot of discussion on whether the Embassy members should even be included in the meeting. But in the end, they conclude that for them to carry out any threat of travel advisory, it would have to go through the State Department.

After we say our goodbyes, Bryan and I walk along the beach back to the condo.

Waves tumble along the shoreline as we recount different interactions from the meeting. Much like the waves at our feet, our confidence rises and quickly recedes.

In dire situations, it's nearly impossible not to be paralyzed by analyzing every move made.

The one fact we're anchored in is that God is clearly already a million moves ahead of us. His hand has been in everything up to this point.

We're able to place all our trust in how the CODEL will conduct tomorrow's meeting through our conviction in Him.

"Tomorrow's the meeting," Bryan says, staring out at the dark water.

"Yeah."

"Everything changes tomorrow."

"Yeah."

"You think they'll let us go?"

I don't answer right away. Because I don't know. I want to believe. I want to have faith. But I've been disappointed so many times.

"I think God's going to do what He's going to do," I say finally. "And we're going to trust Him either way."

MAY 20TH

The morning ticks slowly by. Each minute feels like an hour. Each hour feels like a day.

Everyone is constantly checking their phones to see if we've received any updates on how things are going. The notifications that come through are mundane—spam emails, app updates, nothing important. Nothing that matters.

It's a strange feeling to know that just a few miles away, on the other side of the island, two governments are debating our fate. Deciding whether we go home or spend the next twelve years in prison. Whether our families stay intact or shatter.

All while we sit here, powerless, waiting.

At one point, my mom asks if we think we should pack our bags.

The question hangs in the air. We all look at each other.

I hate to admit we're actually factoring in superstitions. Whether or not the word "jinxed" is ever actually spoken aloud, we collectively decide not to test our luck.

The bags stay unpacked.

~❖~

After several hours of waiting—checking phones, pacing, sitting, standing, unable to settle—Bryan receives a message from Congressman Reschenthaler.

They've finished their meeting with the resort association and are en route to meet with the TCI government.

Bryan asks about the resort association's response.

Reschenthaler responds that they were extremely concerned and wanted the ordeal resolved ASAP.

This gives us a bit of peace. The government has recently been touting in the local paper how tourism has been flourishing despite all the bad PR. We knew that was a ruse.

Just a couple of weeks prior, #CancelTurksAndCaicos was one of the top-trending topics on Twitter. We'd also heard the resort association had called at least two emergency meetings in response to the press.

We know we're making an impact. We know we're hurting them where it counts—in their wallets.

The question is: will it be enough to make them let us go?

~ ❖ ~

Another couple of hours pass before Bryan receives another update from Reschenthaler.

They've finished the meeting but can't provide any other details because they're in an insecure environment.

We all stare at the message, trying to decode it. What does that mean? Good news? Bad news? No news?

Thirty minutes later, Mullin calls me.

The airport noise in the background and the tone of his voice tip me off immediately.

We're not going to be on that plane back home with them.

I take a deep breath to brace myself for the impact of slamming back to earth. I realize I, once again, let my expectations get carried away. Let myself hope too much. Believe too hard.

"Hey, buddy," Mullin says, and even those two words carry disappointment.

"Hey."

"I wanted to call you myself to give you an update."

"Okay." I'm gripping the phone so tight my knuckles are white.

"The resort association was eager to see a quick resolution to your cases. They understand the economic impact this is having. They're losing bookings. Losing money. They want this over."

"That's good, right?"

"It should be. But the TCI Minister of Tourism kept stirring the pot, demanding that you use your media presence moving forward to apologize to the island and encourage fellow Americans to resume travel."

I can't help it—I start laughing. The absurdity of it. They want me to apologize? Encourage Americans to come here after what they've done to us?

"Yeah, that's not happening," I say when I can speak again.

"That's what I told them." He pauses. "I also met with Premier Misick."

My laughter dies. "And?"

He stammers a bit, and that's when I know it's really bad.

"Buddy, it's clear they hold some unexplainable resentment toward Americans, and they're itching to make an example out of you guys. Misick started the meeting by pounding his chest, saying he was not intimidated by us being there and that he was going to sue the United States."

"Sue the United States?" I can't process what I'm hearing. "For what?"

"For supposedly manufacturing the firearms and ammunition that have ended up in their country."

The logic is so twisted I can't even formulate a response.

"At which point," Mullin continues, "I showed him a detailed report on two Haitian gangs we know are responsible for the actual firearms and ammunition that end up on his island. We know this because our Coast Guard patrols these waters as a favor to the United Kingdom and has intercepted these two gangs on countless occasions."

"What did he say to that?"

"I told him that if he wanted to sue us, we'd pull our Coast Guard and let Haiti have at it with them. The U.K.'s Minister of Foreign Affairs definitely perked up when I said that, but Misick..." He trails off. "Misick is letting his pride and prejudice get in the way of common sense."

Pride and Prejudice. The words echo in my head.

"I'm concerned for you guys," Mullin says, his voice heavy. "We have to get y'all out of there. Know this is only round one, and we won't stop fighting for you guys."

"Okay." It's all I can manage.

"I'm sorry I don't have better news."

"It's not your fault. You did everything you could."

"We're not done. This isn't over."

"I know."

"Keep the faith, buddy."

"I'll try."

When the call ends, I just sit there for a moment, staring at the phone in my hand.

Everyone is looking at me, waiting.

"They're not letting us go," I say finally.

The words fall like stones.

I slide down to the bathroom floor and close the door. I need to be alone. I need to process this. I need to pray.

I sit with my back against the door, my head in my hands, and I pray.

I need some glimpse of God's plan for me. Some understanding of why this is happening. Why senators flying here wasn't enough. Why nothing we do seems to be enough.

God, what are You doing? What is the plan here?

I think about Bryan's sentencing in four days. About twelve years in that prison. About Van and Ellie growing up without me. About Valerie raising them alone.

Is my fight to avoid prison, to get back home to my family, resisting some other plan You have for me in that prison?

The question terrifies me. What if God wants me there? What if there's someone in that prison I'm supposed to meet, someone I'm supposed to help, some purpose I'm supposed to fulfill?

I beg You to see my heart, to know that I'm willing to carry out whatever You need from me. But if that means going to prison, I need to prepare myself mentally. I need You to give me peace about it. I need You to show me it's Your will and not just... this. This nightmare.

MAY 21ST

We try our best to resume our daily routines and ignore the somber cloud hanging over us. But the reality is that our hope was the only thing left with the CODEL the day before. They took it with them when they boarded that plane. Left us here with nothing but four days and the weight of Misick's words: I'm not intimidated.

The morning passes slowly. We make coffee. We check our phones. We pretend to have conversations about mundane things while the countdown ticks in all our heads.

Three days until Bryan's sentencing.

Three days to find a miracle.

Later that afternoon, Bryan receives a text from Reschenthaler.

He's doing a live interview. We need to tune in.

We all huddle around Terry's laptop, crowding around the small screen like it's a lifeline. Like whatever Reschenthaler is about to say might change everything.

The interview begins, and within seconds, we realize this isn't a typical congressional interview.

Reschenthaler goes scorched earth.

He calls out the island for targeting Americans. For the documented history of corruption from the families that run it. For the absolute failure of the State Department on our behalf.

He doesn't mince words. Doesn't soften it. Doesn't play politics.

He tells the truth.

All of our mouths fall open as we watch. When they cut back to the anchor doing the interview, his mouth is hanging open, too. He wasn't expecting this. Nobody was expecting this.

The room is silent when the interview ends. We're all just staring at the screen, processing what we just witnessed.

Then Bryan starts to slow clap.

"Let's. Freaking. GO!" he shouts, jumping up from his chair.

We all join in on the celebration. Clapping. Cheering. Hugging. The energy in the room transforms instantly—from despair to defiance. From defeat to determination.

Someone finally said the things we had to avoid saying in fear of retribution in the courtroom. Someone with power, with a platform, with nothing to lose, just told the world the truth.

That validation reignites the spark in all of us.

The fight is back on.

"Did you hear what he said?" Bryan replays it, pulling up the interview on his phone. "He said 'targeting Americans.' He said 'corruption.' He said the State Department failed us!"

"He didn't hold back," Mom says, tears in her eyes. "He didn't protect them at all."

"Because he doesn't have to protect them," I say. "He doesn't answer to the island. He doesn't answer to the Embassy. He answers to the American people. And the American people are on our side."

Sharitta is smiling for the first time since yesterday. "Y'all have a whole congressman going to war for you."

"For all of us," Bryan corrects. "He's fighting for all of us."

We watch the interview three more times, each time catching something new. The way Reschenthaler's voice gets harder when he talks about Bryan's ninety-six days. The way his jaw clenches when he mentions Sharitta handcuffed to a chair. The way he doesn't give the interviewer any room to defend the island or the Embassy.

This is what we needed. Someone going public. Someone calling it what it is.

A targeting of Americans by a corrupt government, enabled by our own State Department's failure.

"This changes things," I say finally.

"Does it?" Bryan asks. "Misick didn't care about senators showing up. Why would he care about one interview?"

"Because it's not about Misick caring. It's about pressure. It's about the U.K. seeing this. It's about the American people seeing this. It's about making it impossible for them to quietly railroad us."

"Three days," Bryan says. "Three days until my sentencing."

"I know."

"Can this change anything in three days?"

I want to say yes. I want to believe it can. But yesterday taught me not to get my hopes up too high.

"I don't know," I say honestly. "But it's better than nothing."

Later that evening, my phone rings. It's Mullin.

"Hey, buddy."

"Hey." I brace myself, not sure if this is good news or more disappointment.

"I wanted to give you an update. I've spent the past twenty-four hours on the phone with the U.K."

My heart jumps. "The U.K.?"

"Yeah. For weeks, I couldn't get anyone to take my phone call. But now, with the threat of leaving the island they ultimately control unattended—pulling our Coast Guard like I said—they're willing to not only talk but aid in finding a resolution."

"What does that mean? What kind of resolution?"

"They feel like the island understood their message that they don't approve of sending any of you to prison. They're putting pressure on Misick and the government. They're making it clear this needs to end."

Hope flickers in my chest, cautious and fragile. "So what happens now?"

"We all have to trust that their Supreme Court will act accordingly. That Judge Jackson will rule on the constitutional issues Oliver raised. That she won't sentence Bryan to twelve years."

The hope wavers. "But Mullin, the island has proven itself to be anything but trustworthy. Why would we trust Judge Jackson to do the right thing now?"

"Because she's not just answering to Misick anymore. She's answering to the U.K. and the U.K. is watching. The world is watching. Reschenthaler's interview is blowing up. The pressure is mounting."

"Three days," I say. "Bryan's sentencing is in three days."

"I know. I know, buddy. We're doing everything we can. The U.K. is involved now. That's huge. That's what we needed."

"But is it enough?"

There's a pause on the other end. "I don't know. But it's what we've got."

MAY 23RD

The past two days have been full of people arriving back on the island. Ashley. Bryan's parents. Media crews. Friends. Faces that feel like home in this place that feels like hell.

I think we all welcome the distraction. Anything to keep our minds from the only thing that matters—tomorrow.

We know Bryan's sentencing will set the precedent for the rest of us. Will Judge Jackson make a ruling on the unconstitutionality arguments Oliver posed on the twelve-year minimum sentencing? Did the U.K. truly engage the island, and will it have influence? Or will it ricochet off the ego of a tiny island attempting to make a stance?

Our brains aren't equipped to be forced to try and process every potential avenue or wrong turn your fate could take. The moment you do, it starts to fail.

You fall paralyzed. You hear noise but can't comprehend words. You feel like you're suffocating but forget to breathe.

The only survival method is to place every ounce of your trust in God and be 100% present in each moment.

Tomorrow is inevitable, but it doesn't exist yet. Only this moment exists. Only now.

~❖~

Bryan and Ashley have agreed to an exclusive with ABC. Not only have we begun to develop a personal connection with the booking producers, but we also feel like they're genuinely invested in our story.

That leaves Sharitta and me to conduct interviews with the other outlets that came to the island. This obligates us to be in different places at different times for the majority of the day.

Interview after interview. The same questions. The same story. My face aching from holding a smile. My voice hoarse from explaining, over and over, why we're not criminals.

Later that evening, Bryan sends me a message.

"Can you come over? Need to talk."

My stomach drops. Something's wrong.

I walk over to the hotel where he and Ashley are staying. When I finally find the unit, I can see Bryan pacing by himself outside. Back and forth. Back and forth. Like a caged animal.

He doesn't notice me until I'm right next to him.

"You okay, buddy?" I ask, reaching up to put my hand on his shoulder.

He shakes his head no and shows me his phone.

It's a local headline: *Native man sentenced to 16 years for possession of firearms and ammunition.*

My heart sinks.

"Judge Baptiste just sentenced someone to sixteen years today." Bryan's voice is hollow, defeated.

Judge Baptiste is the judge presiding over Tyler's case. He has a reputation for throwing the book at people. This is also why we were trying to get Bryan's case heard first—so Judge Jackson could be the first to set a precedent.

"Well, dude, this guy had a gun, and he was caught while leaving the scene of a crime." I quickly skim through the article on his phone. "He had an actual weapon, and he had intent. Our cases are much different."

I'm trying my best to reassure him, but I can see it's not working. The fear in his eyes is primal. Sixteen years. The number hangs between us like a death sentence.

"Ashley isn't taking any of this well, man." He runs his hand through his hair, looking up at the night sky. "Any chance you can help me put her at ease?"

"Brother, if you think my being there could help, I'm more than happy."

We go up the stairs to their room. When we walk in, Ashley is curled up in a fetal position on the couch. The moment she sees me, she begins to sob.

"Oh, Ryan, I'm not doing well. I'm not doing well at all."

I walk over and hug her. She's shaking in my arms. "God's got us," I say, over and over, like a prayer. "God's got us."

She sniffs and dabs her eyes with the crumpled tissue in her hand. She looks up at me, her face red and tear-stained.

"Has your faith always been this strong? It seems like you're somehow completely unshaken by any of this. How? How is your faith so strong?"

Her question sets off a series of questions in my own head.

Is my faith truly that strong? Why now do I feel so convicted? Am I faking this? Am I just putting on a brave face while I'm dying inside?

"Ashley, don't let me mislead you. I have my moments where I question God's plan. I'm not saying I have faith that God will give me the path I'm praying for, but I have faith that He's an amazing God whose design is always greater."

I pause, choosing my words carefully.

"That design is always much easier for us to see in the rearview mirror than through the windshield. I pray that I get to see what good He brings out of this situation, because I know something good will come out of it."

Ashley nods, dabbing her eyes again. "I'm trying to believe that."

"He's brought us all together to weather this storm together, and that in and of itself is pretty amazing. Look at us—we didn't know each other three months ago. And now we're family. That's God."

She manages a small smile. "Yeah. That's true."

We sit with her for a while longer, talking, praying, just being present. When her breathing steadies and she seems calmer, I know it's time to go.

"You're going to be okay," I tell her, standing up. "Tomorrow's going to be hard. But we're all going to be there. You're not alone."

"Thank you," she whispers.

Bryan walks me to the door. "Thanks, man. I don't know what we'd do without you."

"You'd do the same for me. You have done the same for me."

"Tomorrow," he says, the word heavy with everything unsaid.

"Tomorrow."

"I'm scared."

"I know. Me too."

We hug, and I can feel him trembling—two grown men, holding onto each other like shipwreck survivors, trying not to drown.

I leave Bryan and Ashley's room that night, wondering if I'm truly the most equipped to lead or encourage others through their faith.

Had I somehow oversold myself as someone prepared for that role? Sure, I've spent many Sundays studying the Bible, but I know very little scripture by heart. There would obviously be a much higher bar for God to use someone in that way... right?

By the time I reach the condo, I've nearly convinced myself I'm way over my skis. That I'm a fraud. That I have no business speaking about faith when my own is barely holding together.

But something in my heart silences all the doubt in my head.

I vaguely remember a verse about God equipping the called. I pull out my phone and search Google for it.

There it is, in Hebrews 13:21: "[The Lord Jesus] will equip you with everything good for doing his will, and may he work in us what is pleasing to him, through Jesus Christ, to whom be glory for ever and ever. Amen."

I read it three times, letting the words sink in.

God doesn't always call the equipped, but He always equips the called.

I sit down on the couch and close my eyes. Bryan is scared. Ashley is terrified. I'm barely holding it together. None of us are equipped for this.

But maybe that's the point.

Maybe God uses broken people. Scared people. People who don't have all the answers. People who are just trying to survive one moment at a time.

Maybe my faith doesn't have to be perfect. Maybe it just has to be present.

Maybe that's enough.

MAY 24TH - BRYAN'S SENTENCING

Reuben has to navigate his big Suburban through a swarm of armed police, armored vehicles, and news cameras to drop us off at the Supreme Court.

This is wildly different from any other time we've been here. The island is preparing for war.

It seems they're anticipating the judgment might set off a riot. Machine guns. Body armor. A show of force.

We all pile out of the car and slip through the crowd to the court entrance, which is flanked by two policemen holding machine guns. The barrels gleam in the morning sun. Their faces are stone.

There are too many of us to fit in the small lobby, so we all go upstairs to the main courtroom. We quickly grab our seats as elected officials, locals, and reporters pour into the room behind us. The energy is electric, tense, like everyone's holding their breath.

Bryan stares blankly at the judge's bench at the front of the room. Ashley clings to his arm, her head pressed against the lapel of his suit jacket. She's trembling.

I begin to worry that one or both of them might faint at any second.

Bryan looks over at me. "Can you pray for us?"

"Absolutely, brother!" I stand and motion everyone over.

As people start circling around and holding hands, others notice and join the circle. It grows and grows—locals from the island, local reporters who have written terrible things about us, bailiffs, American reporters, cameramen.

Everyone joining together.

It's one of the most powerful things I've witnessed to this point. The circle has grown so big I'm worried some might not hear the prayer.

I close my eyes and begin.

"God, we praise You. We thank You for bringing us to this moment. We beg You to have mercy on my brother Bryan. We beg You to bring him home to his family. We trust You. No matter what happens today, we trust You."

My voice breaks on the last words.

"We proclaim our faith in Your goodness, Your sovereignty, Your perfect plan. Please, God. Please bring Bryan home. Amen."

"Amen," echoes around the circle.

Something shifts in my heart during that prayer. Every lingering negative or anxious thought is purged. And in the most unlikely of places—this courtroom where we're about to be judged—I feel at peace.

We all hug and return to our seats as Bryan makes his way to the wooden cage.

~✦~

There's a gallery to our left where a number of police officers and elected officials are seated. It's reminiscent of being seated next to the opposing fan section at a sporting event.

Everything about their demeanor makes it obvious they're here for one thing: to see us defeated. To watch the Americans get what's coming to them.

I can feel them staring at us as the bailiff asks us to bow and hail the King when Judge Lobban Jackson enters the room. They're expecting us to either fumble or flat-out refuse the observance.

But much to their disappointment, we all follow along—even Bryan's mother, who is frail from her battle with MS, bows with dignity.

Judge Jackson begins by reading the charges and highlighting the arguments given by the prosecution and defense. It's a dense review of case history that almost lulls me to sleep.

The legal jargon drones on. And on. And on.

At one point, I place my hand over my face to cover my yawn and catch Judge Jackson shoot me a look from over the top of her glasses.

I sit up straight immediately. Appearing bored in front of the judge who will soon be hearing my case is not ideal.

I will myself to wake up and focus. This is Bryan's life. This matters.

Nearly an hour after she started, she says, "In the matter of the question posed by the King's Counsel regarding the constitutionality of the twelve-year minimum mandatory sentencing..."

Ashley grabs both my hand and Mom's hand and begins to squeeze. Hard.

Judge Jackson continues, "Given that all necessary governmental parties were not called to testify, I am unable to render judgment on this matter."

Ashley's hand immediately goes limp in mine.

She struggles to catch her breath and fight back tears at the same time.

My heart sinks. This was our hope. Oliver's constitutional argument was supposed to throw out the twelve-year minimum for all of us.

I lean over and whisper, "He's not out of the fight yet. She still can rule that there were exceptional circumstances."

My words are just as much to calm myself down as they are intended for Ashley.

All of our cases have been hanging in the balance on Oliver's argument of constitutionality. With Jackson refusing to rule, it now means we each individually need to prove exceptional circumstances in our cases.

The pressure is back on. Everything hinges on this next part.

Perched on the bench, Judge Jackson flips through pages of documents as we all wait on bated breath. The rustling of paper is the only sound in the courtroom.

She positions the page she's been searching for in front of her and adjusts the glasses on her face before she begins reading.

"Mr. Hagerich, you have been found guilty of possessing ammunition on February 12th, 2024, at the Howard Hamilton Airport. For this crime, you are to be sentenced to an eighteen-month custodial sentence at Her Majesty's Prison..."

Ashley squeezes my hand and breaks down in tears. "NO," she pleads, her voice breaking.

My mind is jarred from the shock, then quickly flooded with empathy for my friend. Eighteen months. Not twelve years, but eighteen months. That's... that's different.

Everything goes silent. The courtroom fades. I can only hear Ashley's sobbing, feel her hand crushing mine.

I pat Ashley's shoulder as Mom pulls her in to console her.

Then the thought hits me.

I remember reading that a judge can reduce or suspend a sentence in exceptional circumstances if it's for a term of eighteen months or less.

"Hang on," I whisper, giving Ashley's hand a squeeze. "This might be a good thing."

She looks back at me, confused, tears streaming down her face.

We all turn our attention back to Judge Jackson as she thumbs to her next page of notes.

"I have found Mr. Hagerich to be of good character, gainfully employed, with no prior arrests. He purchased the ammunition in Pennsylvania, where he holds a license to possess such ammunition for the purpose of hunting."

I hold my breath. Keep going. Please keep going.

"The court also takes into consideration the written testimony of the family's pediatrician, that Mr. Hagerich's six-year-old daughter has exhibited symptoms of traumatic stress disorder since the arrest."

Ashley's hand tightens in mine again. Different this time. Hopeful.

"The court does find that there are exceptional circumstances in this case."

We all grab hands and lean in with anticipation. My heart is pounding so hard I can hear it in my ears.

Judge Jackson continues reading. "Your sentence will be reduced to a fifty-two-week suspended sentence, and you will be ordered to pay a fine of six thousand seven hundred dollars. Upon payment of this fine, your passport will be returned."

Suspended. He's not going to prison. He's going home.

"Mr. Hagerich, are you able and prepared to pay this fine today?"

Bryan nods his head as he wipes tears from his eyes. He can barely speak. "Yes, Your Honor."

Judge Jackson slams her gavel. *Whack.*

She stands to bow. After Bryan bows, he turns to us.

I start crying tears of joy and reach through the wooden balusters to hug him. "We did it, brother. We did it!"

The next couple of hours turn into a flurry of activity.

Everyone is rushing around to pay the fine and get the proper paperwork back to the courthouse to get Bryan's passport. For good reason, Bryan wants to be on the next available flight off the island. But finding seats for him, Ashley, Jonathan, and the ABC crew adds to the chaos.

The buzz and excitement are contagious, and I'm totally engrossed in helping. Running. Coordinating. Calling. Anything to keep Bryan moving toward that plane.

When Ashley and Jonathan return from the treasury with the paperwork, the courthouse clerk tells us Bryan's passport has been mistakenly left in a safe at the Chalk Sound jail.

Their flight is scheduled to depart in just over an hour. They need to address the swarm of media waiting outside, drive to Chalk Sound for his passport, and then make it to the airport.

Their race against the clock is on.

We rush down the steps of the courthouse. I go to help load their bags into a rental car as Bryan and Ashley make their comments to the media. Questions being shouted. Cameras flashing. Microphones thrust forward.

I have the car loaded and running, ready for a quick getaway.

The crowd of reporters parts as Bryan and Ashley push their way toward the car.

When Bryan gets to me, the smile on his face starts to fade. His eyes well up.

"Brother, I wish you were getting on that plane with me."

"You've been on this island a hundred days too long. You are exactly where you need to be." I force a smile, even though my heart is breaking. "Now get going. Y'all have a plane to catch."

I give them each a quick hug—tight, not wanting to let go, but knowing I have to.

They jump into the car and speed off, a caravan of cars trailing behind them like a victory parade.

I stand there on the courthouse steps, watching until I can't see the car anymore.

He's going home.

And I'm still here.

Shortly after getting to the condo, Bryan and Ashley send a selfie of themselves on the plane. Big smiles. Tears of joy. Freedom.

I stare at the photo for a long time.

I walk down to the beach—the place I've loathed throughout this ordeal. I didn't want any part of what this island marketed itself for. But the condo is now too quiet. The silence is deafening.

As I sit on the beach looking at that photo, I scroll to the beginning of the message thread between Bryan and me.

It all started with a message inviting him to dinner to pitch our "Hail Mary" plan. Then, over the course of thirty-eight days, this complete stranger became my brother.

Proverbs 27:17: As iron sharpens iron, so a friend sharpens a friend.

The verse keeps repeating in my head.

A jet engine soars overhead, and I look up to see the jet stream heading northwest. My brother is finally heading home.

My emotions are at war. Once again, I find myself praising God for sending someone home, but trying to hide from Him the part of my heart that's screaming, What about me?

Why him and not me? Why does he get to go home while I'm still trapped here?

I immediately feel guilty for even thinking it. But I can't help it. The jealousy is real. The fear is real.

I continue to grapple with these emotions throughout the weekend.

The parade has left town with the Hagerichs, and the island falls eerily quiet. Though Mom, Terry, and Sharitta are all still in the condo with me, desolation haunts me.

The scene of Bryan embracing his children at the airport is being re-played on every news station. Every channel. Every hour. His daughter running to him. His son crying. Ashley collapsed in his arms.

My tears of joy are eventually hijacked by fear and jealousy.

Will I have the same fate?

The murmur around me begins to speculate that once Bryan is sent home and the media turns the other way, the island will take everything out on me.

After all, I'm pegged as the whistleblower. If they want a fall guy, I'm the perfect mark.

I'm the one who went to the media. I'm the one who leaked the Usha Pitts email. I'm the one who exposed the Embassy. I'm the one who brought the world's attention to this island.

And now Bryan is gone. The CODEL is gone. The media circus is packing up.

And I'm still here.

TUESDAY, MAY 28TH

Mom, Terry, and I meet Oliver at the courthouse. He's arranged for Judge Jackson to hear our formal request for an expedited hearing before her other cases begin.

That morning, Tyler is at the other Supreme Court on Grand Turk Island for his sentencing. Tyler's attorney filed for his expedited hearing a couple of weeks before Bryan's sentencing—something Oliver was not willing to do. He was adamant we needed to wait until Judge Jackson made a determination on his challenge of the law.

We keep checking our phones for updates as we wait for Judge Jackson and the prosecutors to arrive.

The courtroom that was beyond capacity just a few days prior for Bryan's sentencing is once again empty. The silence is almost oppressive after all that noise and energy.

The latch of the door echoes through the empty room as the DPP—the prosecutor—comes rushing through the doorway. When she gets to the bench, she claims to the bailiff and clerk, who are impatiently waiting, that she had no idea we were having a hearing today.

Everyone just rolls their eyes. Of course, she knew.

The bailiff calls for everyone to rise for Judge Jackson's entrance. Oliver clears his throat and points to his wig, then to the prosecutor.

She's forgotten to put on her wig.

The bailiff waits to open the door to the judge's quarters as she digs through her bag. After several awkward moments, she pulls out her powdered wig and flops it on her head, askew.

Finally, the bailiff opens the door for Judge Jackson.

The prosecutor starts by asking Judge Jackson if she can delay the expedited hearing for further review.

I nearly chip my tooth from gritting my teeth so hard. It's obvious she's just trying to toy with me. Make me wait longer. Keep me trapped here.

Judge Jackson appears to be almost as annoyed as I am. She sternly says, "No."

I sigh in short relief.

I feel a barrage of vibrations coming from my phone in my pocket. While Jackson has her head down, I slip it out and set it in the chair under my lap. I quickly open it and see the news.

Tyler is going home. Time served and a $9,000 fine.

This reignites a little flame of hope. If Tyler's going home, surely I will too. Surely.

I hear Judge Jackson begin to speak and quickly shoot my eyes forward, shoving the phone back under my leg.

"Mr. Smith, you are here seeking to submit a guilty plea for your client and file for an expedited hearing?"

"Yes, My Lord."

She begins to flip through her calendar. Slowly. Deliberately. Each page turn feels like an eternity.

"I will accept your client's plea of guilt, but my calendar is full. Our court will also begin a three-month recess soon. So, I'm not sure when I will be able to hear this case."

My head begins to spin.

Did she just say I won't have my case heard for another three to four months?

Oliver continues, "We ask the court to take into consideration that my client is not from this country and is enduring a heavy burden."

Judge Jackson begrudgingly opens up her calendar. "We will set the hearing for June 19th. Is this ample time for the DPP to put together your arguments?"

The prosecutor begins to stall and look through her calendar. "My Lord, I'm not sure that will be enough time."

"Mr. Watson has already submitted his guilty plea. You need more than a month to prepare?" Oliver questions her, his voice sharp.

She smirks back at him. "Well, there are a lot of things to review."

Judge Jackson questions her again. "Can the DPP have its arguments ready for the hearing on June 19th?"

Oliver leans over and whispers something to the prosecutor. I can't hear what he says, but her face changes. She takes a deep breath and sighs heavily.

"The DPP will be ready."

Judge Jackson slams her gavel. Whack. "Hearing is set for June 19th at 10 a.m."

Then she gets up and leaves the courtroom.

I know Oliver feels like this is a victory—we got an expedited hearing, only twenty-two days away instead of three to four months.

But I still feel defeated.

Not only does another three weeks on this island feel like an eternity, but it also seems like everyone's speculations might be coming to fruition.

In three weeks, the news cycle will have washed me out. With the world looking the other way, they can carry on with turning me into a political sacrifice.

Bryan and Tyler went home. But I'm still here.

And now I have to wait twenty-two more days.

I can't speak the entire way back to the condo. Mom, Terry, and Reuben try their best to lift my spirits, but I'm plummeting. Free-falling into darkness.

As soon as we pull up to the condo, I rush in, change my clothes, and take off running.

I frantically chase after something to take the numbness away. I run for hours, pushing myself harder and harder. But the burn in my chest and the ache in my legs and feet bring little refuge.

At some point, my feet can't keep up. My head continues racing on.

I beg to know what God needs from me. I've already submitted myself to His plan. I'm willing to accept whatever that is. I just can't make sense of His timing in all of this.

Why am I left stuck in this purgatory? Why did Bryan and Tyler get to go home, but I'm still here? What more do You want from me?

I get no answer. Just my ragged breathing. Just the emptiness.

The Darkness.

Most of the world saw Bryan and Tyler return home to their families. It was the perfect bow for the media to put on our story and move on.

Nearly all of the interviews I have scheduled are canceled. My relevance to the world has vanished.

But the attention I've lost from the media doesn't hold a candle to the attention that's slipping from home.

The FaceTime calls with the kids are falling shorter and shorter. I'm losing the battle to the normal things that occupy a seven- and nine-year-old's time and attention.

Talking to a screen about their day has become an obligation. I start to feel guilty strapping them with it.

"How was school today, buddy?"

"Good."

"What did you do?"

"Stuff."

"Van, can you give me more than one word?"

"Dad, I have to go. My show is on."

Oftentimes, after they hang up the phone, I log onto the security camera in the kitchen and listen to the normal daily ruckus. The chaos that I once considered nerve-racking now brings the most peace to my day.

I close my eyes and pretend I'm in the house with them. Pretend I'm making dinner while they do homework. Pretend I'm there for bedtime prayers and tucking them in.

I feel like I've become the ghost of my old life. Haunting my own house. Watching from a distance. Unable to touch. Unable to be present.

A good portion of my days are spent gathering testimony for my case. Bryan's case has given me a blueprint.

I need an FBI background check showing my clean record. An expert witness statement on the unique nature, design, and purpose of the caliber of ammunition in the bag.

And the two most gut-wrenching things: a letter from a psychologist assessing the behavioral effects the trauma has had on Ellie, and reading the character references sent by friends and family.

To read a report of how my child has suffered and will likely be emotionally scarred for life leaves me feeling nauseous. Anger, guilt, and "what ifs" spin out of control in my head.

This is my fault. I didn't check thoroughly enough. I put my family through this. I broke my daughter.

Valerie and Holly set up a Box folder so people in my life can write character reference letters on my behalf. I'm overwhelmed at how many friends, colleagues, fellow church members, patients, and even strangers have written.

Oliver asks that we narrow it down to twenty letters.

Mom and I sit down and read each one.

As I read through each heartfelt letter, I begin to feel like I'm reading my eulogy. They each speak of memories and experiences that describe a man's life I'm familiar with but now almost completely estranged from.

"Ryan has always been the first to help..." "I've never met anyone with more integrity..." "He would give you the shirt off his back..."

Who is that person? Is he still alive? Or did he die in that jail cell?

Would I ever get to know that man again? If I were to return to that life, could I make a greater impact? Or have I become someone else entirely?

Over the next twenty days, I continue to slip into a darker place. Like a broken ship tethered in a harbor, slowly taking on water.

Doubt creeps into every crevice.

The timing I can't understand obscures my memory of all that's been witnessed. I forget the miracles. Reuben putting up his car. The impossible connection to Michael Grim. The billions of media impressions. The CODEL.

All of it fades into background noise as I sink deeper into despair.

God brought Bryan home. God brought Tyler home. Why not me? Did I do something wrong? Is this punishment?

I wake up. I run. I check in at jail. I work on my case. I stare at the ocean. I go to bed.

Repeat.

Twenty-two days becomes twenty-one. Twenty-one becomes twenty. Twenty becomes nineteen.

But each day feels like a year.

The only thing that holds my faith together during these few weeks is the promise Van and Ellie are keeping to me.

They've never forgotten the promise we made on that first FaceTime call—to glorify God through every step of this storm.

Back in April, Van read a version of the Action Bible. It's a comic book version of the Bible that illustrates each story in such a way that it fills a nine-year-old with excitement.

He saved his money to purchase one for his cousin. But after considering my challenge to serve God in some way through this, he decided he'd instead like to buy a copy for one of the kids on the island.

He called my mom—she was originally supposed to take him to buy the one for his cousin—and asked if she could help him buy a copy for a kid in Turks and Caicos.

Unable to have one shipped to the island from the online bookstore, she reached out to her neighbor. Before all the news broke, they'd planned a large family vacation to the island and couldn't back out without losing all their money.

Her neighbor is moved when she hears about Van's wish to share the gospel.

News of Van's quest quickly spreads throughout her neighborhood.

We watch in astonishment as Mom's Ring doorbell camera captures a growing pile of Action Bibles on her front porch. One. Then three. Then ten. Then twenty.

Neighbors. Church members. Complete strangers. All buying Bibles for Van's mission.

Van and Ellie write personalized letters and draw pictures of their favorite Bible stories to include in each of the Bibles. David and Goliath. Noah's Ark. Jesus walking on water.

They stuff forty Bibles in suitcases and take them to my mom's neighbor to fly to the island with.

Once we receive them, we give a majority to the local church we attend. We set one aside to give to Reuben's eleven-year-old son.

He is so proud of that Action Bible that he takes it to school to show it off to his friends. His schoolmates circle around him as he flips through the illustrations, pointing, exclaiming, asking questions.

The stir catches the attention of the school headmaster, who quickly confiscates the book.

My heart sinks when I hear this. Of course. Of course, they took it. This island can't let us do anything good.

But after realizing what it is he confiscated, the headmaster contacts us.

He's surprised at how much interest it garnered from his students. He wants to know if we can provide them with more.

"How many more are you thinking?" we ask.

"Well, we have about three hundred fifteen kids in our school..."

Challenge accepted.

Mom gets to work contacting the publisher, letting them know of Van and Ellie's mission to spread the gospel on the island.

It becomes a full-time job for Mom to figure out how to fund and ship all of the Bibles to the island. She's on the phone constantly. Coordinating. Planning. Fundraising.

Little by little, shipment by shipment, I watch their mission come to fruition.

Three hundred fifteen Bibles. For three hundred fifteen kids. All because my nine-year-old son wanted to share the gospel.

My two beautiful children shed light in a time when I'm tempted to allow the darkness to overtake me.

For this, I am forever grateful.

JUNE 17TH

My heart races as Reuben's car approaches the airport. I'm finally going to get to see Valerie again.

Her returning to the island for my hearing is something we tussled with for days. The questions plagued us both, keeping us up at night, cycling through worst-case scenarios.

Would it put her at risk? The island arrested her once before. What if they do it again?

Was stepping foot back on this island something she could emotionally bear? After everything they put her through. After being separated from her for fifty-six days.

Would it be her last chance to see me for the next twelve years?

That question was the one that kept circling back. The one neither of us wanted to voice, but both of us thought constantly.

In the end, my sister Jessica and her husband Derek, without hesitation, stepped up to fly with her to the island. They wouldn't let her do this alone.

~❖~

Despite the airport being considerably less busy than what I remember, the taxi drivers still clog the street, lurking for the remaining travelers. A sea of cars and chaos.

My eyes dart between the lines of cars, looking for Valerie exiting the airport. My palms are sweating. My leg bounces. I can't sit still.

What if she's not on the flight? What if something happened? What if they turned her away at the airport?

Then I catch a familiar glimpse of a man who stands taller than the crowd, with dark hair and a beard.

"That's Derek!"

I throw the door open and run between the rows of cars, weaving through traffic, my heart pounding.

As I get closer to where he's standing, Valerie appears from behind the car in the front of the line.

When she turns and sees me, she leaves her bag in the street and runs toward me.

Time slows. Everything else fades. The noise. The cars. The chaos. It's just her.

She jumps into my arms, and I catch her, holding her so tight I'm afraid I might hurt her, but unable to loosen my grip.

A chamber of my heart that hasn't functioned for the last fifty-five days suddenly begins to beat again.

The air suddenly has more oxygen. The color of the world around me is brighter. Everything sharpens into focus.

Everything about her is just as perfect as I remembered it to be. More perfect, even. I'd forgotten how she feels in my arms. How she smells. How she fits against me.

The only thing I can say is "Thank you, God. Thank you, God. Thank you, God."

I bury my face in her hair and breathe her in. She's shaking—or maybe I am. Maybe we both are.

"I'm here," she whispers. "I'm here. I'm here."

"I know. I can't believe you're here."

"I had to come. I had to see you."

We stand there in the middle of the airport pickup area, cars honking around us, people staring, and we don't care. We just hold each other like if we let go, this might all disappear.

After I finally set Valerie down—reluctantly, not wanting to lose contact—I see my sister approaching.

As she grabs hold of me and hugs my neck, I'm hit with an emotion that catches me off guard.

I feel like a ten-year-old again, seeking comfort and understanding from my older sister. The one who always protected me. The one who always knew what to say.

Tears come before I can stop them. I'm not the strong brother right now. I'm the little brother who needs his sister.

"It's all going to be okay," she says, and just like a child, I believe her without question.

We were exposed to a lot growing up. A bitter divorce. Family bankruptcy. The loss of a parent. We've been in the fire together many times before.

So her being here gives me comfort that can only be found in a battle-tested relationship. I would walk down any dark alley with her by my side.

And I find peace that she's going to be there with Valerie if I'm not coming back with them.

If I'm not coming back.

The thought threatens to shatter the moment, but I push it away. Not now. Not yet.

Right now, I have Valerie in my arms. I have my sister by my side. I have Derek here supporting us.

Right now is enough.

JUNE 18TH

I shoot out of bed as the sun begins to peek through the window. My heart is racing before I'm fully conscious.

I'm overwhelmed by the feeling that I've forgotten something. But what? What am I missing?

Then I realize—it's not that I've forgotten something. It's that leaving the thoughts that have consumed me for so long unattended seems reckless. Like if I stop thinking about tomorrow, if I stop preparing, I'll somehow lose control of the outcome.

As if I ever had control.

I make a pot of coffee and wait on the porch for everyone to wake up. The sun rises over the ocean, painting the sky in shades of orange and pink. Beautiful. Always so beautiful.

This island that's held me captive for sixty-eight days is still one of the most beautiful places I've ever seen. And I hate it for that.

Jonathan Franks, the ABC crew, and my best buddy J.C. are flying to the island today, and I need to ground myself. Need to prepare.

Going to prison is still a very likely scenario. Maybe even the most likely scenario.

I don't want to allow myself to get carried away in the excitement of reuniting with everyone. My heart needs to be ready for anything.

Ready for celebration or devastation.

Ready for freedom or twelve years.

Ready for everything or nothing.

Later that morning, my brother-in-law Derek asks if he can join me on my daily run to check in at the jail.

"You sure?" I ask. "It's five miles round trip. And it's hot."

"I'm sure."

The heat that blankets the island in late June is suffocating. It doesn't allow for much dialogue—we're both too focused on breathing, on putting one foot in front of the other, on not collapsing.

But the sound of falling feet beside me speaks a thousand words.

I have people who are willing to step into the fire with me. Who are willing to suffer alongside me, even in small ways. Who shows up, even when it's hard.

And that means the world.

When we finish the five-mile loop back at the condo, Derek looks at me while trying to catch his breath. His shirt is soaked through. His face is red.

"Bro," he pants. "You have gotten in shape."

I laugh off the compliment, but when I look down at myself, I realize he's right. I haven't given much thought or assessment to my physical state, but running miles every day out of necessity has left me over twenty pounds lighter than I was when I got to the island.

My clothes hang differently. My face is leaner. My body has changed.

It makes me wonder: how much more of me has changed in the last sixty-seven days?

Am I still the same person who landed here in April?

Or have I become someone else entirely? Someone forged in fire. Someone who knows what it's like to fight for your life. Someone who learned to survive when everything was taken away.

I don't know the answer. Maybe I won't know until I'm home—if I get home—and I try to fit back into my old life.

Maybe I'll never fit again.

J.C., Jonathan, and Nic from ABC all arrive on a flight later that afternoon. When I see J.C., my best friend pulls me into a hug without saying a word.

"I'm here, brother," he says finally. "Whatever happens tomorrow, I'm here."

It's like receiving a huge boost of confidence. ABC's willingness to send someone back to the island signals to everyone that the world is still watching. That if they try to railroad me tomorrow, people will know.

We spend the evening gathering B-roll footage and recording short interviews. As awkward as I still find all of this, I'm grateful the story is recirculating.

But now the pressure is immense. Tomorrow, I face Judge Jackson with millions watching—either celebrating my freedom or witnessing my family's destruction in real time.

JUNE 19TH - DAY OF MY HEARING

Panic snatches me from sleep once again. It's hearing day.

I feel as if I've left my mind running through the night. It needs me to get out of bed and move. But I battle the urge and continue to lie quietly in the dark.

Valerie's warm body next to me and the rhythmic sound of her sleeping breath bring a type of peace I can no longer take for granted. I lie there for a couple of hours and pray God's protection over her, praising Him for the time He's allowed me with her.

I memorize the sound of her breathing. Just in case.

The clank of glassware and thump of the cupboard door tip me off that others are up. I sneak out of bed and, to no surprise, find J.C. in the kitchen pouring coffee.

J.C. has a work ethic I've always admired. I often call him on my way to work in the morning to find he's already been grinding away for hours. So, him being the first one up is the obvious choice.

He pours me a cup of coffee, and we sit out on the patio. The sun is just starting to rise over the ocean. Day sixty-nine on this island. Possibly my last day as a free man.

I try to distract from the nerves I know are crawling on my face with my usual joking banter.

He can see right through it and leans in toward me. "How can I pray for you this morning?"

My soul thanks him for being direct. It needs what I've been avoiding.

I explain to him the thing I've wrestled with most the past three weeks—God's timing. I know He has a reason for all of this, and I'm willing to accept going to prison if that's where He needs me, but why the delay in any of it? Why did Tyler get to go home after weeks, while I've been here for over two months?

J.C. sends out a message to the other guys in our Bible study group, asking if they can jump on a quick call. Given how early it is, I don't have much expectation that anyone will respond.

J.C.'s phone lights up within seconds. Nearly all of them jump on the call.

They all take turns praying over me through the phone. Voices I know so well. Friends from home. Normal life that feels like it exists in another universe.

J.C. finishes by asking God to reveal His design and help me understand the perfection in His timing.

After the call, we sit there for a while and watch the rest of the island wake up.

I can't stop thinking: This is what being a friend looks like. I can only hope that one day, I can somehow show up for him the way he's showing up for me.

~❖~

By 8:30 a.m., everyone is rushing around to finish getting ready. The chaos is borderline humorous. Everyone is worried about whether their attire for a British court is appropriate.

I laugh and reassure everyone they're adequately dressed for the occasion. I'm pretty sure no one trusts what I'm saying—they're just trying to be coaxed out the door and into the car.

Once loaded in the car, everyone's conversations screech to a halt. The drive over starts to feel like we're in a funeral procession.

The occasional pothole rattling the dash and the hum of the air conditioner are the only noises to be heard.

I grab Valerie's hand when I hear the blinker begin to tick as we approach the courthouse.

She squeezes back, hard.

The courthouse is relatively quiet. No signs of Oliver yet, so we all wait in the lobby.

I can tell everyone is grasping to find words of encouragement for me. I struggle to find words to ease the obligation they feel.

We all wait quietly and watch out the window for his silver sedan.

We've waited around for about ten minutes when I see a glare reflect off his windshield as he pulls into the parking lot. He slowly gathers his things from the backseat and makes his way up the steps.

When he gets in the lobby, he turns and sees us all packed in. He takes off his glasses, flashes a smile, and says in his soft Caribbean accent, "Hello, everyone!"

He sets his things down and motions me over.

I walk over, curious about what he seems eager to share. My heart is pounding. Is this good news? Bad news? Last-minute strategy?

He digs his phone out of his pocket and hands it to me.

It takes me a second glance to realize what I'm reading.

Notice of Amendment to the Firearms and Ammunition Mandatory Minimum Sentencing Law - Judicial Discretion Now Permitted

"Wait. Is this now in effect?" My voice cracks.

Oliver smiles at me and nods. "It went into effect at 9:00 a.m. this morning."

Tears start to fall from my face as I look out the window at the blue sky above, replaying the hundreds of times I begged God to help me understand His timing.

This morning. The law changed this morning—the day of my hearing.

"Yes, God," I whisper. "Your timing is perfect."

J.C.'s prayer two hours ago echoes in my head: Help me understand the perfection in His timing.

And here it is. The answer. The reason for the delay. The reason I had to wait while Bryan and Tyler went home.

Because if my hearing had been three weeks ago, the law would still have required twelve years. But God held me here. Held me in this purgatory. Until this exact day. This exact moment.

When the law changed.

I turn to everyone gathered in the lobby. "The law changed. This morning. The Judge is no longer required to sentence me to twelve years. The judge has discretion now."

Valerie's hand goes to her mouth. Jessica starts crying. J.C. just nods, a knowing look on his face.

God's timing is perfect.

Oliver starts his arguments that morning by drawing Judge Jackson's attention to the amendment to the law passed earlier this morning, which no longer stipulates a twelve-year minimum mandatory.

I watch her face carefully. Does she look relieved? Annoyed? Is this good for me or bad?

Oliver then reads the expert witness's statement attesting to the unique caliber of the ammunition. He continues by reading my clean background check and highlights a number of character witness letters.

In his closing statement, he reads the physician's assessment of the emotional toll this process has had on Ellie.

My hands tremble. Tears begin to fall uncontrollably from my face.

I know my children are suffering from this, but to hear those words spoken in public—nightmares, separation anxiety, symptoms consistent with PTSD—makes it real in a way I can't bear.

And to see the DPP, Clement Joseph, incredulously shake his head as they're read makes me sick. Like my daughter's trauma is a joke to him. Like her suffering doesn't matter.

Despite Judge Jackson acknowledging the change in law, Clement Joseph still feverishly argues that I broke the law prior to the amendment and urges her to impose the twelve-year minimum mandatory sentencing.

Of course he does. Of course.

Joseph continues flailing about, making erroneous claims about me being a threat to society. His tantrum makes it obvious this is personal to him. He's losing the sparring match, and he knows it.

In a final act of desperation, he looks over and gives a head nod to one of the officers in the courtroom.

The officer stands up and marches over to the evidence bag that contains my ammunition.

I catch a glimpse of the bag as the officer walks by me to present it to the judge.

And I immediately notice something different with one of the rounds.

It's disassembled. The bullet is in its original form. The casing separated.

Wait. They had to take it apart?

Clement Joseph stands. "Your Ladyship, we would like to submit the recovered evidence to the King for consideration."

She turns to Oliver and asks, "Mr. Smith, do you have any objection?"

Given I'm in the back of the courtroom, I try my best to get Oliver's attention. But he doesn't recognize I'm trying to signal him.

"Psst, Oliver."

Nothing.

"Oliver!"

I finally speak out loud—the entire courtroom, including Judge Jackson, locks eyes on me.

Oliver seems confused as he walks back to me. "What?" he says in a perturbed manner.

"Allow it."

"Are you crazy? Those bullets look deadly! He wants her to see how deadly they look."

I lean in closer, speaking quickly. "I read somewhere that they have to test-fire the ammunition here to ensure it's live ammunition. Is that true?"

"Yes, that's true."

"They had to take apart the ammunition!" I'm almost whispering, but urgent. "That's such a rare caliber; they didn't have a firearm on the island that could fire that ammunition. So, they had to take it apart to test it!"

Oliver's eyes light up. He nods his head as he spins to walk back to address Judge Jackson.

"Your Ladyship, we would like to allow the submission, but we ask the King to make notice of how the ammunition was tested. There is no firearm on this island capable of firing that ammunition, so they had to disassemble it to ensure it was a live round."

Judge Jackson raises her eyebrows and begins nodding her head.

Yes. Yes. She gets it. They couldn't even fire it here. It's that specialized. That harmless to this island.

Clement Joseph slumps in his chair, swivels around, and shoots me a massive glare.

I just flash him a grin back.

Checkmate.

Judge Jackson says, "Sentencing is scheduled for 10 a.m. Friday."

She slams her gavel. *Whack.*

Everyone stands to bow before she leaves the courtroom.

As we're leaving the courthouse, it dawns on me that today is Mom's birthday.

Not only do I feel terrible that I'm just now realizing it, but also that she had to spend her day watching her son in court. Watching me fight for my life on her birthday.

I speed up to catch up with her and grab her hand, spinning her back into my arms for a hug.

"Happy birthday, Momma!"

"My only birthday wish is to get to see you go home!" Her voice cracks.

I smile back at her and give her another hug. She's a walking example of what being a selfless parent looks like.

I can only pray to have an opportunity to give so much of myself to my children. To love them the way she's loved me through this nightmare.

JUNE 20TH

The first shipment of Action Bibles we're donating to the school arrived this morning. Our contact at the school says it's okay for us to swing by around 1 p.m.

Everyone wants to see Van and Ellie's plan come to fruition. To witness what my nine- and seven-year-old started from three thousand miles away.

We all meet up at the school and wait for the headmaster in the lobby. The building is modest—concrete walls painted bright colors, tile floors worn smooth from years of small feet.

As we wait, Jonathan looks over to Nic, one of the ABC producers. "I've worked on countless cases of wrongfully detained Americans, but this is the first time I've ever been a part of them donating Bibles to the country detaining them."

"I know, right?" Nic gushes back.

"All of the credit goes to Van and Ellie!" I say, smiling. "They're showing us all how to be the hands and feet of Jesus."

Even in the middle of fighting for my freedom, even facing sentencing tomorrow, my kids found a way to serve. Found a way to spread light in darkness.

~❖~

Shortly after, the school's headmaster meets us in the lobby. He thanks us for being there and tells us they've selected the fifth-grade class to receive the first round of Action Bibles.

Valerie looks at me with tears in her eyes. "Fifth grade... This is perfect!"

Valerie teaches fifth grade back in Oklahoma, so it makes it extra special to get to interact with and deliver such a personal gift to other fifth graders. Kids the same age as the ones she teaches every day—kids who could just as easily be her students.

After a couple of minutes, the fifth-grade class, adorned in their school uniforms—khaki pants and skirts, white shirts—files quietly outside where the headmaster introduces us as "special American visitors."

We tell them how meaningful it is for us to meet them and that our son and daughter thought this version of the Bible was an engaging way to spread the gospel among kids their age.

They all line up as we pass out the Bibles. One by one. Small hands reaching out. Eyes wide with curiosity.

One of the kids anxiously opens the book and starts flipping through the illustrations. David and Goliath. Noah's Ark. Jesus walking on water.

"Wait, these are ours to keep?"

"Yes, they're yours to keep!" Valerie says, matching his excitement.

The kids break formation and begin celebrating—hugging Valerie and me, jumping up and down, showing each other their favorite pages.

The happiness and laughter are inexorable. Contagious. Pure.

I look over and watch Valerie as she bounces along with the kids. Her smile reflects the joy her heart feels. She's in her element—surrounded by children, teaching, loving, serving.

I'm in complete awe.

This is a day our hearts should have been filled with worry. Tomorrow is sentencing. Tomorrow, Judge Jackson decides if I go home or spend twelve years in prison.

But instead, we're all filled with praise. Watching God work through children—both mine and these—to bring light to this dark place.

We take several photos with the kids and their Bibles. A line forms in front of Valerie as soon as they find out she's a fifth-grade teacher. They're all anxious to tell her about what they're learning—math problems they're working on, books they're reading, science projects.

She listens to each one. Genuinely interested. Asking questions. Encouraging them.

She was made for this.

As Valerie takes time to visit with each kid, the headmaster pulls me aside.

The look of elation on his face turns to disapproval.

My stomach drops. What did I do? What did we do wrong?

"What these politicians on television are saying about our country is very concerning."

I'm caught off guard and stammer to find words to diffuse the situation. Is he talking about the senators? About Reschenthaler?

He continues before I can formulate a response. "We don't resent you Americans!" His voice rises slightly. "Despite the fact that it was the American developers who moved in here and bought up our land for pennies on the dollar in the 1970s. They drove up our cost of living and left us only one means for providing for our families... serving you—the Americans—on vacation."

As I listen, I can't help but wonder if he realizes that in his attempt to tell me why the locals don't resent Americans, he's laying out the very reason they do.

His words tumble out, years of frustration finally finding an outlet. And I'm the outlet. The American standing in front of him. The one who represents everyone who's ever come here and taken something.

All I can do is listen.

Debating the matter would only detract from why we're here—to help Van and Ellie spread the gospel. To do something good in this place that's caused us so much pain.

I smile and stick out my hand to offer a handshake. "Thank you for allowing us to be here."

He reluctantly shakes my hand, but his face makes it apparent he hasn't finished saying all he needs to say. The frustration is still there, simmering just beneath the surface.

As we drive past rows of shanty homes and dilapidated buildings back to the condo, his rant replays in my head.

There's an unavoidable truth to what the headmaster was saying.

Hotel and resort companies have carved away the most desirable piec-es of the island—the beachfront, the ocean views, the paradise everyone comes to see. Leaving the remaining interior slivers of land to the locals.

The interior sections are barren, offering little to no resources or means of survival. No beaches. No tourist dollars. Just poverty hidden be-hind resort walls.

Nearly all of the produce is imported from Florida to be sold at an un-believable premium. Goods beyond their expiration dates sell at the local bodegas, providing access to the only affordable food options.

Tourism has become the hand that's simultaneously feeding them and holding them down.

Americans account for nearly 90% of that tourism, becoming the ob-vious party to blame.

The only issue with their line of thinking is that they're holding the consumer liable. The beachfront views Americans are clamoring to experi-ence were sold off by someone else decades before any of these vacationers booked their tickets.

But try explaining that to someone who can't afford to feed their family, while Americans spend thousands on a week's vacation in their homeland.

I think about Reuben. About Dale. About the people who've helped us—locals who risked their reputations, their relationships, to stand with Americans everyone else hated.

I think about the officers who laughed at me. About Wilkie and his newspapers. About Misick pounding his chest. About the locals who want to see us punished.

This island is complicated. More complicated than I understood when I first arrived. More complicated than the media narratives. More compli-cated than "corrupt government targeting Americans."

There's real pain here. Real injustice that predates my arrest by decades.

And I'm just caught in the middle of it. A symbol of everything they resent, even though I never took anything from them. Never bought their land. Never exploited them.

I just made a mistake packing my bag.

But to them, I'm not Ryan Watson, the father from Oklahoma who forgot to check his luggage.

I'm an American. One of the people who took their island and turned it into a playground for the rich, while they serve drinks and clean rooms.

And maybe that's why they're so eager to make an example of us. Why Misick pounds his chest. Why the prosecutors are so vindictive.

Because for once, they have the power. For once, Americans have to answer to them.

JUNE 21ST - DAY OF SENTENCING

I wake up just as the sun starts to break. The nerves I left unattended through the night cause my bones to itch. I need to move.

I roll out of bed, trying not to wake Valerie, but as I get to the edge, I feel her hand on my back.

"I love you, babe."

"I love you too, babe."

I roll back over and kiss her on the forehead. "I need to start packing, though."

Her eyes widen. She understands what I mean.

I get busy packing two separate bags. One for the best-case scenario. One for the worst-case scenario.

I need to be prepared to go to prison.

I fill an old shopping bag with a blanket, pillow, change of clothes, and a toothbrush. Things I'll happily leave behind if I get to go home. Things that will become my entire world if I don't.

Once everyone is packed and ready, we make our way to the court-house.

As we pull onto the street, I reach down and grab Valerie's hand. "God's plan!"

She squeezes my hand, leans over, and places her head on my shoulder.

Whatever happens in the next few hours, we're trusting Him.

One by one, we make our way through the metal detector at the entrance of the courthouse. I recognize that Oliver has beaten us there and is waiting in the lobby.

He pulls me aside. "Are you ready?"

"I guess I'm as ready as I'll ever be."

"I'm hoping it's going to be a similar outcome as Bryan's, but we can't be sure." He pauses. "Judge Jackson can still give you twelve years if she wants to make an example of you."

My stomach drops, but I nod. I know this.

"I did go ahead and book a ticket," I say. "Just in case it does go my way."

Oliver shoots back a look of concern. "What time does it depart?"

"Not till 3 p.m."

"Today is a national holiday, and the treasury closes at noon! It's going to be a stretch to get everything wrapped up by then." He looks at his watch. "You just need to focus on not going to prison. Let everyone else worry about the logistics."

I take a deep breath. "All I've ever had is prayer, so I'll continue with that."

I make my way back to my entourage to let them know the new challenge we face. The clock is already ticking. If Judge Jackson releases me this morning, we'll have maybe two hours to pay the fine and get my passport before the treasury closes.

As we start discussing strategy, the local reporter—Wilkie—makes his way over to us.

We all tense. What does he want? Another photo? Another headline?

"The treasury is going to be packed today." His voice is quiet, almost sympathetic. "I would send someone over there to hold a place in line. This would be your only way of getting a receipt of payment in time."

We all stand there in shock. The reporter who once had it out for me—who handed out newspapers with my mugshot at church—is now seemingly trying to help me get home.

Mom turns to J.C. and Derek. "I need you two in line at the treasury by 10:00 a.m. We'll bring the court documents to you as soon as we get them."

They nod and take off running.

The clock on the courtroom wall echoes as each second passes.

Tick. Tick. Tick.

It's 9:08 a.m. Sentencing was supposed to start at 9. Every passing minute pushes me further from ever making that flight.

KNOCK. KNOCK. The bailiff bangs on Judge Jackson's chamber door.

I turn and face forward as he calls, "All rise!"

Judge Jackson saunters into the room and climbs the steps of the bench before bowing. Her every move feels slower than normal. Deliberately slow. Or maybe time itself has slowed.

I can't pull my eyes off the clock as she reads through the case documents.

I know it's foolish to worry about missing a flight when I should be worrying about going to prison. It just seems like an easier thing for my mind to wrestle with. More manageable. Less terrifying.

The minute hand moves on without regard to the pace at which Jackson is reading.

It's nearly 11 a.m. I wonder how far J.C. and Derek have made it through the line at the treasury. Did they get to the front? Are they still waiting?

"For this charge, you have been found guilty."

Jackson's words eject me from the pettiness of worrying about catching that flight and back to the reality of the courtroom.

This is it.

"Though this charge customarily carries a sentence of twelve years, based on the recent amendment allowing for judicial discretion, I do believe exceptional circumstances apply to your case."

My heart stops. *Exceptional circumstances. She said exceptional circumstances.*

"I hereby sentence you to a six-month suspended sentence and impose a fine of two thousand dollars."

My head falls into my hands, and I begin to weep.

Six months suspended. I'm going home. I'm going home.

I can hear whispers of praise from my family behind me. Valerie's sob. Jessica's "Thank You, Jesus." Mom's quiet crying.

Jackson whacks her gavel to silence everyone and reclaim the attention of the court.

"Mr. Watson, is this something you are prepared to settle with the court?"

"Yes... Yes, ma'am." I struggle to get the words out through tears.

"Once the defendant settles his debt to the court, he may receive his passport and leave our island."

Leave. She said leave. I can leave.

She pauses, looking at me over her glasses one last time.

"Mr. Watson, I know you have taken it upon yourself to garner much attention. I implore you to utilize that attention to urge other Americans to exercise extreme caution when packing their bags to travel to our country."

I nod. "Yes, Your Honor."

Judge Jackson stands to bow and leaves the courtroom.

We quickly hug in celebration before everyone gets to work assembling the paperwork. I have to stay in the custody of the courtroom as Terry rushes the paperwork across the island to the treasury.

The minutes tick by. Each one feeling like an hour.

When Terry gets there, the line is wrapped around the building. He scouts around the crowd and finds J.C. and Derek at the front of the line— they made it there only by bribing other locals with a pocket full of cash.

They pay the fine and rush to return the receipt to the courthouse.

While all of this is going on, I wait anxiously in the lobby of the courthouse under the supervision of two police officers.

I notice a shorter American woman approaching. "Ryan?"

"Yes?" I answer back in confusion.

"We spoke briefly a number of weeks back. We never got a chance to reconnect, so I wanted to come by and say hi before you left."

She shakes my hand and places a business card in it.

I look down at her card, still trying to figure out who she is.

Top o' The Cove Deli: Brenda Branzeno

The Warden?

I look up as she walks out of the courthouse.

Valerie walks up to me to investigate the look on my face. "Who was that?"

"I think that was the Warden." I hand her the card.

"The Warden was a deli caterer?"

We can't help but bust out laughing. To think that this was the woman we thought might rescue us from this situation when all of this chaos began. After everything—all the darkness, all the fear, all the fighting—this tiny absurd moment breaks something open in us. We laugh until we're crying.

~❖~

Terry's rental car comes screeching back into the parking lot. He, J.C., and Derek all pour out of the car and race up the steps with the receipt.

We hand the receipt to the lady behind the counter, and I sign the last piece of paperwork.

She slides my passport to me from under the glass.

I stare at it for a moment. My passport. My ticket home. My freedom.

"Time to go home!" I hold it up as we all cheer.

We exit the building to a handful of reporters waiting at the foot of the steps. Cameras flash. Microphones thrust forward.

"How does it feel?"

"What's the first thing you're going to do?"

They ask pretty standard questions, which I answer without much thought. *I'm grateful. I'm ready to see my kids. I want to hug my children.*

Then one question comes from the back. "Mr. Watson, you fought pretty hard with criticism of our laws. The light you shed on this pushed our country to revise this law, and now there's a revered local woman who was freed from facing mandatory sentencing. How does it feel to know you helped this local grandmother return to her family?"

I pause. I hadn't thought about that. About who else the law change would help.

"God is the only one who deserves any glory from this. I'm forever grateful for His plan."

And I mean it. All of it—the waiting, the suffering, the not understand-ing—it was all for this. For the law to change. For others to be saved from twelve years for a simple oversight.

Not just for me. For everyone who comes after.

The tires screech as the plane touches down in Oklahoma City just after 10 p.m.

My heart is pounding so loudly I can't hear anything else around me. I can't even feel my boots making contact with the ground as we make our way to the baggage claim.

I can see a large crowd gathered on the other side of the glass, but I can't process any of the faces. Friends. Family. Church members. People I recognize but can't focus on.

I'm only looking for one thing. Two things.

Van and Ellie.

The doors part.

And I see their two faces hovering above signs that say "WELCOME HOME DADDY."

My body begins to shake uncontrollably as they run to me and jump into my arms.

Their little voices saying "I love you, Daddy" cut through the cheers of the crowd around us.

I hold them so tight. Bury my face in their hair. Breathe them in.

I'm home. I'm finally home.

Van pulls back and looks at me. "Did you do it, Dad? Did you glorify God?"

I wipe tears from my eyes. "We did it, buddy. We all did it together."

"The Action Bibles got to the kids?"

"All 315 of them."

He smiles—that serious nine-year-old smile that's too old for his age. "Good."

Ellie squeezes tighter. "Don't leave again, Daddy."

"I won't, baby. I promise. I'm home now."

"Forever?"

"Forever."

I look up and see Valerie standing behind them, tears streaming down her face. Our family—broken and scattered for seventy days—is finally whole again.

I reach out and pull her in. The four of us standing there in the middle of the airport, holding each other, crying, laughing, refusing to let go.

Thanks be to God.

I had finally made it home.

~❖~

Seventy days on an island fighting for my freedom.

Seventy days of learning what really matters.

Seventy days of discovering that God's timing is perfect, even when I can't understand it.

I went to Turks and Caicos to celebrate my 40th birthday. A freak accident stranded me on that island and left me fighting for my life. But maybe this was no accident at all.

Because God used that time to:

Change a law that will protect countless Americans

Bring 315 Bibles to children on an island

Show my children how to be light in darkness

Teach me what it means to truly fight for what's right

Expose a system that was failing Americans

Prove that ordinary people can wage war against injustice and win

I don't know what Van and Ellie will remember about this when they're older. Maybe they'll remember the fear. The FaceTime calls. The separation.

But I hope they remember the Action Bibles. I hope they remember that when their dad was trapped on an island, they chose to serve the children there anyway.

I hope they remember that's what it looks like to be the hands and feet of Jesus.

Even when you're scared.

Even when it's hard.

Even when the darkness seems overwhelming.

You bring light anyway.

Because that's what we're called to do.

That's what they taught me.

My children. My heroes. My light.

Thanks be to God.

I'm home.

TWO WEEKS LATER...

We're piled up as a family on the couch. All the interviews and media attention have subsided, and we're trying to reclaim normalcy. Trying to remember what life was like before Turks and Caicos. Before jail cells and courtrooms and fighting for survival.

My phone rings and interrupts whichever Disney movie we're watching.

I look down to see it's Sharitta.

"Hey, guys, Miss Sharitta is calling!" I quickly turn down the television and answer on speaker so we can all say hi.

But I can tell right away that she's upset. Her voice is tight, strained.

I stand up and walk outside to figure out what's going on.

"Ryan, they're trying to delay my case again," she says, and I can hear tears in her voice. "Judge Jackson keeps pushing it back. I don't know what to do."

"I'm so sorry, Sharitta. I wish I was still there to—"

"It's not just that." She cuts me off. "I've run out of my medication. My doctor in Florida can't refill it until he runs my bloodwork. But I'm stuck here. I can't get home to get the labs done. I can't get the medication I need."

My jaw clenches. After everything—after the media attention, after the law change, after the world was watching—they're still playing games with people's lives.

"Sharitta, you need to contact Karen. This is the embassy's responsibility. They need to ensure you have access to your medication. That's literally their job—to help Americans in distress abroad."

"You think she'll actually help?"

"I don't know. But you have to try. Make sure she understands this is a medical emergency. You need those labs. You need that medication."

I give her Karen's number.

"Call me back after you speak with her so we can follow up with an email," I say. "Document everything. We'll escalate if we have to."

"Okay. Thank you, Ryan."

"Of course. We're in this together. I'm not going to forget about you just because I'm home."

About thirty minutes pass before she rings back.

Her voice sounds much less troubled. Almost relieved.

"Ryan, I spoke to Karen. She was actually really helpful this time."

I'm surprised but cautious. "That's great. What did she say?"

"She said she was going to help me. And you won't believe this—she was at a party with Misick when I called, and she asked him to help! I heard her ask him while I was on the phone."

"Wait, she was at a party with Charles Misick? The premier?"

"No, not Charles. Michael Misick. She said his name."

My blood runs cold.

"Sharitta... are you sure she said Michael?"

"Boy, you don't think I have ears?" Her voice gets defensive. "She said Michael Misick! I even heard her say 'Hey, Mike!' when she called him over."

I stand there on my porch, staring at nothing, my mind racing.

Michael Misick. Not Charles.

Michael Misick—the younger brother who was charged with corruption. Allegedly stole millions from the people of Turks and Caicos when he was Premier in 2009. Fled to Brazil after the U.K. disbanded the Turks and Caicos government and extradited back to the island.

But he's not in prison. He's at a party. With the U.S. Consul.

"Ryan? You still there?"

"Yeah. Yeah, I'm here." I try to keep my voice steady. "Sharitta, that's... that's really helpful. I'm glad Karen's going to help you with the labs."

"Me too. I was so worried."

"Keep me posted, okay? Let me know if anything changes."

"I will. Thank you, Ryan."

I hang up and just stand there.

Just as I thought I had closed this chapter. Just as I thought I understood what happened to me on that island.

A new riddle begins.

Was Karen really socializing with Michael Misick?

Why would she go to him for help? How could he influence Sharitta's situation?

I think back to all those empty calls. The times Karen told senators and congressmen that she was doing everything she could when she was doing nothing at all.

I think about the Usha Pitts email. About how the Embassy knew about Non-American travelers being released.

I think about how Karen reported that a prison condemned by the U.N. was fit for us.

And now she's supposedly at a party with Michael Misick.

What else don't we know? What else is lurking beneath the surface?

I walk back inside. Valerie looks up from the couch. "Everything okay?"

"Yeah. Sharitta's having some issues with her case, but Karen's supposedly going to help her."

"That's good." She turns back to the movie.

But I can't focus. Can't settle.

I pull out my phone and start searching. Michael Misick. Embezzlement. Corruption. Turks and Caicos.

The articles come up immediately. Millions stolen. The U.K.'s investigation siting clear signs of corruption and abuse.

But after 16 years his trial has yet to be heard. Instead, he is apparently at parties with U.S. Embassy officials.

That night, I lie in bed next to Valerie, unable to sleep.

I'm home. I'm safe. My family is whole. The law changed. Bryan and Tyler are home. Sharitta will hopefully be home soon.

We won. I should feel victorious.

But instead, I feel like I've only scratched the surface. Like there's a whole iceberg beneath what we uncovered.

And I don't know what to do with that information.

Do I go public? Do I contact more media? Do I reach out to senators again?

Or do I just let it go? Focus on my family. Move on with my life. Be grateful I escaped.

But then I think about Sharitta, still trapped there. About all the Americans who will travel to that island in the future, not knowing the danger they're in.

And I think about Van and Ellie and their Action Bibles. About bringing light into darkness. About not staying silent when you see injustice.

I close my eyes and pray.

God, I thought this was over. I thought I was done fighting. But now I don't know. Is this something You want me to pursue? Or is this a rabbit hole I need to avoid?

Show me. Guide me. Help me know when to fight and when to rest.

Because I'm tired. But I'm also not sure I can just walk away.

Please. Show me what to do.

The fan turns overhead.

Van and Ellie sleep peacefully down the hall.

Valerie breathes steadily beside me.

And somewhere in Turks and Caicos, Michael Misick—with his brother in office—is walking free.

While Sharitta is still trapped, still waiting, still fighting.

The story isn't over.

It was never over.

I just didn't know it yet.

~❖~

AUTHOR'S NOTE

A freak accident with ammunition in my luggage revealed systemic issues that go far deeper than anyone imagined.

The identity of the Jane Doe who was taken into custody on April 15th 2024, then released, has yet to be discovered.

This story isn't just about my seventy days on an island. It's about a pattern of Americans being targeted, a government exploiting tourism while resenting tourists, and an embassy that failed in its most basic duty: protecting American citizens.

But most importantly, it's about God's perfect design in all things.

Sharitta eventually made it home. The law we helped change has protected a number of Americans since. The 315 Action Bibles are in the hands of children who might never have encountered the gospel otherwise.

Good came from this nightmare. God's timing was perfect.

The fight for transparency, for accountability, for justice—that fight continues.

Because when you shine light in dark places, you don't always like what you find.

But you keep shining anyway.

That's what Van and Ellie taught me.

That's what I'll keep doing.

THE END

"The light shines in the darkness, and the darkness has not overcome it."

— John 1:5

www.ingramcontent.com/pod-product-compliance
Lightning Source LLC
Chambersburg PA
CBHW050814050726
47601CB00018B/278/J